First-Time
ASIA

FIRST-TIME ASIA

ROUGH GUIDE CREDITS

Text editor: Jo Mead
Series editor: Mark Ellingham
Production: Link Hall, Susanne Hillen
Maps: Maxine Burke
Proofreading: Nikky Twyman

Acknowledgments

The authors would like to thank Jerry Swaffield, Link Hall, SoRelle Braun, Nick Thomson, Martin Dunford and Jo Mead.

Special thanks to Mark Lewis for compiling the introduction to Vietnam, Nicki McCormick for help with Pakistan, Chris Humphrey for pieces on Cambodia and Laos, and Roshan Weerasinghe for help with Sri Lanka.

Thanks also to Armen Stephen, Paul Lawlor, Barbara Unger and Yau Sang Man.

Thanks to all the following people who sent in anecdotes about their travel experiences in Asia:

Juliet Acock, Shannon Brady, Sasha Busbridge, David Crawford, Jacquelyn Dunn, Jay Golden, Daniel Gooding, Anthony Grant, Roger Hughes, Chris Humphrey, Gerry Jameson, Chris Jones, Debbie King, Peter Lawrence, Karen Christine Lefere, Greg Lief, Laura Littwin, Geronimo Madrid, Colum McAndrew, Nicki McCormick, Shawn McElravy, Jo Mead, Nicole Meyer, Luke Mich, Rosemary Natrajan, Neil Poulter, Aaron Pryce, Xanthe Robinson, Nathalie Salm, Paul Souders, Andrea Szyper, Samantha Tasker, Chris Taylor, Jonathan Tucker, Ross Velton and Bob Williams.

This first edition published October 1998 by Rough Guides Ltd
62–70 Shorts Gardens, London WC2H 9AB
375 Hudson Street, New York 10014
Internet: mail@roughguides.co.uk

Distributed by The Penguin Group
Penguin Books Ltd, 27 Wrights Lane, London W8 5TZ
Penguin Books USA Inc., 375 Hudson Street, New York 10014
Penguin Books Canada Ltd, 10 Alcorn Avenue, Toronto, Ontario MV4 1E4
Penguin Books Australia Ltd, PO Box 257, Ringwood, Victoria 3134
Penguin Books (NZ) Ltd, 182–190 Wairau Road, Auckland 10

Cover pictures Front cover: top right Floating Market, Bangkok, Thailand; bottom right Taj Mahal, Agra, India; bottom left and spine Swayambhu, Kathmandu, Nepal; top left Beach, Maldives. Back cover: top Great Wall of China.

Typeset in RoughSerif and RoughSans to an original design by Henry Iles. Printed in England by Clays Ltd, St Ives PLC

336 pages; includes index
A catalogue record for this book is available from the British Library
ISBN 1-85828-332-9

First-Time
ASIA

A ROUGH GUIDE SPECIAL

Written by

Lucy Ridout and Lesley Reader

with illustrations by

Jerry Swaffield

THE ROUGH GUIDES

TRAVEL GUIDES • PHRASEBOOKS • MUSIC AND REFERENCE GUIDES

 We set out to do something different when the first Rough Guide was published in 1982. Mark Ellingham, just out of university, was travelling in Greece. He brought along the popular guides of the day, but found they were all lacking in some way. They were either strong on ruins and museums but went on for pages without mentioning a beach or taverna. Or they were so conscious of the need to save money that they lost sight of Greece's cultural and historical significance. Also, none of the books told him anything about Greece's contemporary life – its politics, its culture, its people, and how they lived.

So with no job in prospect, Mark decided to write his own guidebook, one which aimed to provide practical information that was second to none, detailing the best beaches and the hottest clubs and restaurants, while also giving hard-hitting accounts of every sight, both famous and obscure, and providing up-to-the-minute information on contemporary culture. It was a guide that encouraged independent travellers to find the best of Greece, and was a great success, getting shortlisted for the Thomas Cook travel guide award, and encouraging Mark, along with three friends, to expand the series.

The Rough Guide list grew rapidly and the letters flooded in, indicating a much broader readership than had been anticipated, but one which uniformly appreciated the Rough Guide mix of practical detail and humour, irreverence and enthusiasm. Things haven't changed. The same four friends who began the series are still the caretakers of the Rough Guide mission today: to provide the most reliable, up-to-date and entertaining information to independent-minded travellers of all ages, on all budgets.

We now publish 100 titles and have offices in London and New York. The travel guides are written and researched by a dedicated team of more than 100 authors, based in Britain, Europe, the USA and Australia. We have also created a unique series of phrasebooks to accompany the travel series, along with an acclaimed series of music guides, and a best-selling pocket guide to the Internet and World Wide Web. We also publish comprehensive travel information on our Web site:

http://www.roughguides.com

THE AUTHORS OF FIRST-TIME ASIA

Lucy Ridout has spent much of the last decade in Asia. She lived in Japan for three years, teaching English to high-school children and working as an editor on a monthly listings magazine. Since then she has travelled widely in India and Southeast Asia, both for pleasure and as a researcher and author for several guidebooks. She is co-author of Rough Guides to Thailand, Bangkok, Bali and Lombok, and has also contributed to books on England and Europe.

Lesley Reader has lived and worked in Bhutan and Thailand and travelled extensively throughout Asia. She is co-author of Rough Guides to Bali and Lombok, and to Indonesia. She has also contributed to the *Rough Guide to China* and to *More Women Travel*, an anthology of travel tales from a woman's perspective.

HELP US UPDATE

We've gone to a lot of effort to ensure that *First-Time Asia* is accurate and up-to-date. However, things do change and if you feel we've got it wrong or left something out we'd like to know. In addition, we'd love to hear your Asian travel anecdotes and tips for possible inclusion in the next edition. We'll credit all contributions and send a copy of the next edition (or any other Rough Guide, if you prefer) for those we include. Please mark letters "First-Time Asia Update" and send to:

Rough Guides, 62–70 Shorts Gardens, London WC2H 9AB

or Rough Guides, 375 Hudson St, 9th floor, New York NY 10014.

Or send email to: *mail@roughguides.co.uk*

Online updates about this book can be found on Rough Guides' Web site *http://www.roughguides.com*

CONTENTS

THE BASICS

INTRODUCTION

Every year, millions of visitors set off on their own Asian adventure. Some want to see for themselves a few of the world's greatest monuments – to stroll along the Great Wall of China or stand beside India's Taj Mahal. Others are drawn by the scenery – the soaring Himalayas and the chance of viewing Everest at close quarters; the kaleidoscopic coral reefs of Southeast Asia, where you'll find yourself swimming amongst sharks, manta rays and turtles; the steamy jungles of Malaysia and Indonesia with the prospect of spotting orang-utans, elephants, even tigers. Few people would say no to a week or two on the dazzling white-sand beaches of the Philippines or pass up the chance to watch the sunrise over the Khyber Pass.

But perhaps the greatest draw is the sheer vitality of daily life in Asia, much of it played out on the streets. You can watch Thai boxing in Bangkok and trance dances in Bali; learn yoga in India and drink rice whisky in Vientiane; eat dim sum in Shanghai and satay sticks in Penang; buy silver in Mandalay and bargain for mangosteens in Manila.

Nearly all these things are affordable even for low-budget travellers, because most of Asia is enticingly inexpensive. Western money goes much further here than it does in Africa or South America. Not surprisingly, this has put

Asia firmly at the heart of the backpackers' trail, and many cities and islands already boast a lively travellers' scene, attracting young adventurers from all over the world. Few travellers leave Asia without experiencing at least one of its fabled hot spots: the beaches of Goa, for example, the guest houses of Kathmandu, or one of Thailand's notorious full-moon parties.

●●

FIRST IMPRESSIONS

I flew into Bangkok from Calcutta. I remember the light, diffuse and glowing, and the smells – exhaust fumes, jasmine, and garlic edged with chilli. I checked into *Charlie's Guest House*, sat downstairs and ordered fried chicken and chillis with rice. It was late afternoon and tuk tuks screamed past on the street. And just like that, in a revelatory moment, I was in love with Southeast Asia.

Chris Taylor

●●

However, Asian travel can also be a shocking and sobering experience. Few people forget their first sight of a shantytown slum or their first encounter with an amputee begging for small coins. Many first-timers are distressed by the dirt, the squalor, and the lingering smell of garbage and drains in some Asian cities. They get unnerved by the ever-present crowds and stressed out by never being able to mingle unnoticed amongst them. And then there's the oppressive heat to cope with, not to mention the unfamiliar food and often unfathomable local customs. There's no such thing as a hassle-free trip and, on reflection, few travellers would want that. It's often the dramas and surprises that make the best experiences, and we all learn by our mistakes.

Preparing for the big adventure

We've both made plenty of mistakes and faux pas during our fifteen years of travels in Asia, and this book is a distillation of what we've learnt. *First-Time Asia* is full of the advice we give to friends heading out to Asia for the first time, and it's the book we both could have done with before setting off on our own first trips. Since then we've returned again and again, backpacking across India, China and Southeast Asia, living and working in the Himalayas, Thailand and Japan, and researching and writing guidebooks to Indonesia, Thailand and Tibet. And we still choose to go back to Asia for our holidays, attracted by the chaos and drama of daily lives that still seem extraordinary to us; by the food, the landscapes and the climate; by the generosity and friendship of the people; and by the sheer buzz we get from hanging out in cultures that are so different from our own.

This book is intended to prepare you for your big adventure, whether it's a fortnight in Malaysia or twelve months across the continent. It is not a guidebook: it's a book to read before you go, a planning handbook to help you make decisons about where to go and which ticket to buy; to advise on what gear to pack and how long you can afford to stay away; and to fill you in on some of the highs and lows that lie in store. And, because we can't pretend to have explored every single corner of Asia ourselves, we've also included tips, advice and funny stories from lots of other travellers. We can't guarantee that you'll avoid every problem on the road, but we can prepare you for the unfamiliar and steer you past many common frustrations. And, when you come back from your trip, be sure to send in your own anecdotes for inclusion in the next edition. We can promise you'll have plenty of great stories to tell.

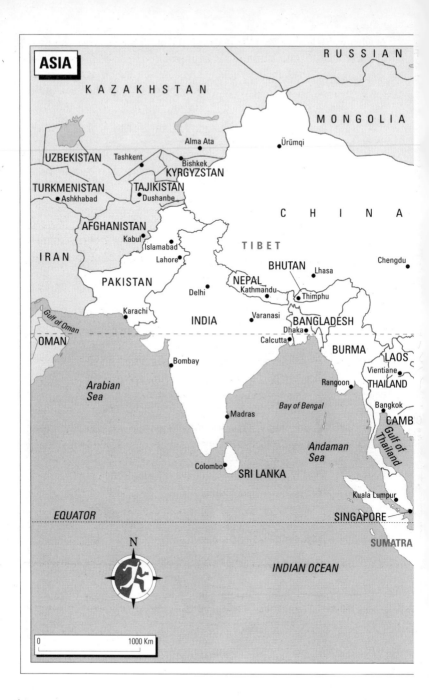

ASIA

RUSSIAN

KAZAKHSTAN

MONGOLIA

UZBEKISTAN   Tashkent   • Alma Ata   • Ürümqi

• Bishkek
KYRGYZSTAN

TURKMENISTAN   TAJIKISTAN

• Ashkhabad   • Dushanbe

CHINA

AFGHANISTAN

Kabul•   TIBET

IRAN   Islamabad•   Chengdu •

Lahore•   BHUTAN   Lhasa•

PAKISTAN   NEPAL   • Thimphu

Delhi•   Kathmandu

Varanasi   BANGLADESH

Karachi•   INDIA   •

Gulf of Oman   Dhaka•   BURMA

OMAN   Calcutta•   LAOS

Bombay•   Vientiane•   THAILAND

Arabian   Rangoon•

Sea   Bangkok•

Bay of Bengal   CAMB

Madras•   Gulf of Thailand

Andaman
Sea

Colombo•   SRI LANKA

Kuala Lumpur•

EQUATOR   SINGAPORE •

SUMATRA

N   INDIAN OCEAN

0   1000 Km

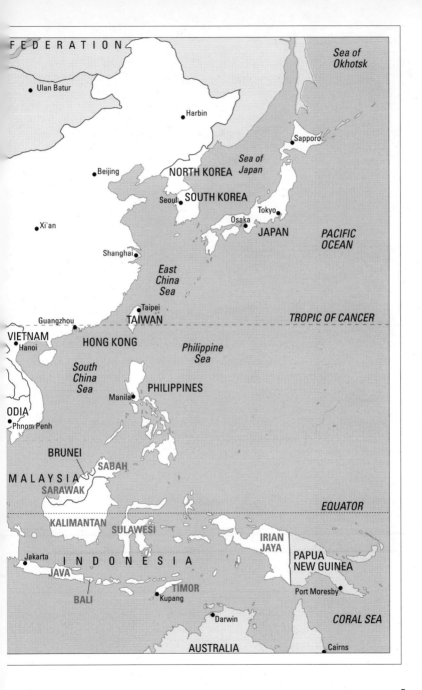

CHAPTER ONE

WHERE TO GO

How do you decide between India and China, or the Himalayas and the Indian Ocean? Would Tioman Island be more fun than Bali? Can you afford Singapore? Who goes to South Korea? Is riding the Karakoram Highway more adventurous than boating up the Yangtse? Is it still hip to head for Thailand?

Over the next few pages we've given you an opinionated taste of what the major destinations in Asia hold in store for first-timers. We've focused on the most accessible and most visited parts of Asia; in other words, the countries that welcome independent travellers. The most remote parts of the continent, north and west of Pakistan, rarely feature on first-time itineraries and so don't belong in this book. What follows is a roundup of country-by-country highlights. They are personal recommendations and generally include some major sights as well as a few little-known gems. Hopefully they'll inspire you to find out more.

The next step should be to immerse yourself in tourist brochures, travel literature, picture books, magazines and, of course, guidebooks (see Chapter Six for specific advice on that). And don't forget to talk to other travellers about their experiences, too.

BANGLADESH

With its reputation as a country of overpopulation, poverty, political instability and annual devastating floods, Bangladesh is not on many Asian itineraries. However, with extensive rivers, lush vegetation, the longest beach in the world, some fine archeological sites and excellent wildlife, the more adventurous may wish to consider it. You should expect even more attention here, especially out of Dhaka, than elsewhere in Asia – tourists are still rather rare.

Tips

◊ Try not to visit between April and September. The humid build-up to the **monsoon** is followed by torrents in June, which put large tracts of the country under water.

◊ Bangladesh is an interesting option for cyclists. Much of it is flat and the **bicycle** is as ubiquitous here as in the rest of the subcontinent. Anything which helps avoid the overcrowded and disaster-prone public transport system is a good idea.

◊ Both men and women should **dress** exceptionally modestly.

◊ Expect to be asked for **money**: the rural people are extremely poor.

Highlights

◊ **River life**. Much of the country is dominated by a huge river system. Travel by boat and see all of Bangladeshi life as you sail past.

◊ There are only two cities in the whole of Bangladesh. The population here is predominantly **rural** – a refreshing change from struggling through the mega-cities of much of Asia.

◊ The **Sunderbans** area, the last preserve of the Royal Bengal tiger, is also inhabited by crocodiles, elephants, gibbons, turtles, deer and the Ganges River dolphin.

◊ **Chittagong Hill Tracts**. An atypical area of Bangladesh with steep jungle-covered hills and tribal people from more than a dozen groups, all of whom are Buddhists of Tibeto-Burmese descent. However, be prepared: this is a restricted area and permits take ten to fourteen days to get in Dhaka.

- ◇ **Cox's Bazar**. Bangladesh's only beach resort lies within reach of other, more stunning, beaches and offshore islands.
- ◇ **Madhupur Forest**, a rare deciduous forest, is home to primates, civets and birds, and contains villages of the tribal Mandi people, originally a nomadic group from eastern India.
- ◇ **Srimangal**, centre of the tea-growing area of Sylhet, has great scenery and tea estates plus forest reserves to visit.
- ◇ **Bagerat**. Awash with historical Hindu and Muslim monuments, including the famous fifteenth-century Shait Gumbad mosque.

BURMA

Described by one commentator as "the most politically incorrect destination on earth", the question with Burma (renamed Myanmar in 1989) is not where, when and how to visit, but whether to go at all. The 26-year rule of General Ne Win (1962–1988) came to an end when the pro-democracy movement forced his resignation, only to have the military authorities refuse to accept the election results and establish their own rule over the country under the name SLORC (the State Law and Order Restoration Council).

The pro-democracy leader, Aung San Suu Kyi, who won the Nobel peace Prize for her attempts to get SLORC to see the error of their ways, used "Visit Myanmar Year" in 1996 to call for a boycott of the country by tourists and investors alike. This seems to have raised awareness, but it is uncertain whether it is having much effect on tourist figures or modifying government thinking. Clampdowns on political dissidents continue, as does confrontation with the large number of insurgent groups who are fighting for independence from Burma. In addition, the government has fairly shamelessly used forced labour from the population to build tourist infrastructure and rebuild temples, monuments and palaces.

Highlights

✧ Burma is famous for its **Buddhist pagodas**. In the capital Rangoon (Yangon is the new name, but not widely known outside the country), Shwedagon pagoda is the main draw. Probably the best known, though, is Kyaiktiyo Paya, a golden stupa perched dramatically on a cliff in the southeast of the country.

✧ The plains of **Pagan** (Bagan) have the most visited temple ruins. Nearby Salay is quieter, while those at Mrauk U, further towards the west coast, are fewer in number, but equally grand.

✧ **Mandalay** is an important centre for many Burmese crafts including puppets, tapestries, jade, silverwork and stone and wood-carving.

PUTAO

MANDALAY

•PAGAN

RANGOON

•MOULMEIN

TAVOY•

BURMA

CAMBODIA

Thanks to warring political factions, continued Khmer Rouge guerrilla activity, smuggling rackets, bandits, kidnappings and gunpoint muggings, Cambodia can be a dangerous place to travel. Consult newspapers, state department travel offices and travellers' newsgroups on the Internet (see *Basics*) before deciding to go.

If the political situation is relatively calm then your answer should probably be yes. You can restrict yourself to the safest and most popular tourist route, which involves flying in and out of Phnom Penh and Siem Reap, the town closest to Angkor. The ninth-century ruins of Angkor are utterly compelling and well worth stretching your budget for. There are plenty of cheap guest houses in these two centres, and tourists generally get a good reception from the amazingly resilient Khmer people. Most of Cambodia's other memorable sights are associated with the horrors inflicted by the murderous Khmer Rouge regime between 1975 and 1979.

As for attractions in the rest of the country – hill tribes, villages, trekking, Mekong river trips, beaches, and so on – do your homework first! Large areas of Cambodia are out of bounds to foreign travellers, and other parts are just plain scary to travel through.

Must-sees

◇ **Angkor**. You can spend several days exploring the ruined temples and palaces of this ancient Khmer city, built between the ninth and fourteenth centuries and now shrouded in jungle. Its crumbling walls, intricate carvings and phenomenal size make Angkor as spectacular and important as Machu Picchu in Peru.

◇ **Phnom Penh**. Cambodia's ravaged riverside capital is a crazy, eye-popping place to explore, with plenty of markets, temples, bars, restaurants and museums, and a small but thriving travellers' scene.

◇ **S-21 Prison**. The thousands of black-and-white mug shots of ordinary Cambodians who were tortured and killed at this former interrogation centre will stay with you for a long, long time.

CAMBODIA

- ANGKOR
- MEKONG RIVER
- PHNOM PENH
- KOMPONG SOM

◇ **The Killing Fields, Choeung Ek.** A continuation of the misery seen at S-21, this is where the torture victims were brought to be shot. The focus of the memorial here are the 8985 skulls piled high inside a huge glass stupa.

◇ **Kompong Som.** Cambodia's main beach resort offers good snorkelling and diving.

Things to avoid

◇ **Travelling by rail or road.** The railways are currently off limits to foreigners because of muggings and kidnappings. Some roads are open to foreigners, but they're not much safer.

◇ **Exploring off the beaten track in Angkor.** The place is still littered with unexploded mines.

◇ **Walking round Phnom Penh at night.** Muggings at gunpoint are not uncommon, so you're better off taking a *cyclo* (rickshaw).

CHINA

The most populous country on earth, encapsulating much of the mystique of the East, China exerts a huge pull on anyone planning a trip to Asia. Closed to Westerners for decades, its mystery is compounded by a language that is impenetrable to all but serious students. It isn't an easy country to get to know and bureaucracy is rampant. Whatever the difficulties of Asian travel, in China they're magnified tenfold – buying a train ticket can be an achievement in itself. Time, planning and a bit more than a rock-bottom budget will make your trip more enjoyable. Force yourself to make some tough

decisions about your itinerary, though – you won't see it all, even on a hundred trips, so scale down your plans and avoid too many expensive and exhausting journeys.

Star attractions

◇ **Beijing** offers China's grandest remnants of the imperial age – the Forbidden City, Temple of Heaven – and some of the only nightlife in the country.

◇ The skyline of **Hong Kong**, especially at night, is one of the modern wonders of the world. The Star Ferry is a must, the outer islands a bonus, and it's worth a visit just to marvel at the most densely populated area on the planet.

❖ **Chinese cuisine** is reason enough for a visit. Try to sample the four major traditions: Northern (featuring hotpots, Peking duck and bird's nest soup), Eastern (seafood and river-fish delicacies), Sichuan (pungent and spicy using lots of chillis) and Cantonese (which uses just about any ingredient imaginable, from guinea pig to dog).

❖ **Harbin**, in the old region of Manchuria, where Russian influences are still obvious, hosts an annual Ice Lantern Festival. This lasts a month, during January and February, with magnificent ice sculptures filling Zhaolin Park.

❖ **Xishuangbanna** in Yunnan province, a tropical area of rainforest and paddy fields along the Burmese and Laotian borders has a fascinatingly diverse ethnic population and some exciting wildlife reserves – and it's summertime here when the rest of China freezes.

❖ **Sichuan**, China's largest province, combines remote mountain scenery and the chance to see pandas in the wild with a rich Buddhist heritage embodied by the holy mountain of Emei Shan and the giant Buddha statue at Leshan.

❖ **Putuo Shan**, a quiet little Buddhist island near Shanghai, offers superb beaches, rural walks and monasteries.

Be warned

❖ The **Terracotta Army** guarding the tomb of Emperor Qin Shi Huang just outside the ancient capital city of Xi'an *is* enthralling, but the complex itself is a huge tourist circus and the city is a highly polluted manufacturing centre of five million people. Try ancient Qufu, the birthplace of Confucius, or the Song capital of Kaifeng instead, both of which have retained a more intimate scale.

❖ The scenery around **Guilin** along the Li River is some of the most magnificent in China, dominated by strangely shaped limestone hills. The town, however, is a tourist nightmare of hassle and overcharging. Head instead for Yangshuo, ninety minutes down the river. You get the same scenery, a small tourist infrastructure and the chance to enjoy it.

❖ Whilst the outside world debates the issue, the annexation of **Tibet** is a *fait accompli*. You should go – the scenery is unsurpassed and the people welcoming, yet nowhere else in China is the might of the state so apparent.

INDIA

For many travellers, India epitomizes the Asia experience. It brims over with bizarre rituals and extraordinary characters; it holds a wealth of temples, ruined cities and dramatic landscapes; and for tourists everything is bargain priced. It is also more crowded, more hassly and seems to have a greater share of poverty than its Asian neighbours.

With seven major faiths and over fifteen regional languages, India is impossible to pigeonhole. A long, slow journey from the north of the country to the south can seem like a trip across a dozen different countries. More than almost any other destination in Asia, India is a place to return to again and again and not somewhere that rewards a whistlestop tour. And, because distances are phenomenal and public transport notoriously tardy, it also makes sense to confine yourself to two or three smallish areas. Many travellers make a beeline for the beaches of Goa and Kovalam, but others head for spiritual centres like Rishikesh and Dharamsala, for the palaces of Rajasthan, or for the hiking trails in the Himalayas.

First-time visitors to India usually worry most about poor sanitation and the prospect of getting sick, but so long as you're sensible and follow the advice outlined in Chapter Twelve, you shouldn't find health is much more of an issue here than anywhere else in Asia.

Some highlights

◇ **Jaisalmer**. Built entirely of sandstone and surrounded by desert, this honey-coloured Rajasthan town makes the perfect backdrop for the fluorescent saris, flamboyant turbans and curly-toed slippers worn by its residents.

◇ The seventeen-kilometre trek to the **Gangotri Glacier**. The sacred frozen source of the River Ganges is spectacularly positioned amidst spiky snow-clad peaks at 5000m above sea level, but is fairly easily reached along a pilgrims' route.

◇ **Varkala**. Low-key travellers' beach resort with great fish barbecues, no ravers, and few hawkers.

◇ The ghostly ruins of **Hampi**, where the remains of intricately carved fourteenth-century Hindu temples lie scattered over a vast boulder-strewn area, attracting a stream of blissed-out refugees from Goa.

◇ **Shopping** – for silver earrings, Kashmiri rugs, mirrorwork furnishings and shimmering textiles.

◇ The camel races, parades and general festivities at the **Pushkar Camel Fair**, held every October/November (see Chapter Four for details).

INDIA

DELHI •

• AGRA

VARANASI

CALCUTTA •

BOMBAY •

GOA •

• MADRAS

◇ The sacred ghats of **Varanasi**. Watch the sun rise and set over the River Ganges, and observe pilgrims immersing themselves in the waters and cremating their dead on the banks.

◇ A visit to the **crafts museum** in Delhi will really whet your appetite for the rest of the country. You'll find some of India's most unusual arts and crafts in this big outdoor compound – and they're all displayed in reconstructions of traditional Indian homes, from simple mud huts to intricately carved wooden palaces.

◇ **Conversations on trains**. Educated Indians love to discuss world affairs with tourists and, uniquely in Asia, they enjoy doing so in English.

Worth investigating

◇ **Calcutta**. This famously warm-hearted and literary city has dozens of bookshops and a reputation for intellectual liveliness, which makes it a stimulatingly relaxed place to hang out.

◇ **Chai**. Horribly sweet and milky, Indian tea is nonetheless invigorating and strangely addictive.

◇ **Christmas on Anjuna beach**. Thousands of European clubbers, round-the-world backpackers and expat techno-heads converge on Anjuna, the most alternative of Goa's numerous beach resorts, for the biggest beachfront raves of the year.

The jury's out on . . .

◇ **Boating through the Kerala backwaters.** The famous tourist boat rides are uninspired and, at eight hours, far too long. It's much better to take the local ferry bus, which winds through narrower waterways, gives you intriguing glimpses into riverside homes, and takes less than three hours.

◇ **Hindi films**. At least three hours long and peppered with ludicrous song-and-dance sequences, but they make perfect distractions on long bus journeys (unless you're trying to sleep).

◇ **Dharma bums**. You may or may not be eager to hear – for the tenth time – your new chum's account of his most awesome spiritual experience.

◇ **Sikkim**. Though this remote Himalayan kingdom sounds intriguingly similar to nearby Bhutan (which is closed to independent tourists), Sikkim feels disappointingly akin to other parts of India.

INDONESIA

The fabulously varied scenery (from equatorial rainforest and volcanoes to idyllic white-sand beaches and desert terrain), the equally diverse flora and fauna, and generally friendly and welcoming people make Indonesia one of the most rewarding Asian destinations. However, as the largest archipelago in the world with more than thirteen thousand islands, you're best advised to restrict yourself to certain areas or fly between your main destinations. With too little time and too much travel your trip could turn into a miserable, stressful race between islands and along ghastly roads.

Sumatra

✧ Indonesia's largest island, 2000km from end to end, has everything from mountains, lakes and orang-utans to culturally distinct ethnic groups and surfing. It's big enough that you can get off the tourist trail very easily. However, Western women can experience unpleasant harassment in some areas, and during Ramadan this strictly Muslim island observes the rules carefully.

Java

◇ The most populous and affluent island, Java is home to the capital, Jakarta. In its cultural centres, Yogyakarta and Solo, you can take courses in traditional dance, music and batik., while Bromo is one of Indonesia's most amazing volcanoes, and Borobodur one of the country's most spectacular Buddhist monuments. Beware the Yogyakarta touts, however, who are some of the worst in Southeast Asia, especially at the train station. The island is simply too crowded.

Bali

◇ Long the jewel in the Indonesian tourist industry crown, Bali now gets around one and a quarter million tourists each year to soak up its beaches, volcanoes, temples, stunning scenery and cultural wealth. You'll find a full range of tourist facilities in every price bracket here. Be aware that the southern areas, including the infamous Kuta Beach, are extremely developed with resultant hassles and a significant gigolo scene.

Nusa Tenggara

◇ This chain of islands stretches between Bali and Irian Jaya. The most westerly, Lombok, is developing a significant tourist industry to cope with the Bali overspill, but the further east you

SULAWESI

MALUKU

IRIAN JAYA

FLORES

TIMOR

WHERE TO GO

go, the less tourist infrastructure there is, the rougher the travel and the more time you'll need. Highlights include Sumba's unspoilt beaches and traditional ikat weaving, Komodo's lizard dragons and the coloured lakes of Flores. East Timor, at the furthest end of the chain is the scene of Indonesian government might at its most repressive.

Kalimantan

✧ The Indonesian bit of the island that also comprises Sabah, Sarawak and Brunei, this is the land of jungles, rivers, extraordinary wildlife and oil towns. Travel here requires time and money. Highlights include the orang-utan rehabilitation centre at Tanjung Puting; however, logging and recent forest fires have decimated vast tracts of jungle.

Sulawesi

✧ Tortured in shape and rough for land travel, Sulawesi has a developing tourist industry based around the central highlands of Tanah Toraja and the spectacular dive sites off Manado in the north. The Christian Torajan people are known for their distinctive architecture and burial practices, but avoid visiting in July and August when the Toraja areas get very crowded with tourists.

Maluku

✧ The fabled Spice Islands, numbering over 1000, are spread out across a vast area of ocean. Most visitors stick to Ambon and the Banda Islands as inter-island transport can be expensive and time-consuming. Some of the country's most recently established diving and snorkelling sites are here as well as many of the country's best beaches.

Irian Jaya

✧ Innumerable tribes inhabit the interior, much of it thick jungle inaccessible except by boat and plane. Independence fighters are still struggling against Indonesia here, travel is highly controlled and visitors need a permit to visit many areas. The scenery and people of the Baliem Valley (the most popular tourist area) live up to all expectations.

JAPAN

Beneath the hi-tech veneer, Japan is still a very traditional society and culturally there's heaps to investigate, from Zen temples to fire festivals, and tea ceremonies to sumo wrestling matches. There's good hiking too – in the Japan Alps, in the mountains, gorges and lakes of Hokkaido, and in the dozens of national parks.

Tourists are rare outside the main cultural centres and are welcomed warmly. Language is a problem, but communication is usually possible. Public transport is fast, efficient and extensive and hitching is quite easy.

Very few backpackers make it to Japan, however, for the simple reason that they can't afford it. The standard of living is so high that one of the best ways to experience the country is to get an English-teaching job here for a few months; see Chapter Five for advice. Otherwise, buy a train pass, bring a tent and don't hang out in too many coffee shops or pinball parlours.

Highlights

◇ **Kyoto**. Japan's loveliest historic city has Buddhist temples, Zen gardens, wooden houses, geisha girls, traditional theatre performances, good clubs and restaurants, as well as hill-walking on the outskirts.

◇ **The Kodo drum festival on Sado Island**. The world music and dance event held over three days every summer makes the perfect excuse to visit this remote island.

◇ **Nikko**. Set in a huge forested park of mountains, lakes and waterfalls, this complex of elaborately carved and gaudily painted shrines and temples looks especially fantastical in the snow.

◇ **Hiroshima Peace Museum** – sober and moving.

◇ **Ryoanji Zen garden, Kyoto**. You'll be amazed how inspiring a stretch of gravel and a few strategically positioned rocks can be. Abstract philosphical art at its best.

◇ **Traditional inns** (*ryokan*). Rooms have tatami mat floors, sumptuous futons, sliding paper doors and views onto traditional Japanese gardens.

♦ A few days' walking in **Kirishima National Park**, which boasts the most dramatic volcanic scenery in the country – 23 peaks in all. There are plenty of bracing mountain trails, plus waterfalls, an impressive gorge and an outdoor hot spring.

♦ **Hot saké**. After a hard day's temple-spotting, a carafe of warm rice wine, drunk from an egg cup, will restore your inner fire very quickly.

♦ Every park and garden looks great **during cherry blossom time and maple leaf season** (see Chapter Four for details).

Lowlights

♦ **Climbing Mount Fuji**. Due to persistent haze, the views are rarely spectacular, the mountainside is strewn with unattractive volcanic debris, and the tracks are always heaving with hikers.

♦ Being **hassled for your photograph** by crowds of Japanese schoolchildren at almost every major sight. It's fun and flattering the first few times, but soon becomes very irritating.

♦ Watching the **Japanese rockabillies** gather in Harajuku at weekends. The tourist literature makes a big fuss about this spectacle, but actually it's just a group of bored Tokyo kids who like to dress up as Elvis.

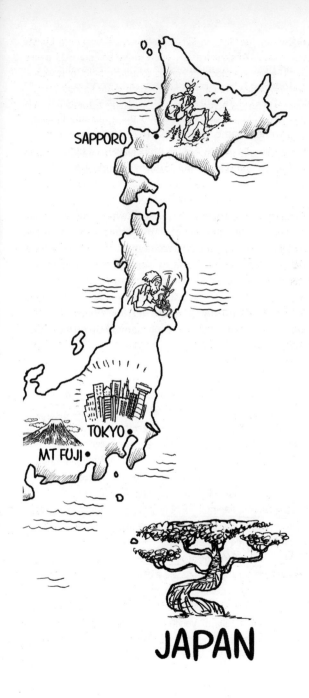

SAPPORO •

TOKYO •

MT FUJI •

JAPAN

LAOS

With no beaches, unmemorable food, and few historical gems to write home about, Laos is not everyone's idea of a great holiday destination. The country's appeal lies largely in its easy-going, unhurried pace of daily life, and most travellers come here simply to rest and take time out before resuming more hectic itineraries in neighbouring Vietnam, Thailand or China. And, with less than five million people living in an area the size of Great Britain, there's plenty of space to relax in.

Because tourists have only been allowed into Laos since 1989, you get a real sense of unadulterated Southeast Asia here, quite different from the melting-pot cultures of Thailand and Vietnam. Hardly anyone speaks English, though you should be able to get by in French, and there are few tourist facilities outside Vientiane and Luang Prabang. Travelling through the rest of Laos is hard, not least because of the bad roads, but for many people that's part of the appeal.

Highlights

◇ Strolling through the outskirts of **Luang Prabang** and admiring the ancient capital's golden spires from a distance.

◇ **Cruising the mighty Mekong**. Any trip up Southeast Asia's biggest river will take you through great scenery, but if you want a focus for your meanderings, head for the riverside Pak Ou caves which are packed full of Buddha images.

◇ **The morning market at Muang Sing**. This remote northwest town is the trading post for at least six different local hill tribes, and the best time to admire their wares – and their outfits – is at 6am in the marketplace.

◇ Eating out in **Vientiane**. The bakeries, fruit-juice bars, Laotian, Thai and Indian restaurants are a definite bonus after the poor-quality food you get in other parts of Laos.

◇ **Being a novelty.** Because tourists are far rarer in Laos than in Vietnam or Thailand, you'll get an enthusiastic reception nearly everywhere you go – and lots of waving and smiling practice.

◇ **Sinhs**. These traditionally woven cotton and silk wraparound skirts are worn by almost every woman in Laos. They're colourful, flattering, and inexpensive and one of the best souvenirs you can pick up.

◇ Flying from Vientiane to **the Plain of Jars**. You may not be that stimulated by the hundreds of mysterious two-thousand-year-old stone pots that lie scattered across the uplands of Xieng Khuang. But you will certainly be gripped by the view from the plane window as you fly over dramatic karst scenery and some of the most scarred landscape in Laos – the result of relentless bombing, mostly by the Americans, in the 1964–73 war.

Dangers and annoyances

◇ **Travelling by road**. Lao roads are buttock-crunchingly potholed and definitely don't make for a comfortable ride; worse still, bandits render some roads too dangerous for tourists to use.

◇ Finding a bed in **Udom Xai**, where guest-house managers have a habit of pretending they're full, when they're blatantly not.

MALAYSIA

An ideal destination for first-time overlanders, Peninsular Malaysia has good transport connections with Thailand, Singapore and Sumatra, and a well-developed tourist infrastructure. Most visitors head for the beaches, particularly on Tioman and Langkawi islands, as the cultural attractions are less interesting than in Thailand or Indonesia.

Thickly forested East Malaysia (Sabah and Sarawak) is a much more adventurous destination: travel here is mainly by river and visits to tribal longhouses are a major feature. Most travellers to Sabah attempt a climb up Mount Kinabalu.

Things to do

◇ Hang out on the peaceful island of **Perhentian Besar**, whose shoreline reefs are perfect for snorkelling.
◇ Trek for nine days through the remote rainforested ridges of **Taman Negara National Park**, camping out every night and finishing with the hike to the summit of Gunung Tahan.

- ◇ Chill out in **Cherating**. Hippie-ish, low-key travellers' beach resort with village-style accommodation in huts on stilts.
- ◇ **Ride the jungle railway**. A fourteen-hour meander through the mountainous landscapes of the peninsula's jungle interior.
- ◇ Watch the baby orang-utans learning to swing and swagger at **Sepilok Orang-Utan Rehabilitation Centre**.
- ◇ Admire the sunrise over the jungle from the summit of **Mount Kinabalu**. The perfect climax to the day-and-a-half's climb up Southeast Asia's highest mountain (4101m).
- ◇ **Take a longboat up the Baleh River** and spend the night at the traditional longhouse of the Kenyah people.
- ◇ Consider a makeover at **the Museum of Enduring Beauty** in Melaka. Gruesome, but gripping, exhibitions on worldwide trends in tattooing, body-piercing, foot-binding, body-stretching, cosmetic surgery and scarring.
- ◇ Pig out at **the night market in Kota Bahru**. Gorge yourself on freshly barbecued chicken in coconut sauce, fried purple rice, banana pancakes and sugar-cane juice at the nightly gathering of hawker stalls.

NEPAL

Sandwiched between Tibet and India, Nepal contains a huge stretch of the Himalayas, the highest mountain range in the world. Trekking is the main draw, but other attractions include Kathmandu, the ex-hippie-trail capital of the East, Buddhist and Hindu festivals, tigers and rhinos in the wildlife reserves of the south, and whitewater rafting on the Trisuli River. Many visitors also come in pursuit of bodily calm and spiritual truth. There are plenty of practitioners of massage, Ayurvedic and Tibetan medicine and astrology, plus courses in meditation and yoga.

As one of the poorest countries in the world, Nepal is tackling a population explosion and experiencing enormous environmental degradation. Ever-expanding tourism provides an important source of foreign

exchange, but has also added to the problems, especially the deforestation of much-tramped treks.

Top treks

◇ **Annapurna**. Sixty percent of all trekking permits are issued for this area, which includes nine mountain peaks over 7000m. The most popular treks are both moderate to strenuous: the Annapurna Sanctuary at nine to twelve days, and Annapurna Circuit at sixteen to twenty-one days.

◇ **Jomsom**. Despite being highly commercialized there is a huge variety of scenery and plenty of small, ethnically diverse villages along the route. The full trek takes around fourteen days, but there are several shorter options.

◇ **Everest treks**, which get you close to the fabled peak, are very strenuous and unless you fly in one direction you'll need to allow three or four weeks of walking.

NEPAL

KATHMANDU   MT EVEREST

CHITWAN

BIRATNAGAR

PAKISTAN

Relatively few tourists make it to Pakistan, but those that do generally describe the feel of the place as either being like Nepal without the crowds, or like India without the hassles. Most overland routes between Europe and Asia pass through Pakistan, but the country has many attractions in its own right, including spectacular mountain and desert landscapes, ancient ruins and fabulous mosques.

Travellers generally head for the north, either along the Karakoram Highway and its offshoots, or west to Peshawar, the Khyber Pass and Chitral. Hiking and trekking in Hunza and Gilgit are the most popular activities. Parts of the south – including Karachi and the whole of the Sind region – are currently considered too dangerous to visit, but safety shouldn't be a problem elsewhere.

PAKISTAN

DARRA

ISLAMABAD

QUETTA

LAHORE

KARACHI

The tourist industry is embryonic: facilities are basic (hot water and 24hr electricity are luxuries), but inexpensive; trains and buses are generally slow and can be uncomfortable. English is spoken by most educated Pakistanis, and foreigners who respect the local culture are warmly welcomed as honoured guests. Women should dress appropriately for a Muslim country, in long loose clothes.

Things to do

◇ Go hiking in the **Hunza Valley**. There are hundreds of enticing trails along the irrigation channels up to fortified villages. Next morning, watch the sun rise over Rakaposhi and the entire valley from a rocky vantage point above Altit village.

◇ Take **a flight from Gilgit to Skardu**. On this route, the plane flies between rather than above the peaks, so you get fantastic views – especially as the pilots are only allowed to fly in fine weather.

◇ Accept the inevitable invitation to test fire home-made **kalashnikovs** in Darra, centre of illicit arms manufacture near the Khyber Pass.

◇ Go **whitewater rafting** along the River Indus.

◇ Hang out in **Lahore**. Pakistan's cultural capital offers a stimulating mix of parks, bazaars, museums, forts and mosques.

◇ Do some bargain-hunting in **Quetta's bazaars**. Marble, onyx and carpets are all good buys.

◇ Spend an afternoon at a **polo match** – much more raucous than it sounds.

◇ Restore yourself in the healing waters of the **Garma Chasma hot springs**.

Not recommended

◇ **Karachi**. Ongoing ethnic and sectarian violence make this a scary and dangerous place. Avoid it.

◇ **Smugglers' Bazaar in Peshawar**. Despite its romantic name, this turns out to be a disappointingly Westernized complex of late twentieth-century shopping malls. Come here for hi-fi equipment, not spices and bejewelled curios.

PHILIPPINES

Easy-going and inexpensive, the Philippines is a major outdoors destination, with world-class – and good-value – diving off nearly all its seven thousand islands, plenty of white-sand beaches, and hundreds of hiking trails across its lush volcanic terrain. Because of its colonial history and Catholic heritage, there's less cultural stimulation here than in Indonesia and Thailand but, on the plus side, English is widely spoken, the food tastes comfortingly familiar, and the transport system is generally easy to fathom. Despite all that, it's still a relatively unusual backpackers' destination, mainly because you can't get here overland.

Highlights

✧ The **sculpted rice terraces** of Ifugao Province. A stunning landscape of mountains, steep-sided valleys, rivers and waterfalls.

✧ **Diving** among the spectacular walls, drop-offs and coral arches off Moalboal, and joining hammerhead sharks and manta rays near Cabilao Island.

✧ The eight-kilometre boat ride through the spooky, bat-infested caves of the underground river in **Saint Paul Subterranean National Park**. Plenty of above-ground attractions too, including jungle hiking, snorkelling and wildlife watching.

✧ Sunrise and sunset over the **Chocolate Hills**, a cluster of more than a thousand limestone mounds in a karst-like landscape.

✧ Sundays at **Manila's Chinese cemetery**. Literally a ghost town, this cemetery has streets and two-storey houses for the departed, many of them furnished with kitchens, bathrooms, electricity and air-con. On Sundays relatives come to the houses to picnic and do the housekeeping.

✧ **Jeepney art**. The elongated jeeps used to ferry people around cities are painted up with gaudy cartoons, pious sayings, religious images and plenty of glittering mirrorwork.

✧ The **exuberant Filipino attitude** to life, once summed up as "that rare blend of Asian grace and Latin fire".

✧ The exceptionally sweet and succulent *lanzone* (lychee) fruits of Camiguin Island. And, while you're there, explore the island's volcanoes, waterfalls, sugar-fine beaches and coral reefs.

PHILIPPINES

SINGAPORE

As *the* transport hub for Southeast Asia, most visitors to the region pass through modern, gleaming Singapore at some point. It isn't cheap, though, and anyone on a tight budget should try to stay as short a time as possible. While many will love the orderly efficiency of the place after a few weeks in wilder parts, others miss the feel of "real" Asia among the high-rises, shopping centres, seamless transport systems and booming economy. However, this is the Asia that most Asians and Asian nations aspire to.

Tips

◇ Make sure you follow the **regulations** for survival in Singapore: don't bring in any chewing gum, don't jaywalk and always flush the toilet after use – heavy fines are meted out to those who disobey. It's easy to mock, but there is no doubt that Singapore is a relatively well-ordered and safe environment both day and night for residents and foreigners alike.

◇ Check if your visit coincides with a **Chinese festival** (such as New Year, Qing Ming, the Moon Cake Festival, the Dragon Boat Festival) or with a Hindu one (Deepavali, Navarathiri, Thimithi), when the island is at its colourful best.

Highlights

❖ The remaining ethnic enclaves of **Chinatown, Arab Street and Little India** are relatively untouched by modern development, although towered over by the new Singapore skyline. The Chinese and Hindu temples are especially atmospheric and picturesque.

❖ Take a trip on the **river** for the cooling breeze, the old colonial sights and to get a glimpse of one of the busiest ports in Asia from sea level.

❖ Singapore's **zoo** is a shining example of the best of such places, offering an after-dark **Night Safari** for viewing nocturnal animals.

❖ **Food**. Head for the hawker stalls and food courts. The surroundings may be pretty uninspiring, but the range of ethnic cuisines on offer is amazing. If you're missing more familiar tastes, Singapore offers everything from Italian and French to Mexican. In addition, American coffee bar chains have hit the city big time.

❖ The **Gateway Building**, the work of architect I.M. Pei, who seems to specialize in dramatic one-dimensional-looking skyscrapers (the Bank of China Building in Hong Kong is another).

❖ **Bukit Timah Hill**, Singapore's highest, is home to the island's last pocket of primary rainforest. Look out for macaques, butterflies and flying lemurs.

❖ Travelling anywhere on **public transport**. The government does everything it can to deter car ownership and usage, and Singapore's public transport system is clean, fast and efficient, placing pretty much the entire island within easy reach. Even taxis are reasonably priced and all vehicles have meters.

Overrated

❖ A visit to **Raffles Hotel** is considered a must for tourists. However, much of the site has been turned into a shopping arcade, the more luxurious areas of the hotel are reserved for residents only and a Singapore sling in the bar costs more than a night in one of the city's budget guest houses.

❖ **Shopping**, or at least cruising the shopping centres, is the number-one Singaporean hobby. If you're on a wider trip through Asia, though, you'll usually get better prices elsewhere.

SOUTH KOREA

Overshadowed as a tourist destination by neighbouring China and Japan, South Korea features on backpackers' itineraries more as a place to find work than as somewhere to explore for its own sake. English-teaching jobs are fairly easy to land in Seoul and Pusan (check the local English-language newspapers), and the cost of living is less prohibitive than in Japan. The most popular sights are traditional Buddhist temples, but South Korea's chief attractions are its thousands of hiking trails through the forests of the mountainous national parks.

Some recommendations

◇ Hiking through Sorak-San National Park into **Inner Sorak**, a tranquil stretch of forested peaks, rivers, waterfalls and temples.

◇ **Kyongju**. Korea's ancient capital holds abundant relics of its two-thousand-year history, including fifth-century tombs, a seventh-century stone observatory, royal gardens, pagodas and temples.

◇ **Autumn**. Huge swaths of South Korea's forests turn a fiery red in late October, making this the best time to visit.

◇ The fifteenth-century village of **Yangdong**, where villagers are forbidden to modify or knock down their 500-year-old wooden houses.

◇ The three-hour **boat ride from Pusan to Yeosu**, with fine views of the crenellated coastline.

◇ The **Buddha's Birthday** in May is memorably celebrated at Pomo-Sa temple, when local people parade up to the temple carrying paper lanterns.

◇ **Chinju**. This small friendly town has an impressive old castle and some of the best night-time food stalls in the country.

◇ **Lacquer boxes**. A Korean speciality, these are exquisitely crafted with mother-of-pearl inlays.

Take a rain-check on . . .

◇ The North Korean border at **Panmunjom**. The most interesting thing about the view of North Korea is that – surprise, surprise

– the landscape looks just like South Korea. Nonetheless the place attracts busloads of tourists, all of whom are required to dress smartly (no jeans or T-shirts) and, if male, to have respectably short hair!

◇ **Weekend expeditions**. Try to avoid major sights, national parks and hiking trails at weekends, when you'll be competing for space with thousands of city dwellers.

◇ **Kimchi**. Korea's national dish is a fiery pickle made from fermented cabbage, garlic, ginger and chilli that is served with everything. Definitely an acquired taste.

SOUTH KOREA

PANMUNJOM

SORAK-SAN
NATIONAL PARK

SEOUL

KYONGJU

PUSAN

SRI LANKA

Sri Lanka is calmer and more manageable than its chaotic neighbour, India. Colombo is the only city, and the rest of the island is dominated by cool hills – ideal for walks, spectacular views and chilling out – and huge tracts of rainforest where you have a very good chance of seeing wild elephants. Birds like it here, too, and many species spend the winter on Sri Lanka's southern coasts before returning to more temperate zones. The beaches are quite lovely, and the island is dotted with ruins from ancient Buddhist empires.

However, Sri Lanka is also plagued by a violent religious and ethnic conflict, a civil war between the Tamil minority and the Sinhalese majority that has been raging here since the mid-1980s. For visitors this means that the disputed territories, which essentially cover the whole of north and east Sri Lanka, are too dangerous to visit. The possibility of terrorist attacks in Colombo as well has seriously dented the tourist industry. A good number of travellers do still come here, however, confining themselves to the south and the west. Check with embassies, newspapers and travellers' newsgroups on the Internet before making up your own mind (see *Basics*).

Highlights

◇ Sunrise over **World's End**, a viewpoint over a 2000-metre drop, from where you can admire the clouds several hundred metres below your feet.

◇ **Mirissa**. This tiny sandy beach is always peaceful and has just a couple of guest houses on its palm-fringed shore.

◇ Being the 1997 World One Day Cricket Champions, the Sri Lankans are **cricket** mad and there's often a foreign side on tour. Go to a match and experience the wild atmosphere and loud, exuberant crowd.

◇ Feeding time for the babies at **Pinnawela Elephant Orphanage**.

◇ The **flamingos** of Bundala National Park. From January to April, thousands of flamingos crowd the park's lagoons and wetlands.

SRI LANKA

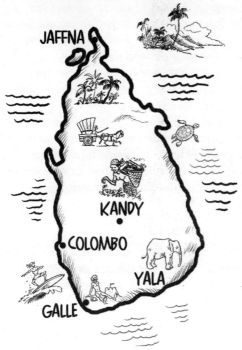

- ◇ **Kandy.** Sri Lanka's cultural capital is set beside a lake in the hills and makes an ideal place to hang out and cool down.
- ◇ The ruined palace of **Sigiriya**, a fifth-century fortress built on top of a massive 200-metre-high granite monolith. Water gardens have been gouged from the summit of the rock and there are fifth-century rock paintings here as well.

Think twice about . . .

- ◇ Going elephant-spotting in **Yala National Park**. You're likely to see more tourist jeeps than elephants in this over-visited park.
- ◇ Swimming very far from the shore. Because of its location right at the tip of the subcontinent, Sri Lanka's coast has fearsome **currents and undertows**, which claim several tourists every year.

THAILAND

The perfect place to start a cross-Asia trip, Thailand is relatively easy to deal with and an inexpensive place to travel in. It has a well-established tourist infrastructure, with good transport links, plenty of backpacker-oriented guest houses and a thriving travellers' scene. Hard-core travellers dislike the place for those very reasons, considering it too easy, too popular, and over-explored – in short, not cool enough.

Bumming around on tropical beaches is the most popular activity, with jungle trekking a close second. There are also plenty of temples to explore, some fine historical ruins and swaths of intact rainforest. English is spoken by Thais working in the tourist industry, but not off the beaten track.

Highlights

◇ The Thailand **beach** experience: Ko Samui for resort attractions, Ko Pha Ngan for raves and chill-outs, Ko Phi Phi for spectacular scenery, Ko Lanta for solitary sunbathes, and Ko Samet for an easy break from the city.

◇ Sleeping in a treehouse under the limestone karsts of **Khao Sok National Park**, waking to the sound of hooting gibbons, and spending the day at the park's eleven-tiered waterfall.

◇ The ancient Khmer temple of **Phanom Rung**. This exquisite pink sandstone complex was built in the tenth century as a blueprint for Angkor Wat across the border in Cambodia.

◇ Having a **traditional Thai massage** at Bangkok's Wat Po temple.

◇ Snorkelling and diving off the remote **Similan Islands**. Turquoise water, powdery sand, banks of coral, plus sharks, rays and turtles.

◇ **The food**. Pungently laced with chilli and delicately flavoured with lemongrass and coconut; your stir-fries will never be the same again.

Hot tips

◇ Instead of **trekking** the hugely oversubscribed routes from Chiang Mai and Chiang Rai, start your hike from Mae Hong

Son, Kanchanaburi or Umpang instead; trails are quieter and more rewarding.

◇ Travel by boat in **Bangkok**. To cross Bangkok in a bus you need three hours and a gas mask – ferries and canal boats are faster and a lot more scenic.

VIETNAM

Currently one of Southeast Asia's hippest destinations, Vietnam arouses in visitors an edge of excitement that Malaysia and Thailand are increasingly hard-pressed to deliver. Burgeoning numbers of travellers are waking up to the country's varied pleasures, but an appealing sense of treading new ground remains.

Inevitably, the war impacts heavily upon tourist itineraries. But when you've had your fill of crawling through tunnels and posing beside downed helicopters, there are tribes, temples, beaches, historic ruins and islands galore to check out.

Though the public transport system is as slow as it is extensive, budget tour operators are taking up the slack and reducing journey times between major attractions. English is widely understood.

Highlights

⬥ The **Vietnamese people**. Starved of contact with the West after a decade and a half in the wilderness, they're welcoming and full of fascinating stories.

⬥ The captivating riverside town of **Hoi An**. Spend the morning browsing through Hoi An's antique shops, and the afternoon sipping tea beside the drowsy Thu Bon River.

⬥ Taking a boat tour round the dramatic **Ha Long Bay**, peppered with hundreds of bizarrely shaped limestone karsts and yawning caves.

⬥ **Pho** – a noodle soup served with sprigs of fresh mint – may not sound anything special, but it sure hits the spot on a cool Hanoi morning, especially when spiced up with a spoonful of chilli relish.

⬥ Meeting **the "mad monk" of Da Lat**. Artist, Zen poet and Buddhist monk Vien Tuc welcomes visitors to his pagoda-cum-art gallery, which houses thousands of his own abstract watercolours.

⬥ **Ho Chi Minh City**. Venerable temples, absorbing museums, classy restaurants and hundreds of bars – Vietnam's full-tilt southern capital hardly gives visitors time to breathe.

Lowlights

◇ **Grim accommodation**. For every comfortable room in a quaint French colonial villa, there are five faceless cells in austere Soviet-style hotel blocks.

◇ **Crossing the road**. Hesitate for a moment and you will be sunk in a maelstrom of bikes, cars, mopeds and *cyclos*.

◇ **Public buses**. Bring a cushion, say a prayer and hold on tight – unless you're heading up to the Highlands, in which case walking might well prove the quicker option.

CHAPTER TWO

PLANNING YOUR ROUTE

Hopefully, Chapter One has given you a taste of what's on offer in Asia. Now you have to decide which countries to head for, which ones to leave out, and what order to see them in. Later in this chapter you'll find some suggestions of popular and creative itineraries across Asia, and in Chapter Six there's a roundup of recommended guidebooks, travel literature and other travel publications that should also be a good source of ideas.

✧ Your first task is to decide on the length of your trip. If money is the main consideration, check out Chapter Five to find out how far your budget will stretch.

✧ Do some research into the climate. Is it the right time of year to go trekking/whitewater rafting/snorkelling and diving? Will it be raining all the time, or too hot to enjoy yourself? See Chapter Four for advice on this.

✧ Make some preliminary investigations into different ticket options, and check out relevant visa requirements, described in Chapter Three.

✧ Think about the pace of your proposed trip. Are you going to be whizzing through places so fast that you won't have any real sense of where you are or what each country is like? Are you allowing yourself enough time and flexibility to add new places to your itinerary or linger in spots that you like a lot? Cramming too many destinations into your schedule means that you'll see far too much of the worst bits of a country, namely its bus stations and airports.

◇ Is your itinerary nicely balanced? Will you get bored if you see nothing but beaches for the next few months? Might you start longing for some hill walking after weeks of museums and temples?

A shared experience?

Now is also the time to think about who you want to go travelling with, or if indeed you want to share your trip with anyone at all. There are obvious pluses and minuses to both options. Travelling with one or more companions means you always have someone to chat to and plan things with; you can mull over your experiences together and share your enthusiasms and worries; and you may well feel braver about exploring and experimenting if you're with someone else. On a practical level, you will save money because double and triple rooms are better value and taxi prices will 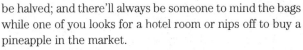 be halved; and there'll always be someone to mind the bags while one of you looks for a hotel room or nips off to buy a pineapple in the market.

However, travel is a surprisingly stressful activity: the heat, the hassle and the sheer strangeness of things are bound to fray your nerves, and guess who's going to bear the brunt of your irritability? Expect to get on each other's nerves and to fall out every so often, and be prepared to split up during the trip – either for a few days because you've got different priorities, or for good because your differences seem to be insurmountable. Bearing this in mind, you and your prospective companion should take a long hard look at your friendship and try to imagine it under stress. Will one person be making all the plans and taking all the responsibilities, and will that annoy both of you? Do you have broadly the same expectations of the trip and share a similar attitude to mishaps and hassles? Does one of you have a lot more money than the other, and will that cause tension?

If travel puts a strain on friendships, then imagine what it does to relationships. A disconcerting number of romances crack during a long cross-Asia trip, but then perhaps they weren't meant to last anyway. If you do survive it, you will have been brought closer together and will have lots of great stories and photos to coo over for many years to come.

Going solo

Solo travel is a more extreme and intense experience. You have to face up to everything on your own, and find the motivation to move on, explore and be sociable all by yourself. There will be lonely times for sure, and scary ones, and you'll probably get tired of eating out on your own every night. But you will also be a lot more open to your surroundings and you'll make more effort to chat to new people – as indeed they will to you (twosomes often put people off because they seem so self-contained). Some people find they're more alert and receptive on their own, and most single travellers write much more interesting letters and journals simply because they're desperate to blurt out all their experiences. And, of course, you have no one to answer to but yourself, which means you can change your plans at a moment's notice or slob around without feeling guilty.

Finding a travel companion

If you're nervous about going on your own, but can't find anyone to accompany you, all is not lost. Travel magazines, university noticeboards, newspaper personal columns and Internet newsgroups are full of advertisements from people looking for travelling companions. Most advertisers have specific itineraries in mind and will want to meet and discuss plans quite a few times – if you don't find an ad that fits your bill, why not place one yourself? Travelling with an unknown person will bring its share of unpleasant surprises, so you should definitely discuss ground rules before you go and perhaps even set off on a dummy trip – a weekend away, for example – before the big departure. But it can also be unexpectedly fun, and with any luck you'll have made a new friend by the trip's end.

Alternatively, you might consider starting your trip by joining an organized tour from home for a few weeks, then branching off on your own when you've gained more confidence and Asia know-how. This is fairly common practice on the youth-oriented overland tours (run by Exodus, Encounter Overland and Explore Worldwide, for example; see *Basics* on p.299 for addresses), and gives you a good grounding as well as the chance to meet potential onward travel companions.

Finally, you will find it remarkably easy to pick up travel companions when you've actually arrived in Asia. The backpackers' scene is well established in major Asian towns, cities and beach resorts, and guest-house noticeboards are usually thick with requests for travelmates. Bangkok's Khao San Road, the Paharganj area of New Delhi, and Thamel and Freak Street in Kathmandu, are all fruitful places to look.

Where shall I go first?

You probably won't have much trouble deciding where to start your trip – there'll either be an obvious geographical option, or your travel agent will twist your arm with offers of significant discounts if you go with their recommendation.

For Europeans, the usual gateway cities are Kathmandu, Delhi and Bangkok. These are the nearest entry points to Asia and generally the cheapest places to fly to. Australians generally begin somewhere in Indonesia, typically in Bali, but a more adventurous opener would be Kupang in West Timor. Flying to Asia from America is a more long-winded process. From the East Coast most flights go via London, Amsterdam or Frankfurt, and then on to Kathmandu, Delhi or Bangkok. If you're starting from the West Coast, the cheapest routes will probably be to Seoul, Taipei or Tokyo.

Saving money should not be the only consideration, though, and you'd be wise to think about the stress factor of your first days and nights in Asia:

◇ Start yourself off gently. Many travellers find the poverty, chaos and crowds of India, for example, a very tough introduction to Asia, so you might want to begin your cross-Asia trip somewhere calmer, like Malaysia or Bali.

◇ For the gentlest introduction to a new country, consider arranging international flights to towns other than the capital cities. You can fly from Europe directly to Phuket in south Thailand, for example, which means that by the time you've worked your way up to Bangkok (or down to Kuala Lumpur) you'll be blasé about big noisy cities and will exude the confidence of an old Asia hand. Similarly, you can fly direct from New York to Goa, from Perth to Bali, from London to Kunming, and so on. See Chapter Three for more details.

◇ If you've had a long flight, you'll probably be worn out when you arrive, so plan an easy schedule for the first week. Two or three nights in a pre-booked hotel near your place of arrival will give you a chance to sleep and acclimatize; then you might want to chill out on a beach somewhere, or relax in a smaller town or resort. See Chapter Eight for advice.

Asia by air

Most people choose to do their cross-Asia trip by air simply because it's faster and easier than going overland. Travel agents sort out all the details for you and everything is booked in advance (which is reassuring for anxious relatives and one less headache for you). Advice on buying the best plane ticket for your trip is given in Chapter Three.

The best approach is to work out your ideal route before you have your final session with the travel agent (see below for possible ideas), picking a few well-placed destinations that you're absolutely determined not to miss. Once you've got your core must-sees, be prepared to be flexible about the in-between bits, bearing in mind that some routes are a lot cheaper than others. If possible, leave some extra free time at strategic intervals so that you're able to follow up other travellers' recommendations once you're on the ground.

Before making any firm decisions about your ticket, check out the section on overland routes within Asia beginning on p.55. There are all sorts of intriguing bus, train and ferry routes between countries in Asia, and this can save you a lot of money on your air ticket, as well as enhancing your adventure.

Round-the-world classic: UK–India–Nepal–Thailand–Malaysia–Indonesia–(Australia)–UK

This is a classic first-time Asia itinerary for anyone starting in Europe, giving you the run of the best of south and Southeast Asia with the added option of rounding off your trip in Australia. The route can be done on a round-the-world ticket, a multiple-stopover ticket or even on an open-jaw return – see pp.78–86 for details on which ticket would be most suitable for you. For Australians, the same route applies, but in reverse, with the option of extending to Europe if you want.

Delhi is not necessarily an easy first port of call, but many Brits start here as it's only ten hours' flying time from London. Delhi is well positioned for trips to Rajasthan and the Himalayas, but if you're going to head south to the beaches of Goa opt for Bombay instead. Calcutta is a more unusual alternative, but a useful one as you can get cheap routings to Bangkok via Dhaka in Bangladesh.

From any point in India you have the choice of flying or overlanding to Kathmandu, but to continue east from there you'll have to fly into Bangkok because it's currently impossible to enter Burma overland. If you decide to leave out the Indian subcontinent altogether, your trip will begin in Bangkok.

From Bangkok you have a choice of flying in short hops through Thailand, Malaysia, Singapore and Indonesia (Sumatra, Java and then Bali), or making the long trek south overland. Travelling from Bangkok to Bali by bus, train and boat will save you heaps of money, but is obviously a lot more time-consuming. If you want to stop off for a while in all four countries then allow yourself at least two to three months for this part of the trip. There's a lot of ground to cover – Sumatra, for example, is the fourth largest island in the world – and the whole adventure becomes a real slog if you're trying to cram it all into three weeks.

In fact, the most popular route south is a combination of flying and overlanding. You can either weave a couple of flights into your round-the-world ticket before you go (for example, between Malaysia and Sumatra, and between Java and Bali), or buy flights in Asia as and when you get tired of long bus journeys. Bangkok is a good centre for cheap flights, and internal flights within Indonesia are both inexpensive and extensive. Long-distance overnight trains and buses cover the Thai–Malaysian–Singapore peninsula, and boats can get you from Malaysia all the way to Bali if you don't mind waiting a fortnight for the right sailing.

Overland routes into Asia from Europe and Australia

For some travellers, the process of getting to Asia is a crucial part of the whole adventure. Time is the major factor here, of course, and the expense may be off-putting too – though trains, buses and boats are generally cheaper than

flights, you will have spent a fair bit on accommodation and food before you even arrive in Asia.

The overland routes listed below are just a handful of the possible options. Though we've described them as routes *into* Asia, they're also quite feasible when done in reverse. It's almost, but not quite, possible to travel all the way from Australia to Britain (and back) without resorting to an aeroplane; the only hiatus comes when you need to cross the sea between northern Australia and Timor (the easternmost island of Indonesia) – unless you cadge a ride on a yacht or a cargo boat, you'll have to get a flight from Darwin to Kupang, after which you can island-hop all the way to Singapore.

On the whole, it's less hassle to organize overland trips from your own country, particularly if using your own transport. The bureaucracy involved in riding an Enfield motorbike back from India, for example, is so over-whelming that some travellers give up before they even get started. That said, however, riding a motorbike back from India is still a popular thing to do: see the box on p.55 for details.

Once in Asia you have the option of continuing your travels by road, rail and river (see "Overland routes within Asia", p.55), or you can buy a series of air tickets as you go.

The Trans-Siberian Railway

The Trans-Siberian Railway is *the* classic overland route into Asia. All trains begin in Moscow and there are three possible routes. The Trans-Mongolian route and the Trans-Manchurian route both end up in Beijing and take about six days to get there. If you are patient, have lots of time and have paid meticulous attention to visa requirements you can then continue your train journey from Beijing to Hanoi in Vietnam; this takes about five days. For access to Japan, take the Trans-Siberian route from Moscow, via Khabarovsk, allowing seven days to reach Vladivostok; from here it's a two-day boat ride across to Niigata in Japan.

Providing you arrange relevant visas, you can stop off pretty much anywhere you like en route, so the trip can last for several weeks if you want. For a full rundown of everything you need to know about visas, life on the train and ideas for stopoffs, see the *Trans Siberian Handbook,* published by Compass Star.

The hippie trail: from Europe to Kathmandu via Turkey, Iran, Pakistan and India

The most common way to do this route is by car or motorbike, which obviously involves some serious preparation, both for yourself and your vehicle. The paperwork is the biggest headache – visas need to be sorted out well in advance of your departure date (especially for Iran) and you will also need a special document for your vehicle known as a *carnet de passage*. Bikers should check out *The Adventure Motorbiking Handbook* (Compass Star), which contains full details on all these requirements, but the closest equivalent for car drivers is currently Bradt's *Russia and Central Asia by Road*, which includes advice on vehicle preparation and necessary documents. If you put your foot down and ignore the temptations of the countries en route you can reach Delhi in 21 days.

Some tour operators (such as Encounter Overland and Exodus) organize group overland trips along these routes in converted lorries. The trips take from four to thirty weeks, the age range is generally between 18 and 35, and the all-inclusive cost is quite reasonable. If you're nervous about setting off for Asia on your own, then this could be a good way to start. It's not uncommon for travellers from Europe to join an overland tour to Kathmandu and then continue on through Asia either alone or with a companion.

It's quite possible, if very time-consuming, to do the hippie trail by public transport. For specific advice, consult Trailblazer's *Asia Overland: A Route and Planning Guide*.

●●

DELHI TO LONDON ON A MOTORBIKE

After six months exploring India on an elderly Enfield Bullet, bought in Delhi for £600, I thought the bike would make a good souvenir. Shipping it was an option, but somehow riding the 10,000-odd miles home across Asia seemed a lot more interesting . . .

My route was a fairly standard one, taking me through Pakistan (with a side-trip up the Karakoram Highway into the northern hills), and then on to Iran and Turkey. Over the next five months, I rode through some of the most stunning and least-touristed areas of Asia, beneath soaring mountains, through barren deserts and across fertile plains. All the way along, people were exceptionally hospitable – there was always someone around to help me decipher squiggly road signs, direct me to a mechanic or, frequently, invite me home to stay with the family.

The gradual transition from East to West was fascinating: the culture, climate and terrain changed imperceptibly day by day. On top of that, there was something immensely satisfying about tracing a line on the map across two continents and actually following it on the ground.

Nicki McCormick

●●●●●●●●●●●●●●●●●●●●●●●●●●●●●●●●●●●●●

Overland routes within Asia

Before fixing your ticket routing, think about spicing up your flight itinerary with some overland routes in between. It's a great feeling to watch from a train window as one country slowly metamorphoses into another – far more satisfying than whizzing over international borders at thirty thousand feet – and in nearly every case it will be a lot cheaper than flying. Sometimes it's also quicker and more convenient than backtracking to the airport in the capital city.

Having the right paperwork is absolutely essential for overland routes, as most countries demand that you specify the exact land border when applying – see Chapter Three for more advice on this, and be sure to check out the viability of your proposed overland route before making any firm flight bookings.

Overlanding under your own steam can also be an exhilarating way to travel across the continent. Some crazed intrepids do it by bicycle – see Josie Dew's *The Wind in My Wheels: Travel Tales from the Saddle* (Warner) – or even on foot, but it's far more popular to zip around on a motorbike or in a car, as outlined on p.55.

●●

BE PREPARED

My trouble was I thought I could just go where I liked when I liked. I'll go to Cambodia today. What do I need? Visa. Get that at the border. Bus ticket. No problem. Can I have a single to Phnom Penh please?

Ho Chi Minh bus station: No. Your visa says leaving Vietnam from Hanoi. This bus crosses the border at Moc Bai. Go to the Ministry of Interior and change your visa.

Ministry of Interior: Not possible. Go to the Foreign Commission.
Foreign Commission: Can't do it. Go to Vietnam Tourism.
Vietnam Tourism: Nope. Show me your Cambodian visa first.
Cambodian Embassy: Come back the day after tomorrow!

Chris Humphrey

●●

An interesting alternative: (UK)–India–Pakistan–China–(Tibet)–Vietnam–Laos–Thailand–(Malaysia–Indonesia–Australia)–UK

This unusual cross-Asia route is longer and more adventurous than the classic version through India and Southeast Asia, the most challenging stretches being Pakistan and China, where travel is relatively difficult and travellers rare. This, of course, is a major part of the route's appeal.

The Pakistan–China–Indochina route can be woven into all sorts of Asian and round-the-world itineraries. It can feature as the middle section of a major overland trip from Europe to Indonesia, following on nicely from the Trans-Siberian route to Beijing (see p.54), or from the hippie trail to Pakistan (see p.54). It can be the challenging preamble to a more light-hearted Southeast Asian trip: the route from Thailand, through Malaysia, to Indonesia (see p.51) will almost certainly seem like a picnic after the bureaucracies of north Asia. Or you can treat it as the surface sector of an open-jaw return or a circle-Asia flight (described in Chapter Three), buying a plane ticket that flies you into Delhi and then takes you out of Bangkok or Singapore a few months later, giving yourself the option of buying some internal flights en route if necessary. This is the version described below.

Delhi is the obvious entry point to India if you're heading up to Pakistan, but it may be worth flying into one of the regional airports instead, such as Madras or Calcutta, if you want to explore southern or eastern parts of India first. You can either cross into Pakistan overland (via Amritsar) or fly into Hyderabad from Bombay or Calcutta, or into Lahore and Islamabad from Delhi.

From Pakistan you can take a bus into China via the spectacular Karakoram Highway, which starts in Rawalpindi and goes via Gitgit to Kashgar in far northwest China. This should take about four days but is only feasible from May to October when the Karakoram Highway is not snowbound.

The direct overland route from Kashgar to Ali in western Tibet is closed to foreigners, so if you want to make a side-trip into Tibet you'll have to head east from Kashgar to Golmud and then southwest to Lhasa. From Lhasa you can fly east to Chengdu.

From China there are overland crossings into Vietnam at Dong Dang and Lao Cai, and into Laos at Bian Mao Zhan. Once in Laos, it's a simple hop over the border into northeast Thailand.

In Thailand, your options are wide open again. You could fly back to Delhi and then return to Europe, or you

OVERLAND BORDER CROSSINGS

All the border crossings listed below are served by public transport. In most cases you will have to get off the train or bus to physically walk over the border and show your relevant paperwork to both sets of immigration officials. Burma and Sri Lanka are currently the only two countries that are inaccessible to all overlanders. Except where stated, all the following border crossings are accessible from both sides, but rules do change, so it's advisable to double-check the situation before making final decisions about your route.

Indian subcontinent

Pakistan–China. By bus via Sust on the Karakoram Highway.
India–Pakistan. Bus or train via Amritsar to Wagha and Lahore.
India–China. No overland crossing allowed.
India–Bangladesh. From Calcutta via Haridaspur to Dhaka by train, rickshaw and bus. Or from Darjeeling via Haldibari to Chiliharti by train.
India–Sri Lanka. Owing to the unrest in Sri Lanka, the ferry service between Rameswaram in India and Talaimannar in Sri Lanka is suspended indefinitely.
India–Nepal. By bus from Delhi, Varanasi or Gorakhpur via Sunauli and Bhairawa to Pokhara or Kathmandu; by bus from Bodh Gaya, Calcutta or Patna via Raxaul and Birganj to Pokhara or Kathmandu; and by bus and/or train from Siliguri, Darjeeling or Calcutta via Raniganj and Kakarbitta to Pokhara or Kathmandu.
Nepal–China (Tibet). Currently not allowed for independent travellers on public transport (though it is legal the other way round). However, foreigners who have booked expensive tours of Lhasa are allowed to cross here as long as they have the required paperwork.

Southeast Asia

Thailand–Malaysia and Singapore. By train or bus from Bangkok or Hat Yai via Padang Besar and Butterworth to Kuala Lumpur or Singapore. By train or bus from Bangkok or Hat Yai via Sungai Kolok and Rantau Panjang to Kota Bharu. By bus via Betong and Keroh to Butterworth; by share-taxi via Ban Taba to Kota Bharu; by ferry from Satun to Kuala Perlis or Langkawi; by ferry from Phuket to Penang or Langkawi.
Malaysia–Singapore. By bus, train or ferry.
Malaysia and Singapore–Indonesia. By ferry from Penang to Medan (Sumatra); from Melaka to Dumai (Sumatra); from Johor Bahru or Singapore to Pulau Batam, Bintan or Karimun (off Sumatra). By bus from Kuching (Sarawak) via Tebedu and Entikong to Pontianak (Kalimantan). By ferry from Tawau (Sabah) to Tarakan (Kalimantan).

Philippines–Indonesia. By boat from Davao City to Manado (Sulawesi). Owing to pirates and Filipino insurgents, the unofficial routes between Kalimantan (or nearby Sabah in Malaysia) and Mindanao are far too risky even to contemplate.

Indochina

Thailand–Laos. By ferry across the Mekong River from Chiang Kong via Ban Huai Sai to Luang Prabang; from Nakhon Phanom via Tha Kaek to Vientiane; and from Mukdahan to Savannakhet. By bus and foot from Nong Khai to Vientiane; and from Chong Mek via Ban Mai Sing Amphon to Pakse.

Thailand–Cambodia. By bus and boat from Trat to Kompong Son, via Ban Hat Lek, Ko Kong and Sao Thong. By bus and/or train from Aranyaprathet to Sisophon, via Poipet. Check with other travellers first, as travel in Cambodia can be dangerous.

Laos–Vietnam. By bus from Vientiane or Savannakhet in Laos via Lao Bao and Dong Ha to Hué or Hanoi.

Vietnam–Cambodia. By bus from Ho Chi Minh via Moc Bai to Phnom Penh.

Vietnam –China. By bus or rail from Hanoi via Dong Dang to Nanning (Guangxi), and by bus or rail from Hanoi via Lao Cai to Hekou in Yunnan.

Laos –China. By bus and boat from Luang Prabang in Laos via Ban Boten to Mo Han in Yunnan.

China and Japan

China–India. No overland crossing allowed.

China–Pakistan. By bus via Tashkurgan on the Karakoram Highway.

China (Tibet)–Nepal. Buses via Zhangmu to Kathmandu, but not allowed going from Nepal into Tibet.

Hong Kong–mainland China. By train, bus or ferry from Hong Kong to Guangzhou (Canton).

China–Laos. By bus and boat from Mo Han in Yunnan via Ban Boten to Luang Prabang in Laos.

China–Vietnam. By bus or rail from Nanning (Guangxi) via Dong Dang to Hanoi; and by bus or rail from Hekou in Yunnan via Lao Cai to Hanoi.

China–South Korea. By ferry from Qingdao or Weihai to Inchon.

China–Taiwan. None.

Taiwan–Japan. By ferry from Keelung to Naha in Okinawa; by ferry from Takao to Naha or Osaka.

China–Japan. By ferry from Shanghai to Yokohama, Osaka and Nagasaki.

Japan–South Korea. By ferry from Shimonoseki or Osaka to Pusan; by jetfoil from Nagasaki to Cheju-do.

could continue south and east to Indonesia, via Malaysia and Singapore, as described on p.51.

Another variation would be to exit China via Hong Kong and fly on to the Philippines, then take a ferry to Indonesia, from where you could overland to Thailand and on into Indochina.

Themes for travel

Rather than hang your trip round tourist sights and famous landscapes, you might consider planning your route around specific activities instead. We've selected some popular highlights below. You'll find specialist guidebooks covering some of these themes, though any decent travel guide should have at least some pointers on a country's most interesting activities.

Trekking and hiking

There's plenty of scope for interesting treks and hikes in Asia and you don't necessarily have to be an experienced walker to enjoy them. In Asia, you'll find the word "trek" used to refer to a long-distance walk, where you will spend the night or several nights en route. "Hike" generally means a walk taking a day or less.

In many cases you can do hikes and treks unassisted, so long as you have a decent route map and are dressed for the occasion. But in some places you'd be foolhardy to go without a guide: jungles, for example, are notoriously hard to navigate, even if you do possess a map, and high mountain passes are usually best negotiated with the help of a local expert. For long, arduous treks you'll probably need to hire a porter as well, to help carry tents and food. Travellers often join forces to arrange cheaper group treks, and in the more established places tour operators organize group treks along standard routes on a daily basis.

Don't forget to check on the climate (mid-June to late September, for example, is hopeless for trekking in the Himalayas), and remember to pack suitable clothes and footwear (see Chapter Seven for specific advice). Here follows a selective roundup of hikes and treks to whet your appetite:

- ✧ **China**. A one- to three-day trek through the alpine scenery of Sichuan to the spectacular tongue of ice known as Hailuo Guo Glacier. Hiking in the hills around Xinjiang's Tian Chi (Heaven Lake), surrounded by snowy peaks and pine forests and staying in Kazakh nomads' tents. Two-day trek through Tiger Leaping Gorge in Yunnan, the world's deepest canyon. Arduous three-day circumnavigation of Tibet's sacred Mount Kailash, stopping at monasteries en route.

- ✧ **India**. Challenging Himalayan treks of two to twelve days through forests and valleys, alongside mountain streams, past remote villages, and over sometimes snowy passes, with constant Himalayan views on all sides. The less difficult routes start from Dharamsala; the more strenuous ones – through the Zanskar and Ladakh regions – begin in Leh.

- ✧ **Indonesia**. Plenty of one-day volcano hikes, including the sunrise walk up Java's Mount Bromo, the trek up to Gunung Rinjani's crater rim on Lombok, and the hike up Keli Mutu on Flores to see its famous three-coloured crater lakes. There are scores of flatter trails to follow in Irian Jaya's Baliem Valley, taking you through cultivated land to interesting Dani villages.

- ✧ **Malaysia**. A two-day hike to Mount Kinabalu's 4101-metre-high summit on Sabah; strenuous day-hikes in Gunung Mulu National Park on Sarawak through rainforest to two peaks, plus exploring parts of the largest cave system in the world.

- ✧ **Nepal**. The Nepal Himalayas are the most popular area in Asia for trekking; there are literally scores of possible options. Independent trekking is quite feasible, but guides, porters and organized tours are also available from Kathmandu and Pokhara.

- ✧ **Philippines**. Highlights include the strenuous four-day climb up the country's highest mountain – volcanic Mount Apo – passing lakes, waterfalls and hot springs en route, plus fine rainforest flora; the steep four-day ascent and descent into sacred Mount Banahaw's thickly forested crater; the picturesque day-long hike through sculptured rice paddy valleys to the traditional village of Batad in Ifugao.

- ✧ **South Korea**. Follow the trails through the craggy peaks and forested slopes of Sorak-San National Park, stopping at waterfalls, temples and hermitages along the way.

◊ **Thailand**. Jungle trekking in the northern hills, mainly to see hill tribe villages but also for elephant rides and whitewater rafting. More remote trekking from Kanchanaburi and Umpang, and in the southern jungles of Khao Sok National Park.

• •

TREKKING IN TIBET

Choosing to trek into the Kailash region of Tibet, I ruled out venturing near the city in order to avoid fellow "travellers". We saw no one for days, with the exception of sheep, yaks, and a few nomads. Not even a trace of civilization. An unforgiving wind swept across the plateau, and there were no trees, just low bushes, random rocks, high mountains and rolling hills. I had known what to expect: I knew the population was sparse, and that we would see no one until we reached Mount Kailash, but the desolate and almost Martian landscape made me long all the more for people.

The rivers we crossed were too cold for bathing, and plumbing was nonexistent. Thinking I was an eco-traveller, I carried plastic bags in which to dispose of my toilet paper. But I soon realized that trash and human waste were not confined to the towns. There was garbage scattered across the land, in the middle of nowhere, like it belonged there. Perhaps it had been dropped by pilgrims on their way to Kailash, or by Western tour groups from the windows of their Land Cruisers.

When we finally arrived at Mount Kailash, the sacred home of the Hindu god Shiva, and the centre of the Buddhist universe, happy pilgrims appeared. Finally, people! Pilgrims older than my deceased grandparents had walked 35 miles in a single day – at altitudes of over 15,000 feet. I was amazed. It took me three days to circumambulate the mountain, following a well-trodden path round the holy peak. Devout pilgrims prostrated themselves as they walked through incoming blizzards. One Hindu pilgrim had walked all the way from Delhi in India. He'd begun his journey two months earlier and had hitched rides, slept out in the open and crossed the Himalayas barefoot. In contrast, I wore heavy winter gear, walked no more than ten steps before having to gasp for breath, and slept inside a tent, wrapped in a down sleeping bag.

Karen Christine Lefere

• •

Wildlife spotting

Asia is home to some of the most unusual animals in the world, including the tigers and elephants of India and Indonesia, the snow leopard of northern Nepal, the yaks of the Himalayas and Tibetan plateau, and the orang-utans of Kalimantan, Sumatra and Sarawak, not to mention scores of extraordinary birds. Many of these creatures are now endangered, as the pressure from an expanding population and the continued trade in rare species threatens their existence, so you're unlikely to happen across many of the above on a random hike in the mountains or the jungle. However, Asia has a fair number of national parks where rare fauna and flora are, at least in theory, protected from poachers, and many of these places are accessible to tourists.

The places listed below are the cream of the crop, highlighted because you've a good chance of seeing wildlife there and you can travel there independently without much trouble. You'll need to be careful about the timing of your visit to any national park, as birds and animals tend to be more social and therefore easier to spot at certain times of the year. For advice on this, and for an overview of Asian wildlife and where to see it, consult the two guides published by Insight: *Southeast Asia Wildlife* and *India Wildlife*, both of which are easy to read and full of colour photos. Or check out *Wildlife Indonesia* and *Birding Indonesia*, both produced by Periplus. As for bird guides to the whole of Asia, try to get hold of *Where to Watch Birds in Asia* by Nigel Wheatley (Princeton University Press), or look at New Holland's *Photographic Guide to Birds* series, which covers China, India, Nepal and Malaysia.

◇ **Bangladesh**. An exceptionally rewarding country for birdwatching, Bangladesh is home to many species normally found either in India or in Southeast Asia, and is also a major wintering ground for migrant birds. The mangrove swamps and coastal wetlands of the Sunderbans are good places to spot cranes and golden eagles (and there's a very remote possibility of seeing a Bengal tiger here, too). The Madhupur Forest Reserve is renowned for its brown wood owl and the dusky owl, and you'll see rhesus monkeys and langurs as well. Several species of pochards and teals visit the Sunamganj wetlands in Sylhet, as do crakes and various fishing eagles.

✧ **Indonesia**. Highlights on Sumatra include the Bukit Lawang orang-utan sanctuary, and the hornbills, Argus pheasants and numerous other birds of Kerinci-Seblat National Park. On Komodo, everyone goes to gawp at the enormous and ferocious monitor lizards known as Komodo dragons; while Irian Jaya is famous for its spectacular birdlife, including birds of paradise (best seen in Pulau Yapen), and the innumerable cockatoos, parrots and cassowaries that can be spotted almost anywhere, along with heaps of gorgeously coloured butterflies.

✧ **Malaysia**. There are common sightings of gibbons, macaques, monitor lizards and hornbills in the easily accessible Taman Negara National Park on the peninsula. In Sabah, the big draws are the Sepilok Orang-utan Sanctuary, the flowers of Sabah's Mount Kinabalu – including a thousand species of orchid, 26 types of rhododendron, and various bizarre insect-eating pitcher plants – and the chance of seeing the proboscis monkey, found only in Borneo and most likely spotted in Sabah's Bako National Park. Gunung Mulu National Park in Sarawak is renowned for its phenomenal birdlife, which includes eight species of hornbill.

✧ **Nepal**. You're almost as likely to spot a yeti in the Nepal Himalayas as you are to catch sight of a blue sheep or a snow leopard, and trekkers rarely see any other interesting mammals in the mountains either. It's much more rewarding to head for the plains of the Tarai, where there's a good chance of seeing rhinos, monkeys and possibly bears at the popular Chitwan National Park. Langurs and wild pig are frequently sighted in Bardia National Park, and you also have a reasonable chance of encountering a rhino, a tiger, or even a Gangetic dolphin. Swamp deer, crocodiles and awesome birdlife, including heaps of cranes, cormorants and eagles, are good enough reasons to visit Sukla Phanta Wildlife Reserve.

Diving

Internationally certified scuba-diving courses are cheaper in Asia than in most other parts of the world and, once you've done your training, the potential for underwater exploration is phenomenal. The reef life is as diverse, prolific and fascinating as anywhere in the world, and as the water tends to be bath temperature you won't always need a full wetsuit. You will find reputable dive schools in all the major resorts listed below, and the same places also organize dive trips and rent out equipment.

Though you can dive year-round in Asia, some

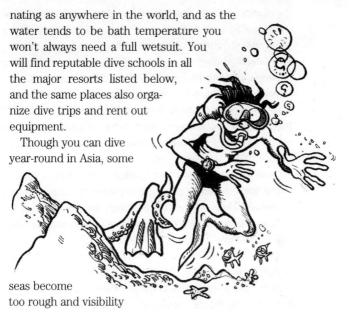

seas become too rough and visibility drops during the rainy season (see Chapter Four), so check with a specialist diving guidebook before fixing your trip. Recommended diving guides, all of which describe and illustrate the marine life as well as detailing the best dive sites, include *Fielding's Diving Indonesia* and *Diving Malaysia, the Philippines and Thailand, Dive! Southeast Asia* and *Underwater Indonesia* (both from Periplus), and the *Dive Sites* series published by New Holland, which covers Thailand, Indonesia, Malaysia and the Philippines.

◇ Boasting warm, clear waters and a breathtakingly diverse marine life, **Indonesia** offers masses of quality dive sites. The most accessible of these are found off Pulau Menjangan, Tulamben, Nusa Penida and Nusa Lembongan in Bali; off the Gili islands in Lombok; and in Sulawesi at the Bunaken-Manado Tua marine park. If you've got plenty of money, live-aboard charters open up areas off Maluku and Irian Jaya.

◇ **Malaysia's** best diving facilities are centred on Pulau Tioman, but there are lots more dive centres on other east coast islands. Aficionados head for Pulau Sipadan off Sabah.

✧ The dozens of islands that make up the Philippine archipelago are ringed by over four thousand square kilometres of reef which, not surprisingly, makes the Philippines one of Asia's most important diving destinations. The main dive centres are at Moaboal, Puerto Galera and Boracay, but the cream of the reefs are off the Palawan Islands and Occidental Mindoro, and there are exciting shipwreck dives off Busuangra.

✧ The most enticing reefs of east-coast **Sri Lanka** are currently too dangerous to visit, but Hikkaduwa in the southwest, and Unawatuna and Polhena near Matara in the south, are rewarding areas for diving and snorkelling.

✧ In **Thailand** there are numerous dive centres at the resorts on Phuket and in Pattaya, but the best reefs are around the outlying islands, particularly Ko Similan, the Surin Islands, Ko Tao and Ko Phi Phi.

Adrenaline rush

For most people, a bus trip on the Trans-Sumatran Highway, a few hours in a tiny, overladen ferry boat in heaving seas, or a few minutes aboard some of the domestic airlines, generate quite enough excitement. But there are all sorts of other ways to spice up your trip, some of which are listed below. If you're planning on doing any of the following adventure sports, be sure to advise your insurance company before signing your policy:

✧ **Jet-skiing and other watersports**. Available at all the big tourist beach resorts, including Sanur on Bali, Pulau Tioman in Malaysia, and Pattaya and Phuket in Thailand.

✧ **Kayaking**. Paddle your own canoe through mangrove swamps, jungle rivers and island caves in south Thailand, north Vietnam and the Philippines.

✧ **Mountaineering**. Whilst most travellers go to Nepal to trek, this country is also the world's centre for serious mountaineering expeditions, as are the entire length of the Himalayan and Karakoram ranges.

✧ **Rock-climbing**. The limestone karsts that pepper the Krabi coastline of southern Thailand and Ha Long Bay in north Vietnam are just crying out to be scaled.

- **Skiing and heli-skiing** in the Indian Himalayas. Take a very expensive helicopter flight out of Manali, then do spectacular runs from around 4000m.
- **Surfing** along the southern and western side of the Indonesian archipelago. The best facilities are in Bali but there are also top breaks off Sumatra, Lombok and Sumbawa. Check out *Surfing Indonesia* (Periplus), or *Fielding's Surfing Indonesia*, for more detail. In Sri Lanka there are surf centres in Hikkaduwa and Midigama and, in the Philippines, Luzon gets reliable waves.
- **Whitewater rafting** in Nepal. Race down choppy Himalayan rivers, through wooded canyons and jungle, past villages and beaches. Or try the rivers of west Thailand, around Umpang.

Spiritual quests

Westerners have been going to Asia on spiritual quests for decades, so there are heaps of foreigner-oriented courses to choose from. We've selected a few of the most popular centres for yoga and meditation instruction, but there are plenty more.

Don't be put off by the fact that courses are designed for visiting foreigners: the truly authentic programmes last for months (if not years), are conducted in the local language, and would be far too rigorous for first-timers. In most cases, the foreigners' courses are quite demanding enough: the daily programme generally starts around 5am, food is healthy but hardly indulgent, sex, drugs and drink are all forbidden for the duration, and some course leaders ask you to stay silent for most of the day. Courses are generally inexpensive and last from a few days to several weeks; most are residential. The usual procedure is to enrol on the spot for the next available course, so, unless you're very short of time, there's generally no need to book a place before you leave home.

With any luck you'll come away in a calmer and healthier state of mind and body and may also have learnt a bit more about the Asian way of looking at the world. It's quite feasible to practise your newly acquired yoga or meditation skills on your travels, especially if you're staying near a beach.

◇ **India** is the spiritual heartland of Asia and the most popular place for travellers pursuing spiritual interests. Established centres for yoga and meditation courses (known as ashrams) include Rishikesh – famous as the place where the Beatles met the Maharishi – and Dharamsala, home-in-exile of the Tibetan Buddhist leader the Dalai Lama and hundreds of his compatriots. The Root Centre in Bodh Gaya (scene of Buddha's enlightenment) and the Shivananda ashram in Trivandrum are also recommended. *Travels through Sacred India* by Roger Housden (Thorsons) is a mine of further information on religion in modern India and includes addresses of ashrams.

◇ **Japan** is the home of Zen Buddhism, and Kyoto is the best place to find introductory Zen retreats catering for foreigners. For specifics, see *Zen Guide: Where to Meditate in Japan* by Martin Roth and John Stevens (Weatherhill).

◇ Like India, **Nepal** also attracts a large number of travellers looking for yoga and meditation courses, most of whom end up at ashrams in the Kathmandu Valley.

◇ In **Thailand**, the most popular meditation course is the ten-day Vipassana programme held every month at Wat Suan Mokh in Surat Thani. Other options include ten-day retreats on Ko Pha Ngan and month-long courses in Chiang Mai. *The Meditation Temples of Thailand: A Guide* by Joe Cummings (Silkworm) is worth consulting if you've a serious interest, or have a read of Tim Ward's first-hand experiences, in *What the Buddha Never Taught* (Celestial Art).

Learning a new skill

With all that time on your hands, why not learn a new skill while you're in Asia? The places listed below are renowned on the backpacker circuit for their short, traveller-oriented courses, where you might learn batik painting in a couple of days, or the fundamentals of Mandarin in a couple of weeks. None of them require any special aptitude or prior knowledge, and most are informal and relatively superficial, but they're a fun way to get a little further under the skin of a country or a region. Backpackers' guidebooks usually carry details about course durations and prices, but you rarely need to book a place in advance, as most people just turn up in the town and find out what the schedule is.

◊ **Arts and crafts**. Design yourself a T-shirt or paint your own wall-hanging in Indonesia by taking a short course in batik design and dyeing in Yogyakarta (Java) or Ubud (Bali). You can also learn batik making at Cherating and Kota Bharu in Malaysia.

◊ **Cookery**. Learn how to recreate jungle curry and chilli-fried fish on Thai cookery courses in Bangkok and Chiang Mai.

◊ **Diving**. There are plenty of dive schools in Indonesia, Malaysia, Thailand and the Philippines, where you can do one-day introductory courses as well as internationally approved certificate courses.

◊ **Language**. It's good to talk – all Asian capitals have language institutes catering for foreign students and interested tourists; contact tourist offices and/or embassies in your own country for details.

◊ **Martial arts**. A course in Chinese self-defence techniques may stand you in good stead on your travels – lessons for foreigners are held in the travellers' centre of Dali (Yunnan), and in Beijing.

◊ **Massage**. Become a hit with fellow travellers by learning the basics of traditional Thai massage in Chiang Mai or Bangkok, or of shiatsu in Kyoto, Japan.

◊ **Music and dance**. You'll get a lot more out of watching cultural performances if you've tried a few steps or banged out a few tunes yourself. Beginners' courses in Indonesian dance and gamelan playing are held regularly in Ubud (Bali) and Yogyakarta (Java).

◊ **Yoga and meditation**. Open up your mind, and loosen up your limbs – a huge variety of yoga and meditation courses are held in India and Nepal; see "Spiritual quests", p.67.

Voluntary work

Doing voluntary work gives you a special insight into a country and its people. As a volunteer you meet people you'd never come across on the tourist trail and may have a chance to do something useful for a community in need. Most international voluntary organizations (like VSO and the Peace Corps) employ people for a minimum of two years and require specific qualifications, but there are some shorter placements on offer.

Concerned tourists, however, can get involved in short-term voluntary projects such as coral surveying in the Philippines, caring for forest monkeys in China or tracking snow leopards in the Himalayas. There are also a few openings for work on archeological digs and community programmes. Projects last anything from a week to six months, and volunteers are expected to pay for their board and lodging and contribute towards the cost of the project. Established organizers of volunteer holidays are listed in *Basics* on p.300.

To get involved with any of these organizations you need to contact them in your home country before you set off. For a more comprehensive roundup, see *The Directory of Work and Study in Developing Countries* (Vacation Work), or *The International Directory of Voluntary Work* (Petersons).

Some local charities are happy to accept volunteers who walk in off the street and have no qualifications except a desire to help out for a few days. A few random examples include Mother Teresa's Missionaries of Charity (hospices for the destitute and the dying) in Calcutta; Mother Teresa's Sisters of Charity (old people's hospice) in Kathmandu; and Empower (education for women in the sex trade) in Bangkok. Consult guidebooks for details on these and other projects.

●●●●●●●●●●●●●●●●●●●●●●●●●●●●●●●●●●●●●●●

A DIFFERENT KIND OF TRIP

When I packed in my job, I decided to go travelling for a while, but I wasn't interested in just bumming around and wanted to try and get under the surface of things instead. Indian Volunteers for Community Service (IVCS) fitted the bill perfectly: a three-week visitors' programme at a small rural development project in northeastern India.

On our first day at the project, the ten new volunteers were all taken to the nearest town to buy traditional north Indian style dress: *salwaar kameez* for the girls and *pajama* for the boys. This was to make us feel and act like we weren't just tourists, and also to help us blend in better with the villagers of Amarpurkashi. Back at the village, we spent the next three weeks following an informal programme of yoga, Hindi lessons and cultural lectures in the morning, and rural development workshops in the afternoon. In between, we got involved with local projects like reorganizing the polytechnic's library and helping with the literacy campaign. And we helped out in the kitchens, and gave regular English lessons at the village school and the rural polytechnic. We also socialized with the villagers and were invited to join their festivities, including one which was held to honour the birth of a baby boy.

I couldn't have asked for a better introduction to India. Though there was quite a big group of us Westerners, we all got involved in community life and experienced things tourists rarely get to see and do. By the end of the three weeks I felt acclimatized, confident and eager to do some exploring, so I spent the next five months making informal visits to development projects in other parts of India, using contacts I'd made at Amarpurkashi.

Juliet Acock

● ●

CHAPTER THREE

VISAS, TICKETS AND INSURANCE

Only a very few countries in Asia actually refuse entry to independent travellers, but in many cases you can only enter via certain air- and seaports unless you've bought a special visa in advance. In other cases you're not allowed to enter by land borders at all, so obviously that will affect your route planning. And some countries (like Burma) impose so many restrictions that you may end up not wanting to go there after all. With all this in mind, it's essential to start researching the visa situation for all your intended destinations as early as possible – before you pay for your air ticket, and before it's too late to get all the paperwork done.

Though you need to find out about the visa situations in all your intended destinations before buying your ticket, you shouldn't actually apply for the visas until you've got firm bookings for your tickets, as most visa applications ask for your arrival and departure dates.

Visas and borders

Lots of Asian countries are crying out for tourists to come and visit, so they make visas easy to obtain and often issue them free of charge as well. Malaysia, for example, gives away thirty-day tourist visas on entry, and Indonesia hands out sixty-day stamps at its major airports and sea-ports. All you need to do is show immigration officials that your passport is valid for at least another six months and that you have a ticket out of the country; sometimes, but not always, you can get by with just showing you've got enough money to buy an onward ticket – see below for details. However, should you want to stay in Malaysia for more than a month, or to enter Indonesia through a non-designated gateway (eg by boat from Malaysia to Dumai in Sumatra), then you'll need to apply for a visa before you reach the border. The table on p.74 gives a broad outline of visa requirements in Asia, but you should definitely confirm details with the relevant embassies by calling the numbers listed in *Basics* on p.290.

Less welcoming nations require visas to be bought in advance whatever the length of your trip and some, like the Himalayan kingdom of Bhutan, refuse visas to any traveller who is not part of an (expensive) organized tour. Rules change all the time, of course, especially in countries where the political climate is more volatile. Land borders are especially unpredictable – at the time of writing it is impossible to travel overland between China and Burma, between India and Burma, or between China and India. And while travellers can currently cross into Nepal from Tibet, they cannot travel independently into Tibet from Nepal. Nor is it legal to enter Cambodia overland from Laos. When planning your trip you should also bear in mind that there's only one border crossing between India and Pakistan (west of Amritsar at Wagha) and that to travel overland between Vietnam and Cambodia, and between Laos and Vietnam, you need to arrange special visas in advance. Details on overland border crossings are given in Chapter Two.

On the whole, it's best to apply for a visa from your home country. A couple of provisos to this, though: most countries require you to start using your visa within three months of purchase, which is clearly hopeless if you'll be hitting India five months after, say, leaving Australia, so

VISA REQUIREMENTS

The following table indicates whether you need to buy a visa before you arrive. It's meant as a planning aid only and applies to entry via the most popular gateways. As rules change quite often, you should double-check by calling the relevant embassies. In the countries that let you in without an advance visa, the number of days you're allowed to stay is given in brackets; you may be able to get a longer visa by applying in your home country before you leave.

	EU	US/Can	Aus/NZ
Bangladesh	no (15 days)	no (15 days)	no (15 days)
Burma	yes	yes	yes
Cambodia	yes	yes	yes
China	yes	yes	yes
Hong Kong	no (90 days)	no (30 days)	no (90 days)
India	yes	yes	yes
Indonesia	no (60 days)	no (60 days)	no (60 days)
Japan	no (90 days)	no (90 days)	yes
Laos	no (15 days)	no (15 days)	no (15 days)
Malaysia	no (30 days)	no (30 days)	no (30 days)
Nepal	no (60 days)	no (60 days)	no (60 days)
Pakistan	yes	yes	yes
Philippines	no (21 days)	no (21 days)	no (21 days)
Singapore	no (14 days)	no (14 days)	no (14 days)
South Korea	no (90 days)	no (US: 15 days, Can: 90 days)	no (Aus: 15 days, NZ: 90 days)
Sri Lanka	no (30 days)	no (30 days)	no (30 days)
Thailand	no (30 days)	no (30 days)	no (Aus: 30 days, NZ: 90 days)
Vietnam	yes	yes	yes

you'll have to get that visa from the relevant embassy somewhere en route. Also, not every nation has an embassy or consulate in every country (Laos and Cambodia, for example, have no representatives in the UK), which means you either have to go through an agency or, if feasible, get your visa in Asia – in Bangkok, for example. Sometimes visas are *easier* to get en route: Chinese visas, for example, are simplest to obtain in Hong Kong; and Laotian visas are quicker to get in Bangkok as all visa applications have to be sent to Laos for approval – considerably speedier when done from Thailand (less than a week) than from Europe (about two months). Getting an Indian visa in Nepal, on the other hand, is ridiculously bureaucratic and much better done somewhere else.

In some countries (like China, India, Laos, Malaysia and Vietnam) you may also need special permits to visit remote or politically sensitive areas. These are usually issued in the relevant country, but it's always worth checking with embassies before you go and maybe applying by post in advance.

Applying for a visa

Even in the most efficient embassies, applying for a visa is a time-consuming procedure. Queues stretch down the hallway, and most embassies and consulates keep unhelpfully short hours. Call the 24-hour phone lines to check opening times, and take relevant national holidays into consideration, too (both yours and theirs); not only will embassies close on these days, but queues will be twice as long on the days before and after. The same advice applies when picking up your visa. To minimize the hassle, find out in advance how many photos you need, how much visas cost and whether or not you can pay by cash/cheque/credit card. Get to the embassy as close to opening time as possible and take a good book.

If you've got plenty of time before your departure it's easier to apply by post, though that might not be feasible if you've got several different visas to collect. Alternatively, you can always use the specialist (but pricey) visa service offered by major travel agents. Points to remember:

◇ Be as accurate as you can about the date of your arrival in the country, as some embassies – eg Vietnam – issue visas with exact dates on them; if you can't be certain, delay applying for a visa until later in your trip.

◇ If there's any possibility that you might be leaving a country after a month and then coming back there a few weeks later (to catch a plane for example), make sure you apply for a multiple-entry visa rather than a single-entry one.

◇ In some countries, writers and journalists are regarded with suspicion by the authorities, so it's advisable to be vague about your occupation on the visa form (they're unlikely to check up).

◇ Some countries are hostile to passport-holders of particular nations. Islamic countries, for example, often refuse entry to Israeli passport-holders; this is true of Indonesia and Malaysia. Check with embassies for details.

◇ When collecting your visa, check that all the details are correct, and that, if necessary it has been signed.

● ●

DÉJÀ VU ON THE KARAKORAM HIGHWAY

We reached the front of the queue and I handed the Pakistani officer our passports, open at the Chinese visa. He glanced casually at the first, then a little more deliberately at the second and finally scrutinized the pair together, side by side. Then he raised his head abruptly and peered over the lectern.

"What is this? These have not been signed! They must be signed, you cannot use them!" he barked.

"What? Surely not!" I protested. "Where?"

"There! Can't you read?"

"Well, actually, no," I admitted. "Not Chinese. Look, it's just an administrative error. These are genuine visas, they'll see that."

But it was no good, he was adamant the Chinese would not let us enter, and therefore he could not let us leave Pakistan.

"You'll have to go back to Islamabad and get them signed. Next!"

Slightly bewildered, I sat down and tried to come to terms with the appalling prospect of going all the way back. We had just spent three weeks exploring the Karakoram Highway and now we had to retrace our steps. In the end it took us four days and a catalogue of hassles, including an unpredicted holiday at the Chinese embassy, a bus breakdown, a randy fellow passenger and an awful lot of déjà vu.

Neil Poulter

• •

Extending your visa

If you know that the statutory number of weeks on a tourist visa is just not long enough for your trip then you could try applying for a special student or business visa. Sometimes it's enough to have a written invitation from someone in the host country; alternatively, try signing up with a language school or a meditation centre and getting a letter from the principal.

All is not lost if you can't get a long enough visa. If you're planning to overrun by two weeks or less, then in some countries you may as well just put aside some money for the fine that you'll be landed with when you fly out – in Nepal it's US$2 per day. In other countries, this is definitely not a great idea – Vietnam charges a whopping US$2000 for overstaying your visa, and Indonesia penalizes anyone who overstays by more than two weeks by putting them on a blacklist prohibiting entry to Indonesia for the next few years.

Some countries offer a legitimate way of extending your visa (the embassy in your home country should be able to tell you this). In Thailand, for example, you can go to any of the provincial immigration offices dotted around the country and get a thirty-day extension for a reasonable fee. You'll probably need two or three passport photos for this and it always helps if you're dressed smartly.

If none of that is possible, you can always do what numerous local expats do and cross the nearest border to get a new tourist visa. In some places this is simple: in Indonesia, for example, you can either fly to Singapore (2hr 30min), or take the two-hour boat ride from Batam Island and then back again. In Thailand you can get a long-distance bus or train down to the Thai embassy in Kuala Lumpur; if you're in southern Malaysia you can zip across to Singapore; while from Japan the cheapest exit is by boat to South Korea.

Buying a ticket

The travel industry is a hugely competitive business, so it pays to shop around when looking for the best fare. It's almost unheard of for travellers to buy air tickets direct from the major airlines – only business travellers can afford the standard airline fares (known as full fares) – which means you'll be buying from a travel agent who offers air tickets at discounted prices. The reason travel agents are cheaper is that they can only sell a limited number of seats on each flight; in other words, they deal in blocks of seats that the airline doesn't think it can sell at full price. See *Basics* on p.295 for addresses of recommended agents.

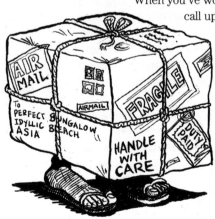

When you've worked out some sort of itinerary, call up one of the major discount travel agents or, better still, go and see them, and ask the travel consultant's advice. Staff at these places are usually young and well travelled themselves; they know what they're talking about and generally aren't out to rip you off.

Having established a price for your proposed route, ring round a few other discount travel agents to see if anyone else can better it. Many newspapers and listings maga-zines carry advertisements for discount travel agents and they usually quote sample fares too. In London, try the *Evening Standard*, *Time Out*, or the free *TNT* magazine; in the US, there's New York's *Village Voice*, *LA Weekly* and *San Francisco Bay Guardian*; and in Australia, try *TNT* magazine. Youth- and student-oriented travel agents give significant discounts to travellers who are under 26, and some places extend their deals to anyone under 35. Student card-holders of any age are often entitled to cut-price deals as well.

Always check that the travel agent you're dealing with is bonded with one of the big travel associations, such as ATOL or ABTA, before you give them any money. If they are bonded you will be refunded if the agent goes bust before you fly out; if not you will lose your money and your ticket. Paying for your ticket by credit card will also protect you against unreliable bucket shops, as the credit card company is obliged to reimburse you if the agent doesn't.

Some eastern and central European airlines offer very cheap fares to Asia, but have notoriously poor efficiency (and, in some cases, safety) records and many major trav-el agents refuse to sell their flights. If you're looking for a rock-bottom fare, it may be worth contacting these air-lines directly; alternatively, look through the classified ads for a travel agent that sells their product.

How to save money on your flight
To help you get the best possible deal for your money, bear in mind the following points:

◇ Ring round a dozen travel agents and write down their quotes so you don't forget them.
◇ Some travel agents have special discount arrangements with particular airlines, so ask several different agents the price of the exact same flight.
◇ Investigate several different types of ticket (see pp.80–86), even if you already think you know what you want.

◇ The early bird gets the worm, so book early. The best deals will be snapped up fast, leaving latecomers on the expensive flights. If you want to fly from Europe to India at Christmas time, for example, you should book your ticket by September to ensure a reasonable fare. And if you're heading from the US to Nepal for the popular October to November trekking season, you need to make your reservations around June.

◇ Be as flexible as possible about your departure date. Airlines have high, low and shoulder seasons and prices vary accordingly, so you could make a significant saving by altering your schedule by a week or two. As a general guide, high season for flights to Asia covers the busiest holiday periods, namely mid-December to mid-January, and July through mid-September; shoulder season wraps around the peak winter season, usually from November through February (when most parts of Asia are enjoying their pleasantest weather); and the remaining months are low season.

◇ Be equally flexible about your routing. It's generally more expensive to fly into less popular regional airports (such as Madras), simply because demand is low and competition slack. Perhaps an inexpensive overland connection (from Bombay, for example) would do just as well, especially if it saved you $150 or more. On the other hand, there's no question that spending your first night in Madras is a lot less stressful than kicking off with Bombay, so the extra cost might be worth every penny.

Which ticket?

Most discounted flights have restrictions on them, which your travel agent should explain. For example, once you've paid for your ticket you probably won't be able to cancel it and you may not be able to change your initial departure date (though return dates and onward segments of round-the-world tickets are nearly always flexible). Most holiday insurance policies cover unavoidable cancellations and delayed departures (see p.86 for advice on insurance). Many discounted tickets also have time restrictions on them, with a minimum stay of seven days and a maximum of thirty or ninety days, though this varies according to the airline.

Sometimes it's worth paying a little extra for your international flight to qualify for special perks. Some airlines offer good deals on domestic flights if you fly in and out of the country on the national carrier. This can apply to a standard return, an open-jaw return or as part of a round-the-world ticket. Malaysian Airlines, for example, sells an inexpensive pass entitling you to five internal flights if you fly to Malaysia with them; Garuda have a similar deal for Indonesia; as do Indian Airlines for India.

One-way tickets

One-way tickets always work out relatively more expensive than a return flight, so this is only a viable option if you're unsure when or how you'll be returning. It can also create problems with visas as most countries require proof that you are actually going to leave their country within a reasonable time limit. In many cases, you will either need to show evidence of onward or return travel plans when applying for a visa in your home country, or at the border when getting a visa on the spot.

The easiest way to bypass this is to decide on an overland route out of the country and make sure you have the information and proof of sufficient funds at your fingertips when getting your visa. This only works of course if it's a legal way of exiting the country – check with travel agents, embassies and guidebooks for details of this before plumping for a one-way ticket.

On the plus side, one-way tickets are adventurous and liberating. Overland transport in Asia is temptingly inexpensive, and airline tickets bought in Asia are good value, particularly in Bangkok, Calcutta, Delhi and Singapore.

Open-jaw returns

Open-jaw tickets allow you to choose different airports for your arrival and departure, which means you don't have to backtrack. One example would be to fly from London into Delhi and then fly back from Bombay to London, making your own way overland between Delhi and Bombay. On some airlines, it's possible to buy an open-jaw that flies you into one country (eg Thailand) and out of another (eg Singapore), leaving you a fairly lengthy overland sector to organize yourself. Open-jaws are usually more expensive than standard returns: prices are generally calculated by halving the return fares to each destination and then adding the two figures together.

Stopover returns

If you're only visiting one or two countries in Asia, then buying a return ticket with a stopover option will probably be your best deal, particularly as most stopovers are offered free of charge. Flying from Sydney to Delhi, for example, you can stop over in Kuala Lumpur, Bangkok or Kathmandu, depending on which airline you use. Flying from London to Kathmandu you could stop in Karachi, Delhi or Dhaka. Most airlines allow you to stop over for up to three months, and you can usually choose whether you stop off on the way out or the way back; you may even be allowed to do both. Not all airlines offer interesting stopover routes, but travel agents will advise on the best options. Don't forget to find out whether you need a visa for your stopover destination.

Circle Asia tickets

If you're planning a multi-stop route across Asia, your cheapest option is almost certain to be a Circle Asia ticket. This is in fact a whole series of tickets, generally put together by a travel agent using the cheapest flights they can find to construct a trans-Asia route via a series of key cities. It's up to you to choose which cities, of course, though agents generally offer very good deals on certain routes, which makes them hard to ignore. Once you've decided on your key cities and paid for your ticket the route is fixed and cannot be changed, although dates of component flights can usually be changed at any point along the way, free of charge. Circle Asia tickets are generally valid for one year.

The cheapest and most popular Circle Asia routes include one or more "surface sectors" where you have to make your way between point A and point B by land, sea or whatever means you feel like; in other words, that section of the journey is not included in your Circle Asia ticket. A typical Circle Asia from London to Bali and back, for example, would include a flight from London to Bangkok, then a surface sector from Bangkok to Singapore, followed by flights from Singapore to Bali, then Bali to Jakarta and Jakarta to London. The idea is that you make your own way between Bangkok and Singapore, either slowly, with several stops on the way, or in one swoop by overnight train or bus – or even local flight – that you organize from Bangkok. The longer your surface sectors, the cheaper your Circle Asia ticket.

Sample Circle Asia prices:

◇ Under £550 for London–Bangkok surface to Singapore–Bali–Jakarta–London.
◇ Under £650 for London–Kathmandu–Bangkok surface to Singapore–Calcutta–Dubai–London.
◇ Under $1200 for San Francisco–Tokyo–Singapore surface to Bangkok–Hong Kong–San Francisco.
◇ Under $1300 for New York–Hong Kong–Bangkok–Kathmandu surface to Hong Kong–Los Angeles–New York.

Round-the-world tickets

A round-the-world (RTW) ticket is a longer and more ambitious version of a Circle Asia ticket, with the added bonus of stops in Australia and the Pacific, North America, Europe or South Africa. RTWs are also put together by a travel agent using the cheapest flights they can find and, as with Circle Asia tickets, most travel agents offer a dozen or so set RTW routes at bargain rates. The route can't be altered after you've paid for your ticket, but again you can usually change the dates of component flights free of charge.

The more surface sectors you include in an RTW ticket, the cheaper the ticket. As internal and short-hop flights are generally cheaper to buy inside Asia than out, you may find it more economical to buy a skeleton RTW with long surface sectors and then add whatever extra flights you need once you've got there.

Sample RTW prices:

◇ Under £700: London–Calcutta–Singapore surface to Bangkok–Perth surface to Sydney–Auckland–Fiji–Tahiti–Los Angeles–London.
◇ Under £950: London–Delhi surface to Kathmandu–Bangkok surface to Singapore–Perth surface to Melbourne–Auckland–Mexico–London.
◇ Under $1600 for San Francisco–Bali–Singapore surface to Bangkok–Cairo–Athens surface to London–San Francisco.
◇ Under $2000 for New York–Amsterdam surface to Paris–Ho Chi Minh surface to Bangkok–Brunei–Perth surface to Melbourne–Auckland–Fiji–Tahiti–Los Angeles–New York.

Special deals: charters and courier flights

Charter flights to major holiday resorts (such as Goa and Bali) can sometimes be cheaper than discounted fares on scheduled flights. Charters are sold through high-street travel agents and sometimes include accommodation as well (you're under no obligation to use the accommodation for any or all of the time if you want to move on), but you're generally limited to a two-week stay – a month at most. Some package tour operators also offer good last-minute discounts on any plane seats left unsold in the last week or ten days before departure. These are advertised in travel agent windows, in newspapers, on the Internet and, in the UK, on ITV's Teletext service.

One other way to get a really cheap flight is to become a courier. A number of courier companies offer heavily discounted international flights to travellers willing to accompany documents and/or freight to the destination for them. There's nothing dodgy about these companies or their goods: it's just cheaper for them to subsidize a traveller's fare than use one of their own employees. Courier deals are advertised in the press and sold through special agents (see *Basics* p.298 for a list); in some cases you'll need to pay a nominal joining fee to qualify.

Courier flights can be up to fifty percent cheaper than advertised rates (eg Los Angeles to Hong Kong return for $350, with last-minute returns sometimes dropping as low as $150), but are only available to certain destinations (chiefly Hong Kong, Singapore, Japan and Malaysia). Most have considerable restrictions attached: you will probably have to come back within a month; you will have to travel alone; and you might only be allowed to take carry-on luggage with you, as some courier companies use your luggage allowance themselves. For the full lowdown on courier deals around the world, have a look at *Courier Air Travel Handbook: Learn How to Travel Worldwide for Next to Nothing* by Mark I. Field (Perpetual Press).

Booking your ticket

Ticket prices fluctuate according to the time of year and are at their most expensive during high season, in other words when most people want to go, which is generally during the school holidays and over the Christmas period. Fares are at their lowest during low season, when the climate at the destination is least favourable (eg during monsoons or deep winter). It's always worth checking with your travel agent whether you could save money by going a week earlier or later than planned.

To make your arrival as hassle-free as possible, try to book a flight that touches down in daylight, remembering that it could take up to two hours to go through immigration and collect your baggage and that it gets dark around 6pm in south and Southeast Asia. This will give you plenty of time to sort out your ride into the city and your accommodation before it gets dark. Though things do not necessarily grind to a halt as soon as the sun sets, everything becomes more difficult – and unnerving – after dark. Not only is it safer to arrive during daylight, but the airport tourist information desk and cash exchange booths may not be open 24 hours a day. For more advice on planning your arrival, see Chapter Eight.

For long-haul flights and RTW tickets, it's nearly always acceptable to make provisional bookings on a ticket, though many travel agents ask for a small deposit, transferable but non-refundable, to deter time-wasters. Or you can just grill the staff for information and then go home and think about it for a few days. Full payment on long-haul tickets is usually only due six weeks before departure.

When you buy your ticket, check with your travel agent about the following things:

◇ Seat reservations. Some airlines let you book your actual seat (window/aisle, smoking/non-smoking, etc) when buying your ticket.
◇ Ordering special food for the flight. All international airlines cater for a range of special diets (such as vegetarian, kosher and diabetic), but these must be ordered in advance, either through your travel agent or by calling the airline yourself.
◇ Non-smoking flights. Many of the major airlines now operate entirely smoke-free flights; if you can't last a longish flight without nicotine, you'll need to choose a different airline.
◇ Reserving a room at your destination. Most travel agents can book mid-range hotels for you (from about $25/£15 a double in Bangkok, for example). Though more expensive than doing it yourself when you get there, this is a good idea for your first couple of nights in Asia as it's one less thing to worry about when you arrive. More details in Chapter Eight.
◇ Travel insurance. Many travel agents offer their own travel insurance to customers (see below for more details on insurance).
◇ Visa service. Major travel agents will get visas for you, but unless you're in a hurry it's much cheaper to buy them yourself.
◇ Vaccinations. The biggest travel agents have on-site health centres where you can get your jabs and buy first-aid kits and malaria pills. These centres give extremely reliable advice and will usually see you without an appointment. But they're not cheap.
◇ Foreign currency. Agents sometimes offer competitive rates.

Insurance

Whatever the length of your trip to Asia and your itinerary, you'll need to arrange travel insurance – both medical and to cover your personal possessions. Recommended agents are listed on p.303. Although some credit cards advertise travel insurance as part of their package, there are usually conditions attached – you must book the holiday using your card, and it is unlikely that overall cover will be adequate. Check your individual policy as some aspects of cover start from when you buy the policy. If you need to cancel your trip due to emergency circumstances (illness, death in the family, civil war at your destination), then you may be covered.

With the huge number of policies on offer, it pays to start your research well in advance to make sure you get the policy you want at a good price. However, don't buy until you have fixed your timing and itinerary. Things to think about when choosing a policy:

◇ If you are planning several trips in one year, consider an annual policy, which usually works out cheaper than buying insurance separately for each trip. Check the maximum allowable length for each trip and the total maximum travelling time allowed. These policies are not suitable for those going on one year-long trip.

◇ For lengthy trips, head for specialist travel insurers who offer longer insurance deals (student insurance companies are worth checking). You don't want to buy a policy from a company specializing in shorter trips and then pay to add on each week or month – it'll be more expensive.

◇ If it's possible that your plans will change, check whether you can add on time once you are travelling or reclaim money for unused time.

◇ Some insurance companies will allow travel companions or home-sharers to buy a policy for a couple, rather than two separate policies.

◇ What does your potential insurance company classify as a "hazardous pursuit"? These are usually excluded from cover and will include activities such as bungy-jumping, paragliding and scuba diving, but some companies have claimed that riding a bicycle or trekking in remote areas come under this heading. If there are activities that you want covered, it may be possible to get them added on for a charge, or you may have to find another insurer, but either way you should think about all the exciting things you may do on your trip and buy your insurance accordingly.

◇ Make sure you note any limits on the value of your possessions. Most policies have single-item limits that won't cover camcorders or expensive cameras. It may be easier to add these items to an existing household insurance policy under an "all risks" clause that covers the item outside the home.

◇ There is generally an "excess" on each claim. This is the amount you have to pay on each claim. So, if the medical bill you paid in Thailand comes to $90 (£55) and the excess on the policy is $50 (£30), you'll only get $40 (£25). Check how high the excess is before you buy.

◇ Any claims won't usually get settled until you get home, so it is wise to have emergency funds – a credit card is the easiest – to cope with reimbursement costs on the spot.

◇ If you have particular needs – are over a certain age or have a medical condition – some insurers may be hesitant about covering you, so start your research early. The chances are that you will find a company who will offer cover, but it may take some time to track them down.

CHAPTER FOUR

WHEN TO GO

I f you've got no constraints on the timing of your trip to Asia, then make good weather your priority. Contrary to the tourist-brochure image, the Asian climate is not all summery days and balmy nights – sometimes it's too hot even to venture outside the door, while in other regions you might get nonstop rain for a week or more, or even snow in the mountains. But with careful planning it's possible to organize an extended itinerary that follows the best of the weather across the continent; "best" here means least extreme, because that's when travel is generally easiest and most comfortable (see the box on p.99 for a list of the best times to visit each country). On the other hand, don't let the prospect of very hot or very wet weather deter you altogether – just be prepared for travel arrangements to be less reliable and for tempers to get more easily frayed.

There is no single time of year when the whole of Asia is out of bounds because of inclement weather, but in the main the northern hemisphere's winter (November to February) is considered to be the pleasantest time to visit the region and is therefore classified as peak season. Prices are at their highest then, for everything from international airline tickets to accommodation; the best-value hotels get fully booked and many places are uncomfortably crowded.

The weather is only one factor, of course. You might want to time your visit around a specific event instead – the metre-wide bloom of the rafflesia, the world's largest flower, blossoms in Sumatra, Java and Malaysia in August or September; the mango season in India (April–August) is well worth a detour, as are many of the major Asian festivals, detailed on p.101. Or perhaps you want to be certain to catch the notorious full-moon party, held every month on the Thai island of Ko Pha Ngan. More prosaically, if you're hoping to pay for your trip by finding a job at the end of it – in either Europe or Australia – remember that timing is important here too. In Europe, May through September is the best time to find work in pubs, on building sites and on fruit farms; in Australia there's fruit and veg picking from November to April in the south, and from May through November in the far north, while in coastal Queensland, there's work available all year round.

● ●

EXTREME MEASURES

Travelling in extreme heat or cold can affect your budget as well as your state of mind and body. Most air-conditioned rooms cost at least 35 percent more than fan-cooled ones, but sometimes that's a price worth paying when daytime temperatures and humidity levels are unbearably high. If your finances won't stretch that far, take refuge in cafés and fast-food joints that can afford their own cooling systems; big supermarkets and modern shopping malls serve the same purpose. At night, wrap yourself in a wet sarong or sheet when you go to bed – that should keep you cool for long enough to get to sleep. Though air-con trains and buses are generally overrated (it's usually much more refreshing to throw the window open instead), taxis, whether air-conditioned or not, can be a real boon in the sweltering midday heat, so that's another expense to consider.

Conversely, you may be glad of heating in certain highland areas; again you will have to pay extra for this, though you might be able to get by with renting extra blankets and ensuring the showers have hot water. A cautionary note on primitive heating systems: it's essential that you check your room for decent air vents before using any kind of heater. In January 1996 a young couple were killed by the carbon monoxide fumes from the charcoal fire they left burning through the night in their room in Darjeeling.

●●●

The climates of Asia

Wherever you are in the world, the local weather is determined by latitude, altitude and continental position (distance from the sea), plus a whole assortment of microclimates. Within Asia, the two annual monsoons (seasonal winds) also play a crucial part.

The further a place is from the equator, the more defined its seasonal differences: northern Japan, for example, which shares roughly the same latitude as southern France or Quebec, has four distinct seasons. Summertime temperatures in Sapporo average 24°C, while winter ones average 2°C. As a general rule, this makes the northern hemisphere's spring and autumn the mildest and most pleasant time to visit the temperate regions of north Asia such as Japan, Korea, China, northern India and Nepal. Summer in north Asia varies from the pleasingly warm to the stiflingly hot, and winter days can get very cold, though skies are often invigoratingly blue.

As you move further south towards the equator, the weather gets warmer and the seasons become less distinct. By the time you cross the Tropic of Cancer – a line of latitude that runs just north of Vietnam and 450km south of Delhi – and enter the tropics (the zone that straddles the distance either side of the equator from the Tropic of Cancer in the north to the Tropic of Capricorn in the south), there is precious little change in temperature at any time of year: Kuala Lumpur is 32°C in December and 33°C in June.

Instead, seasons in the tropics are defined by the amount of rainfall and, to some extent, by the relative humidity. So you get a "cool season" (comparatively low humidity and little rain), a hot season (high humidity and little rain) and a rainy season (high humidity and lots of rain). These are only loose classifications, however, and are explained in more detail later in this chapter. Humidity also intensifies the closer you get to the equator, making central Sumatra and central Borneo, for example, sticky and sultry all year round, while northern Thailand and Burma (which lie close to the Tropic of Cancer) only get really humid just before the monsoon arrives.

Monsoons: tropical Asia

Though the temperature may not affect the timing of your trip to tropical Asia, you will probably want to avoid travelling there during the wet season. Wet seasons are relatively predictable in Asia, as the rains are brought to the continent by seasonal winds, known as monsoons, which follow a particular timetable and itinerary. Asia is hit by two monsoons a year, one of which brings mostly wet weather (May–Oct), the other of which brings mainly dry weather (Nov–April). Monsoons are capricious, however, and though expected to arrive in each place on the exact same date every year, often turn up several days or even weeks late. Worse still, they can bypass whole areas altogether, leaving the farmers battling against drought for up to three or four years on the trot.

The southwest monsoon arrives in west coast regions of Asia at around the end of May and brings daily rainfall to most of Asia (excepting certain east coast areas, explained below) by mid-July. From then on you can expect overcast skies and regular downpours across the region till October or November. To get an idea of just how wet Asia can be during the rainy season, compare London's wettest month (64mm), or New York's (109mm), or Sydney's (135mm), with Bangkok, which gets an average of 305mm of rain every September – imagine what that does to the canals and rivers in the aptly named "Venice of the East".

That's nothing, however, compared to what happens to Cherrapunjee, a small town in northeast India that has been known to get over a metre of rainfall in a single day – for which it earns an entry in the *Guinness Book of*

Records. Across the border in low-lying Bangladesh, monsoons bring devastating floods every year, regularly rendering thousands of people homeless.

The wind direction is reversed during the northern winter when the land cools down, so the northeast monsoon brings drier, slightly cooler weather to most of tropical Asia (east coast areas excepted) between November and February. This period is the best overall time to travel in tropical Asia.

The main exceptions to the above pattern are the east coast regions of Vietnam, Peninsular Thailand, Peninsular Malaysia, and Sri Lanka, and the southeastern region of India. Due to various complicated factors, the most obvious of which is their east coast location, these areas get rain when the rest of tropical Asia is having its driest period, but stay dry during the southwest monsoon.

Much of Indonesia, however, gets the worst (or best) of both monsoons, attracting the west coast rains from May through October, and the east coast rains from November to February. In some parts of the archipelago – like equatorial Sumatra – barely a week goes by without a shower or two, while at the sub-equatorial end of the island chain, in Timor, the annual dry season usually runs from April to October.

Altitude: the Himalayas

Temperatures plummet by 6.5°C for every 1000m you gain in altitude, so the higher you go the colder the air becomes – worth bearing in mind when you're sweltering on the tropical plains (see box on p.95 for suggested upland getaways).

The Himalayas are Asia's major mountain range and, though the climate here is much cooler than on the lowlands, it too is affected by the southwest monsoon. The torrential rain that drenches the Punjab from June to

August falls as several metres of snow in the Everest region – making it an unpredictable and potentially dangerous time to go trekking. At lower elevations, the rains can cause landslides on mountain roads during this time, so it's as well to keep travel plans flexible or to avoid the region altogether.

The snow is heaviest, however, during the cold winter months, and mountain passes above 4000m are usually blocked between December and April, with the snow line descending to around 2500m during this period. October and November are therefore the most popular months for trekking in Nepal and northern India: skies are clear and daytime temperatures fairly warm, especially in the sun (nights are always cold in the mountains). Lower-level trekking is also popular from February through mid-April.

Throughout Asia, mountain areas become inaccessible to vehicles as well as trekkers and mountaineers during the winter months. Heavy snowfall makes the 5000-metre-high trans-Himalayan Manali-Leh Highway impassable between November and April (although the road is officially shut between September 15 and June 15, public buses plough on until the last possible moment). And the similarly dramatic link between Pakistan and China, known as the Karakoram Highway because it crosses a 5575-metre-high pass in the Karakoram Mountains (location of the famous K2 peak), is also closed between November and April.

If you're not trekking or driving at very high elevations, however, the northern winter is a lovely time to admire the snowcapped peaks from a warmer vantage point in the Himalayan foothills and valleys. Though days are brisk and nights extremely cold, the air is crisp and fresh in this season, the skies a lovely clear blue and the mountains at their most spectacular. So long as you're kitted out with the right gear, this can be an exhilarating – and peaceful – time to be in northern India, Nepal and northern Japan.

Continental position: deserts and plateaus

A region's continental position also has a huge effect on its weather. Places far from the sea tend to have extreme climates, with very hot, dry summers, very cold winters, and precious little rain at any time of the year. The high Tibetan plateau and northwestern China, for example, get negligible rain, choking summer dust storms and bitterly cold winters – temperatures in Ürümqi, in Xinjiang, northwest China, never rise above minus 1°C between November and March, sinking to minus 22°C during the daytime in January. In July, however, temperatures average 28°C. Rajasthan, in the Thar desert in northwestern India, experiences a less extreme version of the same climate, so expect some cold nights here in the middle of winter and avoid high summer if you can.

● ●

IF YOU CAN'T STAND THE HEAT . . . GET OUT OF THE CITY

When the mid-morning mercury hits 35°C and the humidity averages ninety percent, it's time to think about cooling yourself down. If you can't get to the seaside, then consider heading up into the hills instead.

During the Raj era, the colonial Brits decamped en masse every summer to the Indian hill stations of Shimla, Ooty, Darjeeling and Kodaikanal, and these old-fashioned resort towns are still pleasant places to visit, many of them reached by quaint steam trains that trundle up through tea plantations to the refreshing forested hills. Further south, in Sri Lanka, the hill resort of Kandy (488m) makes a lovely cool lakeside retreat from the roasting plains, and for a full-on chill-out you can continue up to the former colonial outpost of Nuwara Eliya (1890m), at its best in March and April. In Malaysia, hot season temperatures up on the Cameron Highlands are a good 10°C cooler than down in the sweltering capital. Other popular upland getaways include the hills around Chiang Mai in northern Thailand, the Bolovens Plateau in Laos, Da Lat in south Vietnam, Sylhet in Bangladesh, Baguio in the Philippines, and the volcanic highlands around Berastagi in north Sumatra and Lake Batur in Bali.

● ●

Travelling in the tropics

November to February: the best time to go

The pleasantest overall time to visit tropical Asia is from November through February. This is the so-called cool season, when temperatures at sea level are at their most manageable, the humidity is relatively low, and there is hardly any rainfall. In December, you can expect maximum daytime temperatures of 31°C in Bangkok, 23°C in Delhi, 30°C in Manila, and 28°C in Vientiane. Unfortunately, prices are at their highest during this period, peaking over Christmas and New Year, and the classier hotels add a peak-season supplement to their already inflated rates.

However, certain east-coast areas do get the wet end of the northeast monsoon during this time; namely, most parts of Indonesia, southeastern India, and the east coasts of Vietnam, Peninsular Thailand, Peninsular Malaysia and Sri Lanka. Islands off these coasts are all best avoided between November and February, when boat connections are sporadic, beaches awash with flotsam and waves too high for a relaxed dip. Diving is unrewarding too, because the water gets quite cloudy. Eastern Malaysia (Sabah and Sarawak) is also subject to the northeast monsoon and some roads become impassable during this time. In Indonesia it's unsafe to climb many of the mountains in the wet season.

February to May: the heat is on

By February, the heat is starting to build up right across the plains of tropical Asia, reaching a crescendo in May. During this month, Bangkok temperatures peak at 34°C, and it's 41°C in Delhi, 34°C in Manila, and 32°C in Vientiane. Though travel is perfectly possible during the hot season, it can be hard work, not least because the humidity is so high that it saps your energy and can make you loath to leave the air-conditioning between 10am and 3pm. Heat exhaustion is more likely too.

The weeks before the rains break are a notoriously tense time in tropical Asia: tempers are short, people resort to violence more quickly, and the suicide rate goes up. Depleted water supplies mean many rural households struggle to keep their crops and livestock alive, and electricity in towns and villages is often rationed because there simply isn't enough water to run the hydroelectricity plants all day long. It's especially important to take a torch if travelling at this time of year, as budget hotels rarely have their own generators.

Many Asian cultures believe the rains are controlled by gods or spirits, so the end of the hot season is a good time to catch rain-making festivals. The people of northeast Thailand think that rain is the fruit of heavenly lovemaking, so in mid-May they hold an exuberant rocket-firing festival to encourage the gods to get on with it.

Places to avoid at all costs during the hot season include the Pakistani region of Baluchistan which, by June, becomes one of the hottest places in the world, with peak daytime temperatures averaging 46°C. You won't get much relief across the border in India at this time either, where the Rajasthani town of Jaisalmer swelters in the low forties through May and June.

May to October: wet season travel

As the southwest monsoon brings rain to most of Asia between May and October, this is the overall worst time to travel. Quite apart from getting soaked whenever you leave your hotel, you'll be uncomfortably sticky in any rainproof gear (use an umbrella instead) and may also have to ward off leeches, malarial mosquitoes and other wet-weather bugs. Diseases like typhoid and Japanese encephalitis spread faster in these conditions too (but are mainly confined to rural areas), and you'll be more prone to fungal infections and unhealthy skin.

Diving will be a complete waste of time as visibility will be minimal, surfing will likely be out of the question, and beaches flounder under the garbage washed up by the storms. Some islands are impossible to get to at this time (such as Thailand's Ko Similan and Malaysia's Langkawi), while other regions may be inaccessible because the roads have turned to mud.

Fierce tropical winds are also more frequent during the rainy season. Known as typhoons, these winds hit certain parts of Asia, notably the Philippines, Bangladesh and southeast China, at speeds of over 120km per hour, leaving a trail of flattened crops, dismembered houses and an inevitable toll of human casualties as well. Things can get very hairy during a typhoon, especially on the coastal plains where tidal waves cause additional destruction, so you should always heed local advice about places to avoid during a typhoon. As forecasters usually predict typhoons a few days in advance, you should have plenty of time to prepare and protect yourself (see p.274 for more typhoon advice).

However, rain needn't put a damper on *all* Southeast Asian itineraries. In some places (like west coast Peninsular Malaysia) downpours are limited to just a couple of hours every day for two or three months during the wet season, and these storms are often so regular as to arrive at the same time every afternoon. Waterfalls spring back to life, rice paddies flood picturesquely, and this is often the best time of year for flowers.

The rainy season is usually low season for the tourist industry, and this can have all sorts of advantages, including discounted accommodation and more time to hobnob with local people. Note that, despite the weather, some airlines and swanky hotels treat July and August as a special peak season, because this is the time the northern hemisphere takes its summer holidays.

In most parts of Asia, the coming of the monsoon is cause for celebration – not only is it essential for the crops, but it

THE BEST TIME TO VISIT . . .

A very broad guide to the best season for travelling, assuming you want the weather to be as dry and mild as possible. Mildness is of course a relative concept: a mild maximum daytime temperature in Jakarta is 31°C, in Ho Chi Minh it's 27°C and in Kathmandu it's 26°C. The summary that follows is meant only as an introduction to help with general route-planning and gear preparation. For fuller details, check with guidebooks or tourist offices. To find out what the next four days' forecast is for any major Asian city, call up *www.intellicast.com/weather/asia*

Bangladesh: Nov–Feb.

Burma: Nov–Feb.

Cambodia: Nov–March.

China: March–May; Sept–Nov; **Hong Kong**: Sept–Dec; **Tibet**: April–Oct.

India: Oct–March (except in the southeast); April–Sept (southeast only).

Indonesia: **Bali**: April–Oct; **Java**: June–Aug; **Kalimantan**: May–Sept; **Nusa Tenggara**: May–July; **Sulawesi**: Aug & Sept; **Sumatra**: June & July, Sept & Oct.

Japan: April–Nov.

Laos: Nov–March.

Malaysia: March–July (except peninsular west coast); Dec–Feb (for peninsular west coast).

Nepal: Oct & Nov; Feb–April.

Pakistan: Oct–Feb.

Philippines: Nov–Feb (except stretches of southeast coasts); March & April (for southeast coasts).

Singapore: Feb–Oct.

South Korea: April–June; Sept–Nov.

Sri Lanka: Nov–March (west coast); April–Oct (east coast).

Thailand: Nov–Feb (except peninsular east coast); March–Sept for peninsular east coast.

Vietnam: Sept–Dec; March & April.

also breaks the tension of the preceding weeks and is considered to have both healing and erotic properties (extramarital affairs are said to flourish during the rainy season). In India, middle-class city folk plan their holidays to coincide with the arrival of the first rains in the southwest, and in Bangkok men and women shampoo their hair out on the street in the first decent downpour of the season.

For travellers, east-coast beaches and islands that are not affected by the southwest monsoons come into their own during this time – in Thailand that makes May to October peak season for Ko Samui, Ko Pha Ngan and Ko Tao, and the best time to head for east-coast Sri Lanka; east-coast Malaysia is at its best between March and July. Off season for these coasts and islands is between November and April, during the northeast monsoon.

Special events and local holidays

Many festivals and annual events are well worth planning your itinerary around – or even changing your schedule for. Religious festivals can be especially fun, many of them celebrated with street parades, food fairs (Thailand), dance performances (India) and shadow-puppet plays (Indonesia), which tourists are usually welcome to attend (though you should ask locally first). As Buddhists and Hindus operate on a lunar calendar (as opposed to the Western Gregorian one), these festivals occur on different dates every year, but tourist offices will be able to give you precise details.

The biggest festivals can draw huge local crowds as well, so be prepared for packed trains and buses and over-booked hotels. If possible, reserve transport and accommodation well in advance and expect to shell out up to double the normal price for food and lodging. Occasionally, the volume and exuberance of festival crowds can become quite scary, and so may be best avoided – the water- and paint-throwing festival of Holi, which is celebrated throughout India every February or March, is a typical example, as shown by the box on p.103.

National public holidays tend to be more stuffy occasions, especially the ones commemorating political victories or rulers' birthdays, and are usually marked by military parades and speeches, if at all. Most businesses close on these days, as do markets and restaurants, though popular sights – particularly waterfalls, temples and public parks – will be chock-a-block with local people on their day off.

THE PUSHKAR CAMEL FAIR

Pushkar was hosting its annual fair, a combination of religious festival and huge camel market, with over fifty thousand animals brought in from all over Rajasthan. The streets were heaving with pilgrims, traders and tourists, and the bazaar spilled over into a labyrinth of dim, twisting alleys – market stalls a blaze of colour, the air thick with spices, dust and sweat.

A sea of makeshift tents, camels and assorted livestock stretched far out across the plain. Tall, regal men dressed in waistcoats and long, baggy loincloths wandered among the animals, inspecting, discussing, bargaining. Turbans formed bobbing multi-coloured dots among the ochre-brown mass, and even the camels were decorated with vibrant bridles of twisted cord, tasselled and beaded. Most animals stood or lay quietly ruminating, surveying their surroundings disdainfully, but every now and then a screeching and a swirl of dust would signify a runaway, pursued by groups of stick-wielding men.

Nicki McCormick

Good days . . .

We've chosen some of our favourite festivals, but any guidebook will offer heaps more. Or have a look at *Wild Planet! 1,001 Extraordinary Events for the Inspired Traveler* by Tom Clynes (Visible Ink Press), which includes details of dozens of small- and large-scale celebrations in Asia and the rest of the world.

◇ **Ice Lantern Festival in Harbin, northeast China**. From January 5 to February 5, when temperatures sink to an unbearably chilly minus 30°C, the excess snow and ice in Harbin's Zhaolin Park is carved into extraordinary sculptures and even replica buildings such as life-size Chinese temples.
◇ **Ati-Atihan harvest pageants at Kalibo in the Philippines**. This small town hosts a huge Mardi Gras-style extravaganza on the third weekend of January. The streets are packed with people in outrageous costumes and everyone joins in the dancing.

◇ **Buddhist New Year in Thailand, Laos, Burma and Cambodia.** The Buddhists of Indochina celebrate their New Year in mid-April with nationwide public water fights – once symbolic of a purification ritual, but now more of an excuse for clowning about and drenching total strangers. The most organized people circulate town in pick-up trucks fitted with hosepipes and water cannons, while others limit themselves to more genteel sprinkling. Any passer-by, tourists included, will get soaked, though it's quite refreshing at this time of year, April being the hottest month of the hottest season. The most exuberant New Year celebrations are held in Chiang Mai (Thailand), Luang Prabang (Laos) and Mandalay (Burma).

◇ **Cherry blossoms and maple trees, Japan.** Cherry blossom season begins when the first flowers appear in Okinawa, the southernmost island of the Japanese archipelago, and for the next few weeks national TV broadcasts a nightly *sakura* forecast, showing how far the pink wave has progressed up the country. When the main island of Honshu turns pink (towards the end of April), the parks are packed with blossom-viewing picnic parties. Friends and families settle under the trees, getting drunk on saké, belting out karaoke songs and composing maudlin haiku poems about the fragile petals. Seven months later, the ancient capital of Kyoto flames a brilliant red for the last couple of weeks in November, when the maple trees light up the hillsides in displays bettered nowhere but British Columbia. This is also your one chance to sample the bizarre local delicacy known as *momiji tempura* – maple leaves fried in batter.

◇ **Spring fair in Dali, China.** For five days every April or May, thousands of people from all over Yunnan converge on Dali for horse-trading, wrestling matches, racing contests, dancing and singing.

◇ **Gawai Dayak harvest festival, Sarawak, East Malaysia.** Parties in the traditional Iban longhouses are always riotous, but the biggest celebration of the year happens in June to mark the end of the rice harvest. Expect all-night drinking and heaps of food, plus lots of jokes, pranks and party games.

◇ **Kandy historical pageant, Sri Lanka.** For ten nights every July or August, extravagant torch-lit processions of costumed dancers, drummers and elephants in full regalia parade through the streets of Kandy. It's thought to be one of the oldest historical pageants in the world.

◇ **Pushkar camel fair, northwest India**. For three days in late October or early November all roads seem to lead to Pushkar in Rajasthan as crowds of 200,000 descend on this tiny desert town for India's biggest camel fair. Camels are paraded, raced and entered for competitions and the place brims over with market stalls and street entertainers. At night, tourists are housed in a specially erected tent city where huge marquees are equipped with camp beds and bush toilets.

◇ **Surin elephant roundup, northeast Thailand**. Surin's resident herd of working elephants is rounded up every November for a public display of their talents, and thousands of tourists come to watch them play soccer, engage in a tug of war and parade around the sports ground in traditional battle garb.

● ●

SOAKING UP THE ATMOSPHERE, INDIAN STYLE

It was Holi, the first day of spring, and the townspeople of Puri in east India were celebrating the day in traditional style, by taking to the streets with pails of water and armfuls of paint bombs, and chucking them at passers-by. The owner of the guest house advised us not to go out until after midday, when the water-throwing had to stop. Foreigners were popular targets, he said, and it would not be a pleasant experience.

But we had to go out, to buy tickets from the train station. From the safety of our rickshaw seat, we watched as people on the streets got sprayed, but we stayed fairly dry. Then the rickshaw driver turned down an alleyway and stopped, and the ambush began. A group of young guys rushed towards us, pelting us from all angles with buckets of water and handfuls of paint, which they rubbed into our faces and hair. It was pretty scary, and we got soaked. Our camera was sodden, I had paint in my eyes, and my clothes were stained for ever. Mission accomplished, they backed off and we drove on.

At the train station we stood soggily in the statutory queue. Just as we reached the sales counter, the ticket man's face dropped and we looked round to see another gang of water guerrillas bursting through the doors. This time everyone got soaked, not just the tourists, and files and papers were reduced to mush. Excitement over, the salesman proceeded with his form-filling, and we came away with our tickets.

Jo Mead

● ●

. . . and bad days

Though the tourist industry never grinds to a complete standstill, there are certain public and religious holidays when you'll be hard-pressed to find hotels and restaurants open for business. In Bali, for example, the Hindu New Year is celebrated in March or April with a day of complete silence and inactivity – businesspeople are actually fined if they trade on that day, and the chances of getting a taxi ride from the airport are very slim.

Nor is it a great idea to land in China during the three-day Chinese New Year celebrations (in late Jan or early Feb) as everything will be closed, and you're unlikely to find a hotel room anywhere. The same is true of any town or city with a majority Chinese community – Singapore is an obvious example, but the hotels and restaurants in many Thai and Malaysian cities are also run by Chinese immigrants. If you want to be in one of these places for Chinese New Year (the firework displays can be unforgettable), then get to the city a couple of days early so you can stake your claim on a room and stock up on food. The same advice applies if you're in Sri Lanka over the Sinhalese New Year in mid-April, when lots of hotels and restaurant close down for a whole week.

Similarly, you might want to think twice about visiting an Islamic country during Ramadan, a month-long period of abstinence (on variable dates in Jan, Feb or March), when practising Muslims do without food, water and tobacco during daylight hours. This makes for a very stressed-out population, particularly by the third and fourth week, so you may not get the hospitality you were hoping for. More seriously, you may get abuse, or even stones, hurled at you just because you are a non-Muslim.

Many restaurants stay shut during the daytime throughout Ramadan. If you are in Indonesia, Pakistan, Bangladesh, India, Malaysia or southern Thailand during Ramadan, be sensitive to your hosts and don't flaunt your food, drinks and cigarettes in front of them.

Steer clear of big cities in the immediate run-up to elections too, particularly in India where rallies can turn nasty and curfews may be imposed on and around polling day. It's not unknown for election results to be greeted with riots, so head for safe havens in the hills or by the sea, and get your news from the *Times of India* instead.

CHAPTER FIVE

HOW MUCH WILL IT COST?

This chapter will help you calculate your costs, give you ideas for making your cash go further and provide practical advice on how to take your money with you. However carefully you work out your budget, though, accept that there will be unexpected expenses along the way, and try to take more money than you think you will need. Global incidents such as war and the collapse of stock markets can cause serious currency fluctuations, which will wreck your conversion calculations, while the insatiable urge to ship a divine granite elephant home from Bali or the pressing necessity for a whitewater rafting trip down the Sun Kosi in Nepal will throw inflexible finances into chaos. If you spend half your trip worrying about every penny and unable to do much of what you had planned because of a cash crisis, then you'll have a wretched time. If you are seriously strapped for cash, it's worth planning a shorter trip – we guarantee you'll have a better time than if you embark on a longer, penny-pinching haul.

● ●

EXCHANGE RATES

For an idea of how much your money will be worth once you're on the road, you can check conversion rates for the most popular destinations in the financial pages of newspapers or at the exchange counter of your local bank. On the Web, try *www.oanda.com/cgi-bin/ncc* This web site gives you up-to-date rates for 164 currencies and compiles free wallet-sized conversion tables for travellers. It can also tell you what the rate was on any given day since January 1990, so you can see whether the general trend is up or down.

• •

A realistic budget

One thing to remember is that generalizations are dangerous. "Oh, Asia's cheap," you'll hear again and again. It is true that, compared with the major cost of your plane ticket, other prices can seem cheap. But whilst you can find a basic beach hut in Goa or on the islands off the southeast coast of Thailand for about $5 (£3) a night, you'll be looking at at least $16 (£10) for a bed in Singapore and Hong Kong, and in Tokyo anything less than $35 (£20) is very rare indeed. In fact, you'll find all extremes across the continent. A night in *Raffles Hotel* in Singapore will cost you well over $500 (£300) – this will buy three months' accommodation in parts of Indonesia.

How much you spend also depends on the sort of holiday you want to have. Whilst rock-bottom accommodation, local transport and food from simple food stalls in Vietnam is likely to set you back about $16 (£10) daily, once you start considering a bit more comfort, a few beers and better-quality food, then $25–35 (£15–20) is more realistic. It's relatively easy to sit in comfort at home and swear you'll manage without air-con, bathe in cold water and love it, and never want a private toilet, but after a week in 45°C and ninety percent

PRICES IN ASIA

We have tried to give some indication of costs per day in the most visited countries of Southeast Asia. Prices are approximate, based on budget accommodation, food in local not tourist restaurants, and second-class travel, excluding adventure trips.

However, during 1997, three of the major Asian currencies (the Thai baht, the Indonesian rupiah and the Malaysian ringgit) suffered a dramatic crash against the US dollar and all other hard currencies. In August 1997, for example, the rupiah was trading at Rp2400 to the dollar; by March 1998, it was over Rp10,000 to the dollar. This means that travellers exchanging their dollars and pounds have been, and in many cases still are, very well off in local currency terms. However, rampant inflation often follows such extreme problems and can serve to re-establish prices relative to the dollar, even continuing upwards and making a previously cheap country for travellers into an expensive one. In Burma, inflation is currently running at around thirty percent annually and in Nepal it's twenty percent. Keep a close eye on currency fluctuations prior to your departure.

Top-end countries will cost you $35 (£20) a day upwards:

| China (east coast cities) | Japan |
| Hong Kong | Singapore |

Middle-range countries should be manageable on a budget of $25–35 (£15–20):

Indonesia	Sri Lanka
Malaysia	Thailand
Philippines	Vietnam

humidity, a few cold showers at 3000m or three days with chronic diarrhoea, your perceptions will certainly alter. Even if you plan to have the budget holiday to beat all budget holidays, it makes sense to plan for the occasional splurge. Most first-time visitors to Asia aim for a low weekly budget on living costs, but allow themselves the occasional treat such as a few nights in air-conditioning, some hot water every so often or perhaps a couple of local flights.

Cheapest countries can be coped with on under $25 (£15) a day:

Bangladesh	Laos
Cambodia	Nepal
China (interior provinces)	Pakistan
India	

Three months in India
Staying in the cheapest hotels, eating only rice and dhal and travelling second class on all train journeys, you can manage on around $10 (£6) a day, $70 (£45) a week. If you bump up your luxury quotient, have a room with your own bathroom, vary your diet slightly and throw in a few first-class train journeys, then you'll be looking at $20–25 (£12–15) a day, $140–175 (£85–105) a week. Go further up the scale and book into mid-range hotels, eat in moderately priced restaurants and rent a car and driver for a few excursions, then around $35 (£20) a day, $225–250 (£140–150) a week, is a better estimate. To travel cheaply but realistically we would recommend calculating around half the trip at the lowest rate – say six weeks at $70 (£45) – and the remainder at the middle rate – say seven weeks at $175 (£105) – giving a total and much more realistic figure of $1645 (£1005). If you are planning internal flights, add these on top.

A three-month trip through Thailand, Malaysia and Indonesia
You'll need $3185 (£1820) if you allow $35 (£20) a day. However, long-distance travel costs will increase this figure significantly, especially if you fly, as will the amount of time you spend in Singapore. Allow yourself at least $3500 (£2000) to include some flights, the occasional splurge and some (restrained) souvenir shopping.

Generalizations about individual countries are also misleading. In India, a twelve-hour train trip will cost about $3 (£2) second class and a cup of tea beside the road is just a few cents, but it is equally possible to spend $115 (£70) a night on accommodation in luxury hotels in the big cities or $135 (£80) flying between Delhi and Madras.

Some Asian countries are so vast that you'll find different price "zones" in different parts of the country. East-coast Chinese cities have prices on a par with cities in the

West and you'll be hard pushed here to find a bed for less than $50 (£30). Inland, the picture changes hugely and in Sichuan, for example, there are budget beds available for a couple of dollars. It's worth bearing in mind that throughout Asia peak season prices can escalate sharply and hotel rooms can even double in price. Peak seasons vary locally, but Christmas and New Year are popular pretty much everywhere, while on Bali, June to September, coinciding with the European holiday season, is very busy and, in Nepal, October and November sees a tourist rush to take advantage of the ideal trekking weather.

On a similar note, you may think Japan is out of the question, its high cost of living set to bust all but the most elastic budgets. Whilst the Japan National Tourist Office do their utmost to entice you there with information on economical accommodation, food and travel in all their brochures, the truth is that you can manage there on a New York or London budget but not on a Bangkok one.

Saving money before you go

Windswept and exotic as it may sound, there is actually nothing at all romantic about jetting off to the furthest place you can think of and realizing when you get there that you can't afford to eat, drink or sleep in a decent bed, that you've got a ticket that won't let you go home early and you have to spend the first week working out how you can get money wired out to you. Budgeting is boring, but spending a bit of time thinking about it before you go will leave you more energy to enjoy Asia once you're there, rather than worrying about survival. Some of the biggest savings you'll be able to make are those before you go.

Budgeting is just one part of early preparation – always a good idea. The best flight deals sell early and you'll find that certain routes, eg to Goa for Christmas and New Year, are booked solid several months in advance. If you're rushing to fit visas, jabs and shopping into a few hectic weeks, you'll have to make hurried decisions and may end up paying to cut corners. The following tips may help:

❖ Shop around for your flight tickets and plan your itinerary with your budget in mind; a free stopover in Tokyo may seem like a good idea, but can you afford several days of high city prices? Taking a cheaper ticket that leaves you to travel from Bangkok to Singapore overland can sound appealing, but make sure you budget for the train or bus fare and the extra days on the road.

❖ Although there are plenty of visa services who will arrange visas for you (your travel agent may even offer to do this), it is always cheaper to do it yourself. However, you will need plenty of time, especially if you are applying by post. See Chapter Three for more visa information.

❖ You are probably going to need an armful of inoculations (see Chapter Twelve). Travel clinics provide excellent specialist information and are a time-saving and hassle-free way to get all your jabs. However, many injections are cheaper, and many of them free, from your own doctor.

❖ If you're booking your first couple of nights' hotel accommodation before you leave home (see Chapter Eight), contact a few hotels directly and compare their prices with those on offer through your travel agent.

Insurance

Whatever else you try to save money on, do NOT skimp on your insurance. Knowing that your medical costs and replacement gear will be paid for doesn't make a disaster OK, but it certainly makes it a whole lot more bearable. By all means shop around for a good deal, but don't consider going without insurance, lying about where you are going or what you are intending to do, or underestimating the value of your stuff just to get cheaper premiums – it isn't worth it. You could end up with tens of thousands of dollars of medical bills if you tell the insurance company you are going to Europe but end up being airlifted out of Irian Jaya, or insist you are not taking part in any hazardous sports, but are injured whitewater rafting in the Himalayas. Similarly, don't expect to be able to claim the full amount for your $200 camera if you tell the insurance company it's only worth $50. See p.86 for more details.

Be economical

Don't assume you have to take everything with you from home. Some equipment that will be essential for your trip (see Chapter Seven) such as lightweight clothes, insect repellents and mosquito nets, are cheaper once you are in Asia. Sarongs, those all-purpose coveralls, are cheap across the continent, as are Tiger balm, soap, shampoo, stationery, mosquito coils and detergent. However, sun block, tampons and deodorant are pricey throughout Asia, and hair conditioner is expensive and difficult to find outside tourist areas.

Don't assume everything you bring from home has to be sparkling new: it certainly won't be after a few weeks on the road. Trekking equipment shops often have a board advertising secondhand equipment and outdoor sports magazines usually include a classified ads section. Try local thrift and charity shops for cheap cotton clothes, rucksacks, waterproofs and even boots. However, do check stuff carefully: you don't want a pack with holes, broken zips and detached straps. Look for good value and don't get carried away by cheap prices.

Earning money

Before you go, you may like to think about ways of profiting from your trip. No, we're not talking drug-running or importing gems from Thailand; however, it may be possible to sell the story of your journey and/or photos of your trip when you get back, perhaps to student magazines or local newspapers. You'll be better off with slides rather than print pictures if you intend to try doing this, and you should have a good look at the type of travel articles favoured by different newspapers and magazines. Unless you have a track record or contacts, you'll be unlikely to elicit much interest before you go, but when you come back you can write the articles and submit them "on spec" to the publications you have chosen.

It isn't an easy area to break into, but have a look at *Writing Travel Books and Articles* (Self-Counsel Press) by Richard Cropp, Barbara Braidwood and Susan Boyce, Guy Marks' *Travel Writing and Photography: All You Need to Know to Make it Pay* (Travellers Press) or Louise Purwin Zobel's *The Travel Writer's Handbook: How to Write and Sell Your Own Travel Experiences* (Marlowe) for some tips.

Finding a job on the road

While you are away, you may be able to supplement your money supply with a temporary job of some sort – discretion is the order of the day here, as many tourist visas expressly prohibit employment. Have a look at *Working in Asia* by Nicki Grihault (In Print), a hugely detailed handbook, with contacts and advice on job possibilities ranging from volunteer work, through bar and restaurant work, working as a film extra or model, to English teaching. It also includes tips on acclimatizing to working life in individual countries. You could also check out the Asian sections in *Work Your Way Around the World* (Vacation Work/Petersons Guides) by Susan Griffith or *The Directory of Jobs and Careers Abroad* (Vacation Work/Petersons Guides) by Jonathan Packer. Once you start travelling, look for adverts in English-language newspapers, on noticeboards in travellers' areas, talk to other travellers or approach potential employers directly.

Teaching English

One of the more common jobs is teaching English. Asia is swarming with people learning English who yearn for a native speaker with whom to hone their skills. Most employment for foreigners is in private language schools; you'll find them in every city and they cater for the full range of pupils from beginners up to pre-university students. Classrooms are often small and hours antisocial, as many students want classes after their working day, in the evening or at weekends, but students are invariably eager, especially when they have a native speaker as a teacher. This is a good stepping stone into work as a private tutor or the better-paid jobs in the more established schools or universities. The best pay is to be found in Japan and Taiwan.

Everywhere you will find a TEFL (Teaching English as a Foreign Language) qualification very useful and it will give you access to better rates of pay. The most basic qualification is the RSA/Cambridge Certificate in English Language Teaching to Adults (CELTA), which takes four weeks' full-time study (it is also available part-time) and is recognized throughout the English-teaching world. Courses are widely available in the UK and cost around £950, but are well worth it if you are seriously contemplating teaching while you are away. This qualification is increasingly available in North America and Australasia – consult the *ELT Guide* (EFL Ltd) for details of where to study and how to find work abroad. The ELT Web site (*www.edunet.com/jobs/*) advertises jobs at language schools all over the world, including a good selection in Thailand, South Korea and Japan. *Teaching English in Southeast Asia* (In Print) by Nuala O'Sullivan is also worth a look, and includes language school addresses in every country in Southeast Asia. Don't forget to take photocopies of your qualifications with you and references from previous employers.

In Japan, many Western women get work as hostesses in bars where the male drinkers like to practise their English. Despite rumours, there is nothing dodgy about these places and "hostess" is not a euphemism for "prostitute", although you will probably have to cope with drunken fumblings once in a while.

●●●

GI BLUES

The plan was to travel from London to Perth – I had $400. I sold my camera in Delhi, but by the time I got to Bangkok I was broke. Somehow I had to get to Bali. I wasn't particularly worried about it; something would turn up. And it did – I landed a role in a movie called *Saigon*. The screen test required a crew cut as I was to be a GI, and I got one by marching around and saluting a bemused Thai hairdresser and saying loudly in English, "Shorter, shorter."

Heading to Lop Buri, however, where some evacuation scenes were to be filmed, I was singled out. I'd been surviving on $5 a day in India and it showed. The hard-as-nails American drill sergeant took one look at me and said, "Get him out of uniform." As I sloped off in scrawny shame, he called out, "You can play a civilian, son." Still, I was officially a GI (I had the haircut to prove it), and when the GIs went on strike for higher wages I got a rise too.

Chris Taylor

. . . .

Spending wisely while you are there

Whilst many of the major savings can be made before you even leave home, there are plenty of ways to save money on the road. These tips may be handy:

◇ Take your International Student Identity Card if you have one. The response to this is variable – in some places it'll simply get a bemused look, but in others it can get you reduced entrance fees to museums and performances.

◇ Eat as local people do. Western food and drink cost much more than local food throughout Asia. Many restaurant dishes come in family-sized portions, especially in China and Thailand, the idea being that diners share several dishes. You'll save money by eating in groups of two or more.

◇ Take advantage of the thriving secondhand market amongst travellers on the road. You can sell or swap items of equipment or guidebooks rather than buying them new. Many travellers' hotels and restaurants have noticeboards advertising goods for sale or swap.

◇ Hone your bargaining skills so that you don't pay over the odds for goods and services (see p.117).

◇ Consider taking a water filter if you're going on a long trip (see p.247 for more information on this). The price of bottled water, particularly in tourist resorts, can be surprisingly high and could use up a substantial part of your budget over a long period.

Indulge yourself

However, it's worth bearing in mind that cheapness isn't everything. Asia is probably the best chance most people have of affording some five-star luxury – so why not make the most of the opportunity to join the jet set for at least a few days? For an example, a slap-up buffet lunch in a top-flight Manila hotel will cost around $15 (£10), and a night in the *Lake Palace Hotel* in Udaipur, an exmaharajah's palace on an island in the middle of a lake – one of the world's most spectacular hotels – will set you back $200 (£125). You can see Bali in style with your own car and driver for a day for $35 (£20) or have a tailor-made cashmere suit run up in Bangkok for around $160 (£100).

And, whenever it's a toss-up between spending a bit of extra cash and putting your own safety at risk, you should always part with the cash. Spending money wisely will ensure you have a far more memorable trip than trying not to spend any at all.

● ●

IT'S NOT FAIR?

In several Asian countries there is a two- or three-tier pricing system in operation, so don't be too distressed if you see local people being charged less than you are. In Vietnam there is a three-tier pricing policy with foreigners paying more than local people for accommodation and train tickets, and *Viet Kieu* (overseas Vietnamese) paying somewhere between the two. In China the same principle applies to plane tickets and entry charges for museums and famous sights, while some hotels slap a foreigner's surcharge onto their prices. In Thailand and Sri Lanka foreigners are charged more than local people for entry to all national museums and historic places.

The reasoning behind all this is simple: foreigners can afford to pay more, therefore they should be charged more. It's a philosophy you will encounter time and time again throughout Asia from the woman selling mangoes in the market to the national airline company. There is usually little you can do in official situations (rail and air tickets, entrance charges, etc), except pay up. Some travellers feel it's a fair cop, others fume against it at every turn. However, when dealing with local people on the ground (in the market, in a rickshaw), try to find out a fair price from those around you and endeavour not to pay more (or at least not too much more). If foreigners consistently pay way over the top for something, the danger is either that prices will also rise for local people or that traders providing services will prefer to do so solely for foreigners. Accept that you'll end up paying somewhat over the odds on many occasions, but try not to get totally obsessed and distressed about it and feel you are being "ripped off" at every turn – especially when the amount involved may be just a few pennies.

• •

Bargaining

This is an aspect of Asian life that is very alien to visitors from the West. Some people take to it like ducks to water; others find it hard to cope with, no matter how long they stay on the continent.

It's important to remember that bargaining over the price of something is as much a ritual of social interaction as it is about saving money. Essentially it means that, with a few exceptions, the price of anything on offer is open to negotiation. However, if you offer a price and it is accepted you are morally bound to go ahead with the purchase – so don't get into bargaining if you haven't made up your mind whether or not you really want the item. It's perfectly acceptable, though, to wander around a market asking the prices just to get some idea of the starting figures.

If you're really into bargain-hunting, it can be worthwhile doing your shopping early in the day. In Bali, for example, the vendors believe that a good early sale establishes their fortune in trading for the rest of the day, so start bargaining at lower "morning prices".

HOW MUCH WILL IT COST?

CHAPTER 5

117

●●

SPECIAL PRICE FOR YOU, MADAM

In an Indian market you might like the look of a pair of trousers. You'll enquire the price, the vendor will ask five hundred rupees. You'll shake your head regretfully and offer two hundred (somewhere in the region of a third or a half is a good starting figure for clothing in India). He or she will throw their hands up in horror – they have a family to support, how can you expect them to make a living when you are taking the profit out of their business and the rice out of the mouths of their starving offspring, and how about four hundred? You nod sympathetically, but you notice a tiny fault in the material, can't really see your way to paying that much, but could perhaps go as high as three hundred. The fault is nothing; here, he has another pair that are perfect, three-eighty? Ah, but you have seen some similar ones at a better price down the road, what about three-fifty? He agrees, smiles, this is a special price for you, Madam – the transaction is done. All this may well have taken place over five minutes, an hour or even a week! However, it's always accompanied by smiles, gentle voices and good humour. Even if you can't reach an agreement, and often you can't, you shake your head regretfully and walk away. This in itself can be a useful tool in the process and many a bargain has been struck halfway down the street.

●●

Fixed prices and discounts

The real difficulty in Asia is knowing when and when not to bargain. Basically, prices are fixed (non-negotiable) in restaurants with prices displayed, supermarkets, in large department stores, on official public transport with tickets, in metered taxis and in museums, parks or temples where entrance charges are displayed and tickets are provided. Even in shops with prices labelled, such as CD and tape shops, you may be able to negotiate a better rate for purchases of ten or more or get a free tape thrown in.

As you move upmarket, the jargon changes slightly. So, for example, in a small guest house you might simply enquire whether they can let you have the room they have offered you at 100,000 dong for 80,000 dong, whereas in a luxury hotel you could enquire about the availability of discounts, perhaps producing a business card for a bit of extra effect. You are far more likely to get discounts on accommodation during the low season than when the place is packed out. It's always worth bargaining if you're staying longer than a couple of nights: many places will do good weekly and monthly rates.

How to take your money

However short your trip, NEVER simply take a huge wodge of cash hidden about your person. You'll want flexibility and easy access to your money, but you need security against loss and theft, and ideally some kind of backup or emergency funds. The best solution is to travel with a combination of cash, travellers' cheques and credit cards. It's a good idea to change a small amount of cash into the currency of your first Asian landfall before you leave home, in case the exchange counter at the airport of your arrival is closed or out of cash. This is not always possible. For example, you cannot legally buy rupees outside India; Vietnamese dong are not available outside the country; and other currencies are partially restricted meaning you can only change up small amounts abroad.

Cash

US dollars are the hard currency of choice throughout Asia, as long as the notes are clean and in good condition. Even little hotels at the back of beyond may be willing to change a few dollars into local currency if you get caught short, but they're unlikely to look at any other form of foreign currency. Take small denominations ($1 and $5), as small businesses are unlikely to keep large cash reserves. The other advantage is that cash is usually exchangeable even if you lose your passport. The big disadvantage is its vulnerability – if stolen, cash is untraceable and most insurance policies expressly exclude the theft of cash from their cover.

Travellers' cheques

Travellers' cheques are the long-term stalwart of the traveller and still an essential part of travelling in Asia. They are issued in a variety of currencies, usually at 1–1.5 percent commission, which is essentially the price you pay for peace of mind. However, you do need to be careful about whose cheques you carry. Whatever the other companies say, American Express is the most widely acceptable travellers' cheque in Asia. Every now and again there is a localized scare about fraud involving one brand or another, and if you are relying totally on travellers' cheques you should think about taking cheques from two or more companies. Whilst most major currencies are happily accepted at money changers and banks in tourist centres, you only need to get a bit off the beaten track to find that only US dollar cheques are acceptable.

They also need careful handling. You must record the numbers of the cheques and tick them off as you use them. Keep this record separate from the travellers' cheques themselves, because if the cheques are stolen or lost you must be able to report the missing numbers to the company. Also keep the emergency telephone number separate from the cheques – directory enquiries in a foreign language when you're upset isn't much fun. In general, travellers' cheques will be replaced at the nearest representative within a day or two, provided you have the missing numbers, information about the date and place of purchase and some form of ID. However, if you're exploring the river systems of southern Sarawak in a longboat, the nearest Amex office could be a long trip away. You'll be very glad of a $50 or $100 emergency stash kept somewhere apart from your main money supply should the worst happen.

You will always need your passport as identification to change travellers' cheques, so if your passport gets stolen your travellers' cheques are useless. In addition, some banks, in an attempt to avoid fraud, insist that you also show them the receipt – it has "Agreement to purchase" written on the back.

Plastic cards

The extent to which credit cards are acceptable as payment varies hugely across the continent. Whilst most top-class hotels, restaurants and shops are happy to accept them (and you often get a very favourable rate of exchange when the bill comes in), they're not much use in establishments at the budget end of the market.

You can also obtain cash advances against credit cards. Visa and Mastercard are the most widely accepted throughout Asia, both at banks and money changers. American Express offices provide a cheque cashing service for card-holders free of charge. In China, India, Indonesia, Japan, Malaysia, the Philippines, Singapore, South Korea and Thailand, cities and larger towns have ATM machines that accept debit cards on the Cirrus and Maestro network. There's a charge of around two percent for each transaction.

Even if you don't plan on using it, a credit card is a great emergency standby. Credit cards are particularly useful for major outlays such as internal flights, the occasional hotel

or restaurant splurge or for very large souvenirs and the cost of shipping them home. They can also be useful for booking and prepaying a hotel room over the phone or fax (very handy at peak times of the year), but only at the moderate to top end of the market. Remember that you'll need someone at home to organize the paying of the credit card bill if it's going to reach home before you do. You should also carry with you the phone number to report theft and make sure you NEVER let the card out of your possession. Bear in mind that, if it does get lost, it is likely to take at least four days to get a replacement to you.

Changing money

Whenever you change money you should check the current rate being offered and the commission charged on the transaction. Just as rates vary from bank to bank, so can the commission on the deal. In some cases you'll need to do your sums to decide on the best place to go. For example, $100 of Indian rupees at Rs39 to the dollar with a one percent commission fee is a better deal than a rate of Rs35 to the dollar with no commission. One disadvantage of travellers' cheques is that you pay commission on them when you buy them and you usually end up paying again on exchange. However, the same applies to a credit card: you'll be charged commission when you get the money, but it also attracts a 1–1.5 percent cash transaction fee on your bill.

Wherever and however you change money, be certain that you save your exchange certificates. This is your proof that you changed the money legally and in many countries it's vital if you want to change unspent local currency when you leave the country or want to pay for tourist tickets – for example, on Indian railways or China Airways, with local currency.

Follow a few sensible precautions when changing your hard currency into local money and you'll be a few baht, rupiah or dong better off:

◇ In some countries (China, India, Vietnam) there is a black market in the local currency offering better rates than the banks for hard currency. However, bear in mind that the local police or security forces often "sting" foreigners in this way: they set up the deal and then either arrest you for black market trading or extract a bribe to avoid criminal proceedings. There is also a risk you'll get caught up in a crackdown on local operators, become the victim of sleight-of-hand tricks or receive counterfeit notes. It probably isn't worth it.

◇ The most competitive rates are usually found in travellers' centres, such as Kuta in Bali or Khao San Road in Bangkok, where there's plenty of competition. You'll usually have a choice between changing money at banks, money changers or hotels. Shop around carefully, but don't be unduly suspicious of money changers. They are licensed by the local authorities, offer competitive and often better rates than the banks, have more flexible opening hours and often require less paperwork than banks (see box below). The last resort is to change money at hotels, where rates are usually the lowest.

◇ If you are passing through a country more than once, don't change money as you leave, as you'll only have to get more when you come back.

◇ Get rid of coins before you leave a country, as they are not exchangeable outside.

◇ At border crossings the chances are that rates will be poor. Change only what you need until you can get to a more competitive dealer.

◇ Always count your notes before you leave the cash desk, however long and tedious the process. It's worth it to be sure you've got the right amount. There are plenty of scams in operation – one involves folding notes in two so that you actually get half as much as appears to be being counted out. Another ploy is distracting you while counting out the money, so stay alert.

● ●

READY CASH?

I'd arrived in Sumatra from Singapore, where changing money is absolutely straightforward. I was in Bandar Lampung, a big city of several million people in southern Sumatra and down to my last few rupiah. It was time to hit the bank. I left the guest house saying

I wouldn't be long, but there were a few things I hadn't counted on.

The banks were all closed. Today was a national holiday on account of a Hindu festival in Bali, over 1000km away. Nobody in Bandar Lampung was Hindu, but who were they to turn down a day off? Well, three days off to be precise. Well, really five, if you add the Saturday and Sunday that followed.

I borrowed some cash off other travellers to tide me over and returned to town on Monday to try the bank again – actually several of them. In the first three branches they didn't do foreign exchange and directed me to a main branch across town (funds were getting low again and I had to walk). When I presented my sterling travellers' cheques rather than nice desirable US dollars, however, they didn't want to know, and directed me to another bank, who were equally disinterested in my cheques but took pity on my plight and found me a bank up the street that would exchange them.

By the time I got there it was lunch time. Myself and my rumbling stomach (no money for food) settled down for a long wait. The security guard was very apologetic, but I couldn't wait in the lovely cool air-conditioning – the bank had to be locked. I sat on the steps and dreamed of how many ice-cold drinks and outrageously exotic lunches I would buy when I got my hands on some cash.

When the bank re-opened, I was first at the counter. Did I have my purchase agreement for the travellers' cheques? Owing to some recent frauds, head office insisted that this piece of paper must be presented as well as a passport. I didn't know whether to laugh or cry. Yes, I had it, but it was back in the hotel. I raced back across town, starving hungry and dehydrated, collected the agreement and scurried back to the bank with ten minutes to spare before it closed for the day. Together the bank staff and I negotiated the forms in triplicate, they photocopied my passport and purchase agreement, they phoned head office twice to check the day's exchange rate, the supervisor checked everything and handed it all over to the cashier, who checked it all again and then, finally, handed over the money – six full days after I wanted it.

Lesley Reader

●●

Running out of money

In an emergency it is possible to get money wired out to you from home. However, hefty fees are charged and the efficiency and speed of the service varies across the continent.

Not surprisingly, it is relatively straightforward to transfer money to banks in Hong Kong (even so, it can take the best part of a day to arrange), but more time-consuming and haphazard to those in Nepal and India, whilst in China it can take weeks. It's easier if someone in your home country can make the arrangements or if you think you might need this service, have a chat with your home bank before you leave. You'll need to find a bank in the country you are in that has an agreement with the bank you wish to transfer from at home, and you'll need your passport as ID to collect the money once it has arrived. Most banks charge a flat fee for transfers, which makes it more economical to send larger sums. From the UK, expect to pay £15–20.

More straightforward, but more expensive, is Western Union, who transfer money to their overseas offices in a matter of minutes. This will need to be done by someone at home. Currently they have agents in all the countries covered in this book, except Singapore, Japan, Laos, Cambodia and Burma, but they are extending their network all the time. Charges (around 10–30 percent) depend on the amount sent, with small amounts attracting a larger fee. Call ☎0800/833833 in the UK and ☎1-800/325-6000 in North America for details of their overseas offices.

CHAPTER SIX

GUIDEBOOKS AND OTHER RESOURCES

Once you've planned a skeleton route, you can enjoy filling in some of the detail by scouring guidebooks and tourist brochures, reading travelogues and talking to old Asia hands. Check out the various travel-related sites on the Internet and contact relevant tourist offices. (Web site and tourist office addresses are listed in *Basics* on pp.307 and 287.) And try asking your travel agent for first-hand recommendations – the bigger student-oriented travel agents advertise the fact that their consultants have been all over the world, and advising prospective travellers is part of their job.

Guidebooks and maps

In an alien culture where you can neither speak the language nor read the signposts, a guidebook will be a real comfort to you in the first few days. You don't have to use it slavishly, but a good guidebook can make all the difference to your trip by showing you what to leave out of your itinerary and what to include. Don't buy your guidebook at the last minute, however, as it should also contain crucial advice on all sorts of travel preparations, including what visas you'll need, which inoculations to organize, and what gear to take along.

On the other hand, you could waste a lot of money if you splash out on a set of guidebooks before you've settled on a definite route. It's probably best to start off by borrowing a few guides from a library (even out-of-date editions are usually perfectly adequate for planning purposes), and then invest in a couple of new editions when your itinerary becomes more certain. If you're planning a long trip, there's no need to buy a guidebook for every country you're going to visit: you'll save money and luggage space by buying secondhand guides on the road, or swapping a guide you've finished with for a book on your next destination.

Choosing a guidebook

Personal recommendation is unbeatable, but you can also make your own judgement in bookshops by comparing the way Guidebook Series A describes a certain town and the way Series B does it. Look up a few things you're par-

ticularly interested in – wildlife, for example, or budget accommodation – and see how different books approach the topics. Do not be swayed by sumptuous photographs, and remember that you'll be lugging your chosen book around with you for quite a few weeks, so it shouldn't weigh too much. (Whatever the size of the book, you can save weight by ripping out and discarding the sections you know you'll definitely not need.)

Never expect your guidebook to be infallible: things *do* change, and new editions are generally only published every two or three years; prices rise, and hotels shut down. Guidebook authors also have their own preferences (some series emphasize this, others play it down), so you may not always agree with their choices. And it can be worth getting a second opinion on certain things – for example, the specific direction of a mountain trail – either from other travellers, or from local people, as illustrated by the story on p.132.

Bear in mind too, that there are many types of guidebook. Books that cover several countries in one volume are easy to carry and should include specific information on travelling between the countries contained in the book; on the down side, you may find that the smaller and less mainstream islands, towns, hotels and restaurants have been edited out because of space considerations. If, on the other hand, you know that you'll be sticking to just one city, region or route, comb the shelves carefully to see if there's a detailed guide on that area. The *Rough Guide to Goa*, for example, contains a lot more local information than the general India guide, and also includes access and accommodation details for Bombay. There are also a useful number of activity guides, some of which, like *Leh and Trekking in Ladakh* (Trailblazer), are self-contained and include enough details on gateway cities and accommodation options for you to do without any other guidebooks; others, such as *The Dive Sites of Indonesia* (New Holland), are best used in conjunction with general guides.

•••

THE BACKPACKER TRAIL

Guidebooks can have a huge influence on a town's tourist trade. If a hotel, restaurant or tour agent in a popular travellers' centre is given a favourable review in a Lonely Planet guide, for example, that business is almost guaranteed to receive a steady flow of backpackers. In a north Indian town, a tout runs through the normal routine: "Where you from? How long you been in India? Where you stay? I know cheap hotel". When we say that we've already decided to go to *Dreamland Hotel*, he smiles. "Ah, you must have the Rough Guide. All Rough Guide readers go to *Dreamland*; Lonely Planet readers go to *Uphar Hotel*, next door."

If an establishment does not appear in the guide, it will have to try harder to attract customers, possibly by resorting to touts or by making itself more competitive. On the door of a small restaurant in a tiny, but touristed, Indian village is pinned a sign that reads, "We're not mentioned in the Lonely Planet, but please give us a try anyway."

Lucy Ridout

•••

Lonely Planet

Lonely Planet is by far the best known guidebook series for independent travellers in Asia. *Southeast Asia on a Shoe-string* (first published in 1975) is their longest-running title and is still regarded as the backpackers' bible. They publish a huge number of single-volume guides to Asia, as well as some unusual trekking guides. Lonely Planet's strengths lie in their attention to practical detail, and they're especially good on how to make your money stretch as far as possible. Not surprisingly, you will find Lonely Planet readers dominate the Asian travellers' scene, and that's beginning to have its own drawbacks (see box above).

Rough Guides

Rough Guide authors also pride themselves on giving detailed practical information for independent travellers and include good cultural and contemporary write-ups as well. Some travellers prefer Rough Guides purely because they're not Lonely Planets and are therefore slightly less mainstream. Rough Guides to look out for include guides to China, India, Nepal, Thailand, Malaysia, Vietnam and Indonesia, among others, and a Rough Guide to the whole of Southeast Asia, which is planned for the year 2000.

Footprint

These small, densely packed hardback volumes have a good emphasis on contemporary issues such as politics, economics and ecological concerns, but are not quite as angled towards the budget-conscious traveller as some of the other series. The series covers most of Asia, including Cambodia, Laos, Vietnam, Tibet, Pakistan and Indonesia.

Moon

Moon's *Indonesia Handbook* is regarded as a classic because of its phenomenal attention to cultural detail, but it's not updated very regularly, so you wouldn't want to use it as your only source. Their *Tibet Handbook* is essential reading for anyone intending to trek in Tibet. Other Moon guides to Asia include books on Thailand, Japan, South Korea and the Philippines, all of which feature practical information geared mainly at low-budget independent travellers.

Let's Go

These American guides are written and researched by students and aimed specifically at budget-conscious travellers. Although they carry extensive practical information, updated every year, they can be short on details about the sights and cultural background, and some readers find the studenty tone a bit wearing. Areas covered by Let's Go guides include Southeast Asia, India and Nepal.

Insight

Insight guides are thick glossy handbooks with lovely pictures and text written by cultural experts. They have little practical information and nothing for low-budget travellers, but they do make inspirational pre-departure background reading. The Insight pocket guides are much handier, and livelier, than the parent series, but they are only good for short-stay visits and have no practical information on hotels and transport.

Periplus

Periplus only publishes guides to the various islands of Indonesia and to Malaysia, Brunei and Singapore. If you want a specialist guide to a specific part of Indonesia (eg Sulawesi or Maluku), this is the series to go for. Their activity guides on surfing and diving in Indonesia are also worth checking out. Like Insight, Periplus specializes in combining stunning photographs with thoughtfully written descriptions of sights and local issues, but the books are not that strong on practical detail.

Choosing a map

Most guidebooks include useful enough maps of major towns and resorts, but you might want to invest in a larger, more detailed map of the whole region or country you're planning to visit as well. Buy this before you leave home, where there'll be a larger selection.

Only a few maps cover the whole of Asia and the scale is so small on these (1:12,000,000) that they're only useful for a general overview. Better to invest in one or more of the major regional maps – Southeast Asia, China, the Indian subcontinent – published by Bartholomew, Nelles or Geocenter. The same publishers do maps to a comprehensive range of individual Asian countries as well.

Very large-scale maps for independent trekking should also be bought before you leave home (the best selection of trekking maps for Nepal and Tibet, however, are available in Kathmandu). Detailed town and city street maps, on the other hand, are often best bought on arrival, particularly big city maps that include bus routes.

GOOD GUIDES AND BAD GUIDES

"We're going to die."

"I know," I replied. We sat on the mountain ridge in silence. There was nothing more to say.

Dawn was approaching. The sun was rising leisurely over Lake Batur, northern Bali. I remember thinking it was the most beautiful sunrise I had ever seen. Oranges and purples filled the sky. Down below, specks of brown dotted the white sandy beach: men had risen early to prepare for the day's fishing. Life was going on as usual, unaware of our predicament. I laid back in the sun and closed my eyes.

We had begun to climb Mount Batur in the early hours of the morning, misled by a guidebook which had stated that the route was easy and a local guide unnecessary.

Two hours later, with a bruised back and a twisted ankle, we found ourselves stranded on a rock ledge. A sheer rock face loomed above us, and a steep drop onto boulders lay below. No one knew where we were. I really believed this could be the end.

Some time later, our knight in shining armour arrived in the form of an 8-year-old boy, wearing flip-flops and balancing a bucket of iced drinks on his head. We would have paid anything to have been led off the mountain but, crazily, in true Indonesian style, the bargaining began. We settled on 5000 rupiah, approximately $3; a bargain.

For the next nerve-racking three and a half hours, we scaled precipitous rock faces with no ropes or safety equipment. A couple of times we slipped, but somehow managed to hold on. To this day I cannot believe we made it.

At the summit we learnt that we'd taken the wrong path up the mountain. It was sheer luck that a local villager had spotted us and summoned our guide. I felt someone was watching out for us that day. Guidebooks contain lots of useful information, but local knowledge should always be consulted too.

Sasha Busbridge

Background reading

Other people's travel stories are full of good ideas on where to go and what to do – and will help prepare you for what lies in store, too. What follows is a highly selective list of some of our favourite books about Asia. Other good places

to look for first-hand travel narratives include national newspapers and specialist travel magazines.

If you've got plenty of time, consider genning up on Asian religions before you go – most people's lives revolve around their faith in Asia, and many of the sights and festivals that you'll be visiting will be religious ones. Icon Books publishes two enjoyable cartoon-and-caption introductions to Asian religions: *Ancient Eastern Philosophy for Beginners* and *Buddha for Beginners*. Hodder and Stoughton's *Teach Yourself World Faiths* series takes a more serious approach, but its paperback books on Hinduism, Sikhism, Buddhism and Islam are all clearly written and easy to understand.

Magazines

All the following magazines are aimed at independent travellers and, while none of them deals exclusively with Asia, you're guaranteed to find some sort of feature on Asia in every issue. Unless otherwise stated, they're all monthly publications, and all of them accept overseas subscriptions.

In the UK, *Wanderlust* focuses on fairly mainstream destinations for the independent traveller, with well-written travel stories plus lots of useful items on equipment, visas, tour operators and related TV and radio programmes; it also carries classified ads for people who are searching for travelling companions. As you'd expect, *Adventure Travel* is aimed at the more active and intrepid traveller, so the emphasis here is on hiking, biking, kayaking and the like, though the featured ventures are by no means too extreme for the average independent traveller.

In North America, the long-running *Outside* is a huge glossy tome, with heaps of readable articles on worldwide destinations for backpackers and independent travellers, plus plenty of ads for gear specialists and tour operators. *Escape* centres on more adventurous trips and activities and is a similarly good read. Other mags worth dipping into include the consciously unglossy and low-key *Big World*, and the quarterly magazines *Outpost* and *Trips*, both of which run articles on fairly unusual and adventurous destinations.

In Australia, the wilderness adventure magazine *Wild* covers activities such as climbing, trekking and rafting and has information on training courses and on buying specialist gear. Asian magazines published mainly in Singapore and Hong Kong are also widely available in Australia and these include the activity-specific *Tracks* (surfing), *Asian Diver* (diving) and *Rock* (climbing).

For a more detailed take on the realities of daily life in the countries you're planning to visit, you should browse through some of the special-interest magazines that carry a more in-depth coverage of Asia than national newspapers. The *New Internationalist* focuses on areas such as environmental concerns, women's issues, education and poverty action; *Far Eastern Economic Review* does hard-hitting but readable reports on the political and economic stories in the region; and *Asiaweek* is a lighter-weight version of the *Far Eastern Economic Review*. There are a number of similarly focused web sites too, listed in *Basics* on p.308.

Travellers' tales

❖ *More Women Travel* (Rough Guides). If you're feeling a bit nervous about setting off on your own – or just setting off full stop – this edition of real-life travellers' experiences will cheer you up and give you heart. It's an inspirational collection of travel stories and anecdotes from about sixty different women – tourists, long-term travellers, expats and volunteers – but is as relevant to male readers as to female ones. Though the book covers the whole world, there's a chunky section on Asia.

◇ *Travelers' Tales* (Travelers' Tales Inc) are also highly enjoyable anthologies, full of lively extracts from contemporary travelogues, magazines and guidebooks. They'd be ideal to take along if they weren't so heavy, but make tantalizing pre-trip reading as well. Travelers' Tales Asian titles are Thailand, India and Hong Kong.

◇ Alexander Frater's account of *Chasing the Monsoon* (Penguin) will revolutionize your attitude to rain and make you long to be in Asia during the monsoon. As the author – a self-confessed weather nut – follows the annual rains north through India, he goes to monsoon parties, interviews harassed meteorologists and listens to rainy-season tales.

◇ If you want to know what it's like in the jungles of Southeast Asia, look no further than Redmond O'Hanlon's *Into the Heart of Borneo* (Penguin/Vintage), the hilarious true story of two erudite, but not terribly fit, English men as they search the impenetrable Borneo jungle for the elusive two-horned rhinoceros. There's a memorable passage on a typical Dyak party (involving much drunkenness and buffoonery) and offputtingly graphic descriptions of leeches, Dyak cuisine and jungle trekking.

◇ And for a fine account of trekking in the Himalayas, read Peter Matthiessen's *The Snow Leopard* (Panther), which describes the author's two-month hike into the remote Inner Dolpo region of northwest Nepal. Alongside beautifully written passages on the changing scenery, the tracks, rivers, peaks, bird, animal and plantlife, Matthiessen also talks about his own emotional ups and downs, as he vascillates between exhaustion and exhilaration and tries hard to make sense of his Zen Buddhist training.

◇ Peter Hopkirk's *Trespassers on the Roof of the World: The Race for Lhasa* (OUP/Kodansha) tells the amazing story of how a group of Brits and Indians charted every nook of the vast High Tibetan Plateau, the most inaccessible – and hostile – place on earth, at the turn of the century.

Real lives

◇ For some idea of what it's like to be a woman in India, dip into Elizabeth Bumiller's *May You be the Mother of a Hundred Sons*

(Fawcett). This American journalist spent several years listening to the life stories of all sorts of different Indian women – young brides, housewives, widows, film stars, even a traffic cop – and in this collection she draws together their experiences, putting some into context, expressing her own horror or amazement at others. Well worth reading, even if you're not going to India, as many of the stories have relevance to other parts of Asia too.

✧ You'll get another, more controversial, peek behind the scenes of Asian women's lives in *Patpong Sisters* by Cleo Odzer (Arcade Publishing). This is an American anthropologist's funny and touching account of her life with the prostitutes and bar girls of Bangkok's notorious red-light district. It's an enlightening and thought-provoking read and a surprisingly enjoyable page-turner.

✧ Forget the dry analytical history books and turn instead to Jung Chang's emotionally charged story of her family's experiences in twentieth-century China. *Wild Swans* (Flamingo/Doubleday) paints a harrowing picture, with vivid accounts of her grandmother's days as a concubine, of her mother's struggle to fulfil her obligations to the leaders of the Cultural Revolution, and of her father's victimization under a new regime. It's even more sobering when you realize that this is probably not an unusual story at all, and that the people you meet in China may well have similar histories. Don't take the book with you, however, as it's banned in the People's Republic.

Fiction

✧ There aren't many novels written about the travellers' scene in Asia, but Alex Garland's *The Beach* is a hugely enjoyable exception. It tells the story of a group of travellers living a utopian existence on an uninhabited Thai island. Tensions rise as people start to reveal their true personalities and, when the idyll begins to sour, the book turns into a mesmerizing thriller. Ideal beach-side reading, or fodder for long train and plane rides.

✧ And when you've run out of *The Beach,* get your teeth into *A Suitable Boy*, Vikram Seth's enthralling blockbuster that will have you travelling long distance without so much as a yawn. This is the rollicking saga of a young Indian woman, her extended family and all their acquaintances just after Partition. Hilarious and engaging, it's full of characters that you'll bump into all over India.

Background viewing: Asia on film

Why not round off your Asia education the easy way – by watching a few videos? The films we've recommended have been chosen not necessarily because they're great works of art, but because they evoke the feel or character of a place, or provide an easy or unusual history lesson. In addition, you might want to check out some of the numerous natural history documentaries and travel programmes now available on video. Videos produced by National Geographic and by Lonely Planet are recommended.

China

◇ For sheer aesthetic pleasure you can't beat the films of Chinese director Zhang Yimou, with his stunning attention to visual drama, his glorious use of colour and his alluring portrait of traditional rural China. *Ju Dou* (1989), *Red Sorghum* (1987) and *Raise the Red Lantern* (1991) are all set in the 1920s and are all variations on a similar theme. Each tells the story of a young woman who is sent against her will to marry an elderly and intransigent man, the elderly husbands being symbols of the inflexible Chinese state. Yimou's more overtly political film, *To Live* (1994) follows a single family from the end of the old regime, through the crazy, dehumanizing twists of Communist rule, to the present day. All Yimou's films are censored in China.
◇ *Farewell My Concubine* (Chen Kaige, 1993) takes a more unusual approach to modern Chinese history, filtering it through the melodramatic and often heart-rending experiences of two (male) stars of the Peking Opera; one a sensitive, gay, interpreter of female characters, the other his macho leading man.

Vietnam

◇ Vietnam figures in dozens of movies – from *Rambo: First Blood* (Ted Kotcheff, 1982) to *Born on the Fourth of July* (Oliver Stone, 1989) and *Apocalypse Now* (Francis Ford Coppola, 1979) – but few of these films have anything very interesting to say about Vietnam itself, or about the effect the Vietnam War had on the Vietnamese people. Most focus instead on the American experience in and after 'Nam, and Vietnam is generally depicted as

a land of hellish bug- and mine-ridden jungles inhabited by a
bunch of crazy savages.

✧ Balance out the American view of the Vietnam War with an
attempt to see the conflict from a Vietnamese point of view.
Though *Heaven and Earth* (1993) was made by US director
Oliver Stone, the film is based on the autobiography of Le Ly
Hayslip, who grew up with the war, was tortured by the
Vietcong and forced to flee, eventually ending up in Saigon.
The film ends with Le Ly in rural USA, struggling to cope with
life as the displaced wife of a damaged and violent former GI.

✧ And to complete the picture, you should definitely rent a copy
of *Cyclo* (Tran Anh Hung, 1995), a shockingly graphic thriller set
in 1990s Ho Chi Minh City. Uniquely among all the films about
Vietnam, this paints a recognizable portrait of modern-day city
life – though you're unlikely to encounter the underworld
inhabited by its hero, a desperately poor young cycle-rickshaw
driver who gets drawn ever deeper into S&M prostitution, drug
smuggling and gang warfare. Dubbed by some critics the Vietnamese *Pulp Fiction*.

Cambodia and Thailand

✧ When the Vietnam War spilled over the borders into Cambodia,
and the Khmer Rouge began their terrifying campaign of re-
educating the Cambodian people, journalist Dith Pran was
forced, along with millions of others, to deny his past and work
for the Khmer Rouge in labour camps. His story is told in *The
Killing Fields* (Roland Joffé, 1984), a harrowing, if Hollywood-
ized, portrait of life under Pol Pot's tyrannical regime.

✧ *Swimming to Cambodia* (Jonathan Demme, 1987) makes a
good companion piece to *The Killing Fields,* as it's about – at
least in part – the making of *The Killing Fields,* which was
filmed on location in Thailand. In fact, it's a monologue, a
hugely entertaining *tour de force* by actor and raconteur
Spalding Gray, who had a minor role in the film. He tells some
funny stories – about his first encounter with an hallucinogenic
Thai stick, about the bar girls of Bangkok, and about his perfect moments on the beaches of Thailand – and in between
these anecdotes he tells us what he learnt about the Cambodian War.

- ◇ There are plenty of other films about conflicts in Asia as witnessed through Western eyes. Ones worth watching include *Beyond Rangoon* (John Boorman, 1995), which describes the ongoing struggle for Burmese democracy under Aung San Suu Kyi, and *The Year of Living Dangerously* (Peter Weir, 1982), set during the political conflicts in Indonesia in 1965.

India

- ◇ Richard Attenborough's *Gandhi* (1982) is an epic blockbuster, but none the worse for that. His biography of the famous man of non-violence is both an inspirational tribute to the power of civil disobedience and a very watchable lesson in twentieth-century Indian history.
- ◇ The Raj era has been romanticized, and criticized, by dozens of film-makers, but *A Passage to India* (1984) is one of the most interesting movies about colonial tensions in early twentieth-century India. Director David Lean evokes a tangible sense of unease as the good-hearted but ignorant and suggestible young English heroine becomes overwhelmed by the sheer strangeness of India. It's a fine exploration of (extreme) culture shock (and colonialism), still relevant to modern-day travellers.
- ◇ *Bandit Queen* (Shekar Kapur, 1994) was so controversial that it was initially banned in India and denounced by the woman whose life story it tells. She is Phoolan Devi, a young woman from a village in northeastern India, who endured a forced marriage, domestic violence and several rapes before fleeing to the hills and becoming a much-feared bandit leader. It shows how cruel life still is for some women in caste-ridden rural India.
- ◇ Based on the real experiences of a hot-headed young Western doctor in the slums of Calcutta, *City of Joy* (Roland Joffe, 1992) captures the atmosphere of life on the street better than any other mainstream film about India. The film shows the daily struggles of a rickshaw puller as he races round the city trying to earn enough money for his daughter's dowry, and the frustrations of the Irish nurse as her clinic is repeatedly trashed by the local mafia. And, though the young doctor is a typical Hollywood hero, he is also a typical Westerner in India, angry at

his inability to change things for the better and frustrated at the slum dwellers' apparent acceptance of their lot.

Learn the lingo

Wherever you go, people will appreciate your efforts to speak their language. You'll probably be giggled at, but that's as good an icebreaker as any and, in the more remote spots, knowing a few local phrases can make the difference between having to cope with a plate of beef brains and enjoying a tasty bowl of noodles.

Luckily, English is the language of tourism throughout Asia, so it's quite possible to do a six-month trip without ever consulting a phrasebook. And, in India, one of the greatest delights is the sheer number of Indian English speakers who take great pleasure in debating local and international issues with English-speaking travellers. French is also understood in parts of Indochina by the older generation who lived under French rule, and some elderly Indonesians can speak Dutch.

However, as only a tiny percentage of Asians can speak or understand any Western languages, it is well worth learning at least a few phrases. For travel off the beaten track, a basic vocabulary is essential, and will also give you access to people who are not involved in the tourist industry – a reason in itself for struggling through a few unfamiliar verbs.

Though some languages are guaranteed to turn you into a tongue-tied fool (Mandarin Chinese with its four tones and everyday alphabet of 10,000 pictograms springs to mind), others are relatively simple to master. Bahasa Indonesia, for example, is officially recognized as the easiest language in the world. It's written in roman script, has a straightforward grammar, and is also understood throughout Malaysia and Singapore (where it's known as Bahasa Malay).

If you have the time, it's very satisfying to give yourself a grounding before you go. There's a huge range of teach-yourself language tapes available for most Asian languages now, including Hodder and Stoughton's *Teach Yourself* series, and other options from Routledge, Berlitz, Hugo and Lonely Planet. The Linguaphone tape courses are the most comprehensive, but are also expensive.

Alternatively, fix yourself up with some face-to-face language classes. Expatriate Asians quite often advertise lessons in local papers, or you might try setting up an informal language exchange via a community centre or even a neighbourhood Asian restaurant. Should you be planning a lengthy stay in Asia, the very best way to learn the lingo is to attend a course once you're there – check the local English-language press for details or ask at tourist offices, embassies or universities.

Choosing a phrasebook

The easiest way to make yourself literate in an Asian tongue is to travel with a good phrasebook. Rough Guides, Lonely Planet, Berlitz and Hugo all publish a good range of handy pocket-sized phrasebooks and, as with guidebooks, you should compare several different ones before you buy. Think of a few situations – asking the price of a double room, for example, or saying that you're vegetarian – and look for them in the three or four rival phrasebooks. A user-friendly layout is also important and, where relevant, you'll probably want words and phrases to be written in local script – especially important for China, Japan, South Korea, Laos and Thailand.

CHAPTER SEVEN

WHAT TO TAKE

Y ou could quite happily set off for Asia with all your belongings stuffed into a plastic carrier bag and stock up on clothes and extra bits as and when you need them. Contrary to popular stereotypes, most of Asia is absolutely brimming over with merchandise, so you don't need to pack a lifetime's supply of T-shirts or shampoo. Buying on the road is nearly always cheaper and, more importantly, this means that you'll be able to travel light. A few things are best bought at home, as the quality of Asian goods is variable, and certain items will be difficult to find when you're away. But apart from these essentials, we'd advise you to take the very minimum you can and improvise on the rest.

A heavy load is a real hindrance and can spoil your trip by making you less keen to stop off at places because you just can't face dragging your huge pack along with you. Things really are bad when your pack starts dictating your itinerary, so start how you mean to go on and get your baggage under control right away. A few tips on how to lighten the load:

◇ Mail stuff to the place where you think you'll need it most. For example, if you're doing a three-month overland from Australia to Europe and you're planning to look for office work when you get to London, send your smart work clothes direct from home to a UK poste restante. Use surface mail, as poste restante is usually only held for two months.

◇ Plan to send excess baggage back after you've finished with it (eg your thermal underwear and wool sweater after you leave Kathmandu) or, better still, buy your woollies when you get there and then sell them, junk them or send them home. Surface mail from Asia generally takes about three months and costs around $35 (£20) for 5kg to the UK or the US; a bit less to Australia (see Chapter Thirteen).

◇ Rent or buy any special gear on the ground rather than taking it with you. You can rent diving and surfing gear in Bali and southern Thailand, for example, down jackets and sleeping bags in Kathmandu, sleeping bags (but no down jackets) in Lhasa and Chiang Mai (northern Thailand), and camping equipment in Malaysia's Taman Negara National Park. Consult your guidebook for details. You may also be able to buy secondhand equipment from departing travellers: check guest-house noticeboards.

Rucksacks

If you haven't already got a rucksack, this is the one item that it's worth splashing out on. Choose a recognized brand-name pack (such as Berghaus, Karrimor or Lowe-Alpine) as they are hard-wearing and ergonomically designed. They can cost anything from $80 to $250 (£50–150), but think of it as an investment: a good pack could last you for many years and will certainly make your trip a more comfortable one.

Rucksack capacity is measured in litres or cubic inches – not that helpful really as it's hard to visualize your socks and T-shirts in liquid form. Our advice is to buy the smallest one that looks practical for you: a 40- to 55-litre one if possible, but certainly no bigger than 65 litres. Buying a smaller pack forces you to travel light, and there's no question you'll be grateful for that when you're battling with overflowing Bangkok buses or wandering up and down a roasting Colombo street. Some travellers, on the other hand, claim you should buy as large a pack as you are ever likely to need, presuming that if you don't fill it to the brim on your way out you will certainly pick up enough trinkets on the trip to make it worth its massive size.

In the end, though, it's not the capacity that matters so much as the weight of stuff that you cram into it. Nearly all airlines specify a 20kg maximum for hold baggage, so that should definitely be your limit; a realistic optimum weight lies somewhere between 10kg and 15kg – it's definitely worth jettisoning stuff once the scales go over the 17kg mark.

Once you've decided on size, check out the extra bits, particularly the pockets, compartments and additional strap attachments. Packs with more than one compartment are easier to use. And side- and lid-pockets are perfect for stashing bits and pieces you need to get at quickly – soap and a toothbrush for example, so that you don't have to root right through to the bottom of your pack in the sleeping compartment of an overnight train – as well as your map and guidebook, or your rain gear. Some rucksacks have detachable front pockets which are actually daypacks, of which more below. Bear in mind, though, that the more compact your pack, the easier it will be to lug on and off buses, to squeeze onto train luggage racks and into train station left-luggage lockers. Fully stuffed side-pockets can add a good 30cm to the width of your pack, and attaching boots, sunhat and umbrella to external loops only makes your load more difficult to carry.

Choosing a rucksack

You won't regret the time and care you take in choosing the right rucksack. Always try them on before buying, and think about the following:

◊ **The best packs are made from heavy-duty synthetic fabrics; avoid the ones that feel flimsy and will tear easily. Zips should be sturdy, too.**

◇ Most travellers' rucksacks are constructed round a lightweight internal frame. This gives shape to the pack but, most importantly, it helps spread the load across your back. The smaller packs – under 40 litres – are often considered too small to warrant a frame, but they should come with thickly padded and contoured backs which also help distribute the weight and make the whole thing more comfortable. These days, external frames are the province of serious, long-distance trekkers and backpacking travellers don't need them.

◇ A thickly padded hip belt is essential for carrying any load over 10kg. This transfers most of the weight off your shoulders onto your hips and legs – the strongest and sturdiest part of the human body. By channelling the weight down to your lower body, you're also making yourself more stable: a full load resting solely on your shoulders will quickly tire you out.

◇ If you're not average size and build, check out the packs with adjustable back systems, where you can change the position of the shoulder straps in relation to the frame.

◇ Some packs are designed especially for women, with shorter back lengths and a differently contoured back shape and hip belt.

Is it a rucksack? Is it a suitcase? . . .

. . . No, it's a travel sack. Some rucksacks can also be turned into suitcases: a special flap zips over the straps and, with the aid of a handle, you can carry it like a suitcase or a shoulder bag – a useful feature for plane, bus and train journeys where dangling straps can get tangled up or ripped off. This also means that you can walk into a hotel without looking like a backpacker. Most travel sacks can be unzipped all the way round to open like a suitcase, which is much more convenient than a conventional rucksack, especially for overnight stopovers. They are also easier to lock.

Though all these features make travel sacks versatile, they won't provide the long-distance support of a properly contoured rucksack. If you choose this option, go for a travel sack with an internal frame, not just padding; external compression straps also help to secure the load.

Packing up and locking up

It's worth customizing your pack to make it as user-friendly, resilient and secure as possible. These ideas may be useful:

✧ Most rucksacks are showerproof, but that doesn't make them monsoon- or tropical-storm-proof. To keep your stuff dry, you can either buy a special rucksack liner, or make do with a large dustbin liner or two; alternatively, just wrap your most precious items in individual plastic bags.

✧ Pack your rucksack so that you are not being pulled backwards all the time. This means distributing weight as evenly as possible from top to bottom, and keeping the bulkier stuff as close to your body as possible. Be careful where you pack sharp or angular objects as you don't want them jabbing into your back.

✧ As well as tagging your pack on the outside, stick an address label to the inside of one of the side-pockets, so that there can be no dispute about whose it is.

✧ Though most rucksacks are unlockable as bought, a lot of them come with useful devices like double zips on the side- and lid-pockets so that you can use a small padlock on them. If not, you might think about getting a couple of small holes punched into your rucksack fabric above the zip fasteners, so that you can use a mini-padlock to lock the zip to the hole; shoe-repairers and keycutters will do this for you, and will re-inforce the hole with a metal ring. To lock the straps you can use specially designed little ladder locks or sacklocks (available from camping shops) and attach mini-padlocks to them.

✧ Some travellers take a small chain and a spare padlock for securing their pack to luggage racks on overnight trains and buses (see p.155).

Daypacks

You should be just as fussy about choosing a daypack as your main pack. After all, this is what you're going to be carrying around all day every day, so it needs to be comfortable and well designed. For comfort, you'll need padded, adjustable shoulder straps, a padded back and an overall size and shape that's not too cumbersome. For convenience, you should look at the opening system and the number of pockets.

Some daypacks zip open all the way round. Although this is handy for digging out a wayward pencil or whatever, it also makes it easier to drop things out of when you're opening it up, and can come unzipped if you don't keep it locked. The top-opening drawstring system is a more user-friendly alternative. External pockets can be useful – some are large enough to accommodate a one-litre water bottle on each side – but an internal pocket is more useful, and ideal for documents, a wallet, a map or a bus ticket.

Remember, too, that you will sometimes have to wear both your rucksack and your daypack at the same time. This can be awkward, and a security hazard, so the best solution is to empty your daypack and stuff it inside your main pack. If that's not possible, you're probably best off wearing your daypack across your front; this helps your balance a bit, and discourages pickpockets.

Some main packs are designed with built-in, detachable daypacks, which zip onto the outside of your main pack. If you go for this option, be sure not to carry valuables in the zipped-on mini-pack as you probably won't be able to tell if a pickpocket slashes it when you're on the move.

Advice on what to carry in your daypack on long-haul flights is given in Chapter Eight.

Money belts

Most travellers like to keep their valuables on their person at all times, and the safest and most convenient way of doing this is to wear a money belt. A money belt is essentially a long flat pouch, made of fabric, plastic or leather, attached to a belt and designed to be worn around the waist. It should be worn *under* your clothes, and should be as discreet as possible – preferably invisible – so that it does not attract the attention of muggers and pickpockets. To keep it slimline, it should be used only to carry stuff that you don't need to access every twenty minutes. Keep your passport, your airline ticket, your credit card, travel insurance policy and the bulk of your cash in the money belt, but leave your petty cash, notebook, lip balm and pocket torch for your daypack.

Be sure not to confuse money belts with bum bags. A bum bag is a larger and altogether more ostentatious item; it's worn over your clothes and can usually hold a small camera as well as sunscreen and dark glasses. As a security item the bum bag is useless and may as well be inscribed with flashing lights announcing "Valuable items inside, help yourself". It just takes one deft swipe of a knife for your bum bag to drop to the ground and into the hands of an opportunist thief.

Some people prefer neck wallets to money belts. These are similar pouches, designed to be worn either round the neck or over the shoulder. As with money belts, they should be kept under your clothes and out of sight. The main drawback with neck wallets is that they swing around more than money belts and therefore feel less safe and possibly more uncomfortable.

Choosing a money belt (or neck wallet)

A few points to bear in mind:

◇ It should be wide enough to accommodate your passport and long enough for your travellers' cheques. Take these along with you when making your purchase.

◇ Cotton is the most comfortable fabric: it absorbs the sweat and does not irritate the skin – and you can wash it when it gets dirty or smelly. Nylon and plastic are not recommended. When wearing a cotton money belt, it's a good idea to keep something water-proof – eg your free plastic-coated travellers' cheque wallet – at the back of the money belt nearest your skin, so that any excess sweat will not obliterate vital documents such as airline tickets.

◇ If you're planning to spend a fair amount of time on the beach, consider buying – as a supplement to your money belt – a little waterproof canister that you can wear when swimming. These come in varying sizes (with names like "surfsafe") and should be able to hold your room keys and/or security box key so that you don't have to worry about leaving your money belt with all its valuables unattended on the beach.

Clothes

Once you're on the road you'll almost certainly end up wearing the same two or three outfits week-in, week-out. Ideally you'll want to work that out before you leave home, but there's always parcel post to send back any excess. Nonetheless, it's well worth being brutal with yourself at the packing stage. Ask yourself: do I *really* need five T-shirts and three pairs of jeans?

Your clothes will deteriorate faster than they do at home because of the heat, the extra sweat, and the pounding and mangling they'll go through at local laundries. To some this is a reason for taking new clothes: the newer the item, the better its chance of survival. On the other hand, why waste your money if things are only going to get ruined anyway? Whatever you decide, don't take your smartest gear, or anything that's of irreplaceable sentimental value.

And remember: Asia is full of clothes shops selling stuff that's ideal for the local climate. Note that Asian sizes rarely go above men's UK/US trouser size 36 and women's UK size 16 (US 14), though you can get Western sizes in touristed towns. Also bear in mind that tailoring in Asia is extremely inexpensive, and Asian fabrics are stunning, so you can always get new clothes made up, particularly in Bangkok, Hong Kong, Singapore and almost any big town in India (a tailored cotton shirt costs about $8/£5 in India) – very handy if you happen to be larger than the average Asian man or woman.

● ●

THE MODESTY FACTOR

Most Asians do not enjoy seeing acres of exposed Western flesh displayed in public. They find revealing dress offensive and cheap, so you'll get a much better response from local people if you respect their views and adapt your attire accordingly. This is particularly important when visiting temples, mosques and shrines – if you're unsuitably dressed in these places you'll probably be refused entry.

Prudish (and sweaty) though this sounds, this means wearing long trousers or skirts for most day-to day activities and keeping shorts for beach resorts. Singlets are also considered low-class, especially for women, who will get a lot of unwanted attention if they reveal their cleavages or are obviously not wearing a bra. The notice above the entrance gate to Bangkok's Grand Palace sums up the (usually unspoken) rules; it's illustrated with photos of unsuitably dressed men and women, and forbids "leggings, shorts, singlets, fishermen's trousers, torn and dirty clothing and flip-flops".

Lots of travellers ignore local clothing etiquette and may not even notice that it's an issue. This is quite easy to do if you're sticking to heavily touristed ghettos – Bangkok's Khao San Road, for example, or Sudder Street in Calcutta. But as soon as you deviate from the beaten track you'll almost certainly start to feel more self-conscious. One young female traveller got stones thrown at her in Medan (a Muslim town in Sumatra) for walking around in shorts; another adopted local Indian dress (cotton pyjama-style tunic and trousers) for her six-month stay and found that this made villagers much less nervous of her – in fact, they would often start a conversation by complimenting her for wearing a *salwaar kameez*.

• •

Packing for the heat

For tropical Asia you will need clothes that are long, loose and light:

◇ Long trousers and long sleeves are good because of the modesty factor (see box), but also for sun protection and, curiously enough, for coolness as well. The more skin you expose to the sun, the faster your body moisture evaporates and the more dehydrated and, therefore, hotter you become. You only have to picture the flowing white robes of an Arab sheikh to be reminded of this.

◇ Long sleeves and long trousers are also good protection against mosquitoes.

⬧ Loose, baggy clothing improves ventilation and cuts down on sweat.

⬧ Lightweight fabrics are faster to dry and smaller to pack.

⬧ Cotton and linen are the most comfortable, as natural fibres are absorbent and will let your skin breathe.

⬧ Artificial fabrics such as nylon and rayon tend to encourage sweat and itchiness, and may even cause heat rash and fungus.

⬧ Lycra is a guaranteed heat trap and crotch-rotter – and it contravenes the modesty code too.

⬧ T-shirts are quite heavy to wear and to carry, and take a long time to dry. Consider taking short-sleeved cotton shirts instead – or buy some on the road.

⬧ Jeans are heavy to carry, hot to wear and take a long time to dry, though some travellers find they make them feel comfortably at home.

⬧ Light-coloured clothing will help to keep you cooler (it reflects rather than absorbs the sunlight), but it will also get dirtier faster.

⬧ Asian men and women tend to dress far more colourfully than Westerners and you might feel rather drab in comparison if you wear nothing but sober blues, blacks, greys and browns. Avoid wearing anything yellow if you're in Brunei, however, as it's considered unlucky – and is illegal in the presence of the royal family.

Packing for a cold climate

The best way to pack for a trip that is to include a few weeks in a cooler climate is to go for the layers technique. This means you can make the most of your tropical clothing by wearing it all at once.

⬧ Consider taking a fleece jacket; these are warm and weigh surprisingly little.

⬧ Thermal underwear is a good idea: ideally long johns and a long-sleeved undershirt, but woollen tights or thick leggings and a long-sleeved brushed cotton top will do instead. If you have money to spare, buy some silks (100 percent silk thermals), which feel incredibly light (and slinky) but are extremely warm.

◇ Warm socks are a must: go for the hard-wearing, double-thickness ones sold in camping shops. They're good for wearing with hiking boots in hot places as well.

◇ Woolly hat and scarf, or balaclava, plus gloves are easily bought when you arrive; the yak-wool ones sold in Nepal are especially popular.

A clothing checklist

◇ Two pairs long trousers/skirts/dresses.

◇ Two T-shirts/short-sleeved shirts.

◇ One long-sleeved shirt.

◇ One lightweight fleece jacket, sweatshirt or similar item for moderate warmth.

◇ One pair shorts.

◇ A sarong.

◇ Swimwear. Stripping down for swimming and sunbathing is a Western practice that bemuses most Asians. When the Thais go swimming they walk straight into the water in their jeans and T-shirts; Indian women do the same in their saris or *salwaar kameez*.

◇ Underwear. Natural fibres are most comfortable. Easily replaced all over Asia, except for bras over size 38B. Don't bring too many, as you can wash and dry them in no time at all.

◇ Socks.

◇ Rain gear. A PVC poncho or cagoule might be useful and squashes into a small space. But in the tropical heat that comes with monsoons you'll feel more comfortable using an umbrella instead (PVC makes you sweat). Buy your umbrella when you need it; don't take one with you.

◇ Sunhat. Not many people wear them, but they do keep you cooler and prevent sunstroke. Broad-brimmed straw hats are a pain to carry when you're on the move, so either buy one there and then dump it, or opt instead for a baseball cap or squashy cotton number.

◇ A smarter option. You might find yourself invited to a wedding, a festival, or even a circumcision ceremony, so you'll want to at least look like you've made an effort. Smart gear is also useful when dealing with Asian bureaucracy. Something light that doesn't crumple is best.

CRACKING THE DRESS CODE

A friend of mine and I were in Amritsar and decided to walk from the hotel to the Golden Temple. We were both wearing ankle-length skirts and decently modest tops, but we may as well have been sporting sequinned bikinis for all the anonymity that gave us. No sooner had we stepped out of the lobby than the stares began, levelled unashamedly and unmistakably directly at crotch level. It took us a while to realize that this was not the impolite lunacy of one or two individuals, but rather the local pastime for any male aged between 10 and 80. Our skirts were neither see-through nor hip-hugging, but maybe that was the attraction: what could be hiding behind those draped floral pleats? Which just goes to show that, whatever you wear, as a foreign female you will always be an object of fascination for local men.

Lucy Ridout

Shoes

The footwear of choice for the perfect backpacker is the sports sandal or reef-walker, of which Teva are the best known: a go-anywhere sandal with adjustable straps, and sturdy, contoured rubber soles. With a pair of sport sandals on your feet, you can negotiate rough terrain, go swimming, wade through rivers and wander the streets, without having to take them off. They are, of course, not as protective as walking boots, though not nearly as heavy either. Genuine Tevas are pretty expensive in the UK (from about £30 to £70), although in the States you should find them for $40–80. If you're considering trying one of the numerous copies, be warned that the $8 looka-likes sold in Bangkok and Delhi are nothing more than glorified paddling shoes.

Each extra pair of shoes adds a kilo or two to your load, so, sports sandals or not, you need to keep your shoe quotient down. Ideally this means you should take just one hardy pair for daily walking, plus a pair of thongs or flip-flops for beach and hotel. If you're planning to do any sort of overnight trekking, hiking boots will probably be useful enough to justify that extra space and weight, and you can always wear them rather than pack them whenever you're moving on, though some people find trainers an adequate substitute. A few pedi-points to bear in mind:

◇ You may be wearing these shoes every day for the next six months, so they must be comfortable and strong.

◇ They need to be airy too, as, not only do sweaty feet stink, but they can also fester and give you unpleasant flesh-rot in tropical climes.

◇ Leather sandals (Indian chappals) are the foot uniform of the East: do as most Asians do and wear sandals.

◇ Wherever you are in Asia, you will find yourself forever taking your shoes on and off to go into temples and mosques, and when visiting people's homes. Laces and other fiddly fastenings can become extremely annoying after a while.

◇ If you have big feet (that is, bigger than the Asian maximum size men's 44/US $9^1/2$, UK $8^1/2$; women's 40/US $8^1/2$, UK $7^1/2$), be sure that your shoes will last you the whole trip, as you may not be able to buy any more off the peg. But you will be able to get some made for you – Bangkok, Delhi and Yogyakarta in Java all have reputable shoemakers.

Essentials

An alphabetical list of things you will definitely need.

Batteries

Put new batteries in your watch, camera, alarm clock, flashlight and any other vital item before you leave home. Consider taking replacements as well: although you will be able to get most brands in major cities, you may not be near a major city when yours run out.

Contact lens stuff

You can get standard brand-name contact lens solutions at opticians and pharmacists in Asian capitals and major cities, so you don't have to take a huge supply along with you. Take a pair of glasses as a backup, as your lenses may get damaged by dust and sand and it would be a shame to travel all that way and then not be able to see anything. Also, should you get an eye infection, you'll need to do without lenses until the infection clears up.

Contraceptives
Condoms are available over the counter in nearly every Asian nation, but try to buy them from air-conditioned shops or places where they keep them in the fridge so the latex doesn't perish; women may feel uncomfortable buying them because many Asian women don't. Do not rely on being able to buy other contraceptives in Asia: take enough to last you for the whole trip.

First-aid kit
Basic first-aid kit, medicines, antimalarials and insect repellents: see Chapter Twelve for details.

Flashlight (torch)
Head-torches, which are like mini miners' lamps on an elasticated headband, are much more practical than conventional hand-held ones, leaving your hands free to wrestle with keys and padlocks in the dark, say, or to hold up your skirt while pissing in the pitch black – and they're a godsend for taking out or putting in contact lenses when the guest-house power supply suddenly packs up.

Glasses
Take your prescription with you. Any optician should be able to fit your frames with new lenses, or supply a new pair if required.

Guidebooks, phrasebooks and maps
See Chapter Six for advice on choosing the most useful guidebooks, phrasebooks and maps.

Padlocks and a chain
Small padlocks serve as a good deterrent to anyone considering pilfering stuff from your rucksack, and are also

useful as extra security on hotel doors. Keep two sets of keys in different places, or take combination padlocks instead, so you don't have to worry about losing the key (just about forgetting the number). A chain can also come in handy for securing your pack to luggage racks on overnight trains, or to roof racks on long-distance buses.

Sarong

It's amazing what you can do with a 2m x 1m length of cloth: you can use it as a bath and beach towel, as a sleeping sheet or blanket, as a turban-style sunhat or a temple headscarf-cum-shawl. You can turn it into a shopping bag, an awning on a shadeless beach, or even a rope for hauling your friend up a mountainside. And, of course, like the women and men of Thailand, Indonesia, Burma, Laos, Cambodia and Bangladesh, you can also wear it! Sarongs are easy to buy in the West now, but you'll get a much bigger selection if you wait for your first port of call. You should be able to pick one up for around $8 (£5) anywhere in Asia.

Sunglasses

Tropical light is intense, so you'll be glad to hide behind some dark glasses. The same goes for high-altitude glare in Pakistan, Nepal, Tibet and northern India. Buy them at home, as quality is not as good in Asia.

Sunscreens

Take sun block and a bottle of factor 15 for the first few weeks, plus a lower-factor lotion for use once your skin's adjusted to the rays. Don't forget that you can get burnt just as easily in the mountains as by the sea: do not be deceived by the cooler air, as the UV rays are just as strong and the risk of getting skin cancer just as high.

Tampons

Available in most major cities across Asia, though check with your guidebook. Southern Sumatra, for example, is an exception.

Toilet paper

Toilet paper is rarely supplied in backpackers' accommodation in Asia. You can buy it in tourist centres and big cities, but take a small roll with you anyway.

Toiletries

Unless you have very special requirements, you'll be able to restock your toiletry supply anywhere you go. And there'll be plenty of new lotions to experiment with, too – like the ochre-coloured face powder that Burmese women plaster on themselves to prevent sun damage, or the pure coconut oil used in India to ensure supple skin and lustrous hair. However, beware the large number of moisturizers, very popular with Asian women, that have a "whitening" effect on the skin.

Towel

Towels get disgustingly smelly very easily, take ages to dry and use up far too much valuable rucksack space. Use a sarong instead. Or, if you must, take a tiny hand towel.

• •

THE IDEAL TRAVELLING COMPANION

When I'm travelling on my own, I find it comforting to have a reminder of people at home, so I always take Reggie, a tiny teddy bear, along too. We have shared many adventures, but it was in India that his talent as an icebreaker came to light – children and adults seemed to find him so irresistibly cute that they just had to start talking to me!

The most memorable Reggie-encounter happened when I was trekking in Kinnaur, in the Himalayas. I was following a path up through the forest, heading for the snow line, when I heard a man's voice beckoning from below. I wandered down to the clearing, greeted the old man and his wife, and introduced Reggie, emphasizing that his Hindi was much better than mine. Beaming from ear to ear, the old man immediately grasped hold of Reggie with both hands and began to have quite an animated conversation with him. Ice duly broken, we all sat down and shared a cheroot, after which I helped them with their wood-collecting.

Juliet Acock

• •

Optional odds and ends

An alphabetical list of bits and pieces that you may or may not need.

Alarm clock or watch
For early departures.

Binoculars
Worth considering if you're going to be wildlife-spotting in national parks, or even trekking.

Books
New, English-language books are relatively expensive in Asia (India and Nepal are the exceptions), but secondhand book-stores and book exchanges are usually plentiful in travellers' centres, so there's no need carry a whole library around with you. See Chapter Six for a list of novels and travelogues about Asia that will make enjoyable travelling companions.

Cigarette lighter

Useful even for non-smokers, for lighting mosquito coils, candles (during power cuts), and campfires; matches get soggy from the humidity and are more of a hazard.

Comfort food

Some travellers swear by Marmite, Vegemite, peanut butter or whatever – a little taste of home to soothe their stomach and their taste buds. Whatever you take, it should be small, non-perishable and hard to break or spill.

Compass

Only necessary if you're trekking without a guide.

Earplugs

To block out snoring partners, roaring all-night traffic, video music on overnight buses and other annoyances (see box).

● ●

EARPLUGS

Earplugs are essential for screening out the routine din of Asian hotels. Until you've been to Asia, you just can't imagine how noisy everyone is. We regularly had building work going on in the next door room or in the one directly above us – and it always continued through the night because that's the coolest time to work! Then there's the morning throat-clearing chorus – at 5am – when the night's phlegm is hawked and spat out by every man in the locality. And in Indonesia, it's impossible to stay out of earshot of the early morning muezzin calls at the neighbourhood mosque; in Padang, our hotel had its very own mosque – in the room adjacent to ours!

Jo Mead

● ●

Games

For all those exhausting thirty-hour bus and train journeys. Pocket Scrabble, playing cards, Game Boy and Connect 4 have all been road-tested by the authors.

Gluestick
For recalcitrant Asian envelopes and stamps.

Handkerchief
Hopefully you won't be getting a cold, but you will be sweating a lot – and a hanky is useful for mopping your brow. Also handy for drying your hands after washing them in restaurants or toilets – you'll only find paper towels in posh hotels and airports.

Mosquito coils
Buy them when you arrive, where they will be much cheaper. Some hotels provide them free. See p.245 for more on this form of mosquito repellent.

Mosquito net
Can be useful anywhere in Asia, though most tourist accommodations will provide nets or screened windows. Nets are much cheaper in Asia than in the West, but, if you do buy one from home, choose one which is impregnated with mosquito repellent. They're available from camping shops in the UK for £25 to £50, although you should find them cheaper in the States ($25–40).

Notebook or journal and pens
For all your profound observations and amusing anecdotes. (Don't forget to send in the best ones for the next edition of *First-Time Asia*.)

Penknife
If you take one, make it a Swiss Army knife (or a good cheap copy), as you might be glad of the blade and the bottle opener.

Photos of home
A good icebreaker, and just as weird and interesting to the people you'll meet on buses and trains as a picture of a Dyak longhouse or a Vietnamese rickshaw would be to you.

Radio and personal stereo

If you're away for a long time, a short-wave radio can be a comforting link with home, especially if you're travelling alone. A personal stereo is great for long bus journeys and for entertaining people in the more remote villages. Consider taking a pair of mini-speakers as well. Bootleg tapes are sold all over Asia, often for as little as $3 (£2).

Sewing kit

Safety pins, needle and cotton, plus a couple of buttons for emergency repairs.

Sheet sleeping bag

More useful in tropical Asia than a down sleeping bag, but by no means essential: if you're worried about the cleanliness of the hotel sheets you can always use your sarong instead – or change your guest house. If you do want to take one, you don't need to buy one: either sew two sheets together, or use a lightweight duvet cover instead.

Sink plug

Asian sinks tend not have plugs, so this can be useful, especially for wet shaving. On the other hand, most hotels provide buckets for you to do your laundry.

Sleeping bag

Unless you're going to spend a long time camping (see p.162) or trekking in the colder and more remote parts of Asia, there's no point lugging a sleeping bag around with you. In popular trekking centres (like Kathmandu and Lhasa) you can rent four-season bags for as little as a dollar a day.

Stamps from your home country

No, not because we assume that everyone's a closet collector, but because Asian post is not always that speedy (see Chapter Thirteen), so you might want to give pre-stamped letters to travellers you meet who are heading home in the next week.

String
To use as a washing line and to suspend mosquito nets from.

● ●

TOGETHER FOREVER

The problem with travelling with a keyboard in your rucksack is that you don't have any room for normal things like clothes or insect repellent. But you could never make as many friends with a pair of Levi's as you could with a Casio. My keyboard was a brilliant way of meeting people and a positive effort on my part to communicate in a language other than the ones we speak.

Sometimes I used to carry my keyboard around in a bin-liner. One time, during a hand-luggage check in Laos Airport, they threw my money belt on top of the keyboard, setting off the demo button. Everyone stopped in their tracks and stared as this black bag emerged from the X-ray machine singing Rick Astley's "Together Forever". Naturally, I was arrested.

Chris Humphrey

● ●

Tent and other camping gear
Accommodation and food is so inexpensive in most parts of Asia that you won't need a tent, sleeping bag and camping stove to eke out your budget – and the weather in tropical Asia is so warm anyway that you can sleep out under the stars with no canvas protection. Exceptions include Japan and Hong Kong, where hotel rooms will take a big slice out of your budget and campsites are plentiful (if a bit far from major tourist attractions). Camping gear is essential if you're heading into remote wilderness areas anywhere in Asia and are not planning to take a guide (guides usually provide food and bedding). Before lugging your equipment halfway round the world, check relevant guidebooks for local places that rent out camping gear.

Wallet
Most Asian currencies are based on notes and, in countries where the denominations are very big, you'll find a wallet much handier than a purse because you'll have far more

notes than coins. In Indonesia, for example, there's even a note for 100 rupiah, currently equivalent to about one US cent. Inexpensive leather and fabric wallets are available all over Asia, so you might want to buy one when you get there.

Washing powder (clothes detergent)
Camping shops sell expensive travel-wash suds in tubes, but you're better off buying cheap individual portions of washing powder when you get there.

Water bottle and water purifier or tablets
If you stick to the beaten track, you shouldn't need your own water bottle, as bottled water is sold in all touristed areas. You should definitely take your own water bottle and purifying equipment if you're going trekking or venturing into remote areas. Buy a bottle that holds a litre and has a belt or shoulder-strap attachment. More information on water purification is given in Chapter Twelve.

Wet ones (baby wipes)
Not just for babies, but for sweaty travel-worn adults too. Good for cleaning yourself up on buses and trains, and for wiping hands before eating.

Cameras

Photos are a great way to jog your memory when you get home, and the best way to share your experiences. If

you're buying a camera for the trip, weigh up the advantages of taking a bulky top-of-the range SLR (single lens reflex) with a variety of lenses against a point-and-shoot compact or the compromise zoom-compact option. Be realistic about what you intend to do with the pictures once you get home: if you're planning to sell them for publication or use them in slide shows and lectures, then an SLR is probably essential. But, if you just want them for your personal satisfaction, you may be happier with a smaller and less ostentatious camera. Cameras draw a lot of attention wherever you are and can make you feel self-conscious – they also attract thieves.

Equipment

◇ Take a UV or skylight filter if you have an SLR camera, as the ultraviolet light in the tropics and at altitude can give an unnatural colour cast to pictures that makes them look washed out.

◇ Clean your photo equipment daily: dust will quickly ruin it and your pictures.

◇ Carry some silica gel in with your camera lenses and film. This will absorb excess tropical moisture.

◇ Take spare batteries: they're not always available in Asia.

Film

◇ Take a range of film speeds as the speed of the film determines its ability to cope with different light conditions. Much of Asia is very bright, so ASA100 film is generally fine. But for darker subjects, like a tropical rainforest, or the inside of certain temples, where you may be allowed to photograph but not use a flash, you'll need ASA400 or 800.

◇ You can buy print film all over Asia, but slide film is less easy to find. Do not buy film that looks as if it's been stored in damp or humid conditions.

◇ Many Asian baggage-check machines are film-safe. However, you should always pack your films (new and exposed) in carry-on baggage, as hold baggage gets a heavier dose of radiation, which can fog films. The higher the film speed, the more vulnerable it is to X-ray damage. X-rays are cumulative, so one X-ray incident isn't fatal, though if you are doing a lot of air travel consider keeping your films in a special lead bag (available from all decent camera shops), which will protect them from the rays.

Picture etiquette

Remember that not everyone you see in Asia, no matter how photogenic, will want their photo recorded by you for posterity. Some tribal people in Thailand and Indonesia hate to be photographed as they believe that a tiny fragment of their soul dies with every snapshot taken; and, for many orthodox Muslim women, to be photographed is almost tantamount to being indecently assaulted. You should therefore always ask before taking someone's picture – gestures can usually convey the idea.

Festivals and religious events may also be off limits, so check with local people first: masked festival dancers in Nepal believe they embody the deities during their performance, so taking photos of them is sacrilegious; and filming the sacred burning-body ghats in Varanasi, India, could easily get you lynched by mortified onlookers. Be equally sensitive when photographing temples, mosques and other shrines, and don't whip out your camera at an international border, airport or military checkpoint.

You'll even find that some people – like the Padaung "long-neck" women of Burma, the Ifugao people in the Philippines, and certain Nepalese sadhus – are now so used to having their pictures taken by tourists that they charge a per-picture fee.

Developing film

Film should be processed as soon as possible after being exposed; a couple of months is fine, but you don't want films rolling about in the bottom of your pack for a year before getting them developed. Process-paid slide film can be sent air-mail to the processor for the pictures to be returned to a home address. If you decide to get film developed while on the road, you should definitely check the quality first, either by asking other travellers or by getting just one roll developed first. Sending film, prints or negatives home is often a good idea (see p.262).

Documents

Your most essential documents are passport (with appropriate visas), airline tickets, travellers' cheques, credit card and insurance policy. These should all live in your money belt (see p.147), which should be in permanent residence around your waist. Make two sets of photocopies of all your vital documents, including the relevant pages of your passport, your airline tickets, travellers' cheques receipt and serial numbers, credit card details and insurance policy. Keep one set of copies with you, but in a separate place from the originals (eg passport, etc in your money belt; copies in your rucksack), and leave the other set at home with friends or relatives in case of loss or theft.

Take an international drivers' licence if you're eligible, and a student card and international youth hostel card if you have them. Don't buy a hostel card just for the trip, though, as guest houses tend to be cheaper and more convenient than hostels in most parts of Asia (Japan, Hong Kong and Singapore are the exceptions – see Chapter Eleven). In Bangkok you can buy fake student ID cards and press cards; no one will accept them in Thailand, but you may find them useful elsewhere in Asia. Take eight passport-size photos with you to use for visa applications, visa extensions and any passes you might need to buy while you're travelling.

CHAPTER EIGHT

YOUR FIRST NIGHT

There's nothing quite like a foreign airport for freaking you out and making you wonder why on earth you left home. Illegible signs, confusing instructions, and crowds of unfamiliar people chatting incomprehensibly can be bewildering, even scary, especially when you've just spent a night without sleep. On top of all this, you'll perhaps be anticipating extortionate taxi fares, sleazy hotels, and "friendly" helpers who turn out to be predatory touts or worse.

Rest assured, however, that even the most laid-back travellers find their first night in a new country a challenge, something that needs to be approached with a clear head and a sense of humour. After thirty

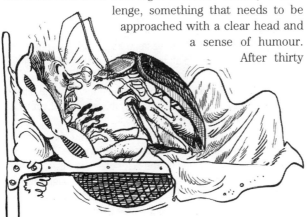

hours on the move you'll probably be lacking both, so this chapter is designed to help you cope without them and ensure that your first experience of Asia is a positive one.

Planning your first night

If you follow only one piece of advice in this whole chapter, then this is it: plan your first night before you leave home. The decisions and preparations you make in advance can go a long way to reducing the chances of trouble once you arrive.

Even if your aim for your trip is to wander where the fancy takes you, it isn't really advisable just to amble off the plane that first night in Saigon, Singapore or Seoul trusting that something will turn up. It probably will, but the chances are you won't like it. You should know where you are planning to stay and how you are going to get there.

Before you read any further, make sure you have all the right paperwork (tickets, passport and visas; see Chapter Three) and a rough idea of how long you intend to stay – you may need to stipulate this on arrival.

● ●

A CAUTIONARY TALE

Three intrepid young men of my acquaintance set off for their year-long travels around the world, first stop Delhi, touching down at around midnight. In their enthusiasm to begin their adventure they abandoned their original plan to wait in the airport until daybreak and rushed outside to join the queue for taxis, which was a mile long. A driver and his friend approached from the side and offered them a cab. They accepted keenly: surely this would be better than hanging around waiting?

Once in the taxi they told the driver they had no idea where to go, but they needed a hotel. He knew just the place. Off they set through the dark Delhi streets. The first hotel was full. No matter, he knew another place. Yet more meanderings through the dark Delhi streets to learn that the second hotel too was full. They became concerned that he would charge them for all this useless ferrying around and pointed out they wouldn't pay for his mistakes. He replied it wasn't his fault and demanded the equivalent of $50 for the trip so far.

Thinking this was too much they eventually, after much heated argument, handed over the equivalent of $30, suggested the cab driver and his chum called the police if they were unhappy, hoisted themselves and baggage into the dark Delhi streets and set off on foot. They flagged down a motorized rickshaw and, having learnt at least one lesson, asked how much it would cost to take them all to a hotel – forty cents! They loaded themselves and luggage aboard and were whisked away to an acceptable hotel where they got a bed for the night.

The next morning they were having breakfast and another foreigner approached them. He was leaving India; did they want to buy his guidebook? They definitely did. They read that the official fare from Delhi Airport to town was less than $8; they also found out about backpackers' places in the city. "Why didn't we buy one of these before?" they wondered.

Lesley Reader

●●

Choosing where to spend your first night

Stage one is to work out in which area of the city you want to spend your first night or two. To have your destination clearly etched in your mind is absolutely essential, whether you decide to book ahead or just take potluck on the ground. Any reliable, up-to-date guidebook will help you decide (see Chapter Six), but here are a few extra tips:

◇ Choose an area that has a lot of budget hotels close together, so that if you don't like the first hotel it's easy to change to a different one.

◇ Select a district that's close to the sights that interest you, and/or convenient for any onward transport connections you might be needing in the next few days.

◇ Check out how easy this area is to reach from the airport and, with the help of your guidebook, decide now what method of transport you plan to use. Bear in mind that the cheapest options (eg some of the youth hostels in Hong Kong) may be significantly less accessible than pricier alternatives.

Deciding on a hotel

Once you've picked your area, draw up a list of three hotels you like the sound of so that you have a ready-made contingency plan should one of them fall through. Consider booking in for two nights, which gives you your first day to sleep, clear your head and plan your next move. Plus, if the hotel's too expensive, or just not right, you've got plenty of time to explore alternative options without having to repack your bags by midday and lug them round the neighbourhood.

You can either book your hotel before you leave home (see below) or sort out your accommodation once you've landed (see p.180).

Booking a hotel room before you leave home

The main disadvantage of doing this is the price. In Asia, cheaper hotels and guest houses rarely accept advance bookings without advance cash payment (youth hostels are an exception; see opposite), so you will probably find yourself booking a moderately priced room for your first night or two. But remember that prices are much lower in Asia than in Europe, the US and Australia, and that you can always move to a cheaper place later. Even though you may be planning to do your entire trip at subsistence level, your first night is not really the time to start – saving money takes time, local knowledge and alertness, and you'll lack all three when you first arrive.

If you want to do it yourself from home, your guidebook should list phone and fax numbers as well as reviews of recommended hotels. Alternatively, ask at the relevant tourist office. Plenty of Asian hotels employ English-speaking staff, so you shouldn't have too much difficulty making yourself understood. Give them your flight number and the approximate time you expect to arrive at the hotel (allowing up to two hours to get through airport formalities, plus whatever time it takes to get into town) – and enquire about hotel courtesy buses as well. You might be asked for a credit card deposit. Once you've made your booking, confirm it in writing by mail or fax.

If you can't face phoning the hotel yourself, you could either make your arrangements online, through Internet-based accommodation booking agents (see *Basics* p.302 for details), or you could use a travel agent instead. Both these options could be a little more expensive, as your choice will probably be limited to mid-range and expensive hotels.

The best budget option may well turn out to be the youth hostel in the city of your arrival (if there is one), some of which can be booked from overseas using the IYHF Booking Network (see *Basics* for details). Women might also consider a homestay with a local woman for the first couple of nights: contact the Women Welcome Women organization for membership details (see *Basics*, p.302).

The plane journey

If you're coming from Europe or America, the flight into Asia is almost certain to be a long slog – NYC to Rangoon, for example, will last a good thirty hours, and London to Bombay can't be done in less than eight. If you're doing things on a budget, chances are your journey will be convoluted, involving several touchdowns and possibly even a couple of long waits while changing planes. There's nothing you can to do to speed the trip up, but here are a few suggestions on how to make it as bearable and comfortable as possible.

Hand baggage

Don't just throw all your backpack overflow into your hand baggage, but think about what you might need for the time you'll be in transit. Too little, and you might freeze or go out of your mind with boredom. Too much, and you might not be allowed to take it into the cabin – many airlines specify a 5kg maximum weight for hand baggage, while others may refuse anything that won't fit under your seat. However, they vary in their zeal in enforcing these rules. Also, if you're wandering round transit lounges for several hours en route, you don't want to be dragging too much with you. Airlines also have regulations about batteries, blades and knives – anything deemed a potential weapon in a hijack will be removed from you, carried by the crew and returned at your destination.

Handy items you might want to include in your carry-on baggage:

◇ Something to read (don't rely on the movies being riveting).

◇ A guidebook so you can plan your arrival strategy (see p.176), plus a map in case you want to follow your route during the flight.

◇ Socks and a sweater. Even planes in tropical climates get cold when they're cruising at 36,000 feet; airline blankets are often in short supply.

◇ All valuables and fragile items, including camera. Your checked-in baggage is more likely to go adrift than your hand baggage and is treated much more roughly.

◇ Films. Checked-in baggage is treated to higher doses of security X-rays, which can fog film.

◇ Some basic toiletries, including a toothbrush: a quick wash and brush can improve how you feel very quickly and put that freshness back into your breath after a surfeit of airline food.

◇ Contact lens case and spare specs so you can sleep without waking to permanent haloes around your eyeballs.

◇ Moisturizer to combat the dry cabin atmosphere.

◇ Chewing gum and/or sweets to help clear your ears during takeoff and landing.

◇ A small bottle of water so you don't dehydrate on the plane (you can fill it up when you run out), or in transit lounges where you might otherwise have to shell out for soft drinks in local currency. Even if transit lounge facilities accept hard currency, you will usually be given local currency as change, which is a waste of time if you're heading somewhere else.

◇ Clothes that will be appropriate for your point of arrival. In other words, it's a good idea to wear or take several layers of clothing so that you don't perish in your home country and boil when you arrive (or vice versa); also remember the modesty factor (see p.149).

◇ One set of clean underwear. You never know when you or your baggage may get delayed or separated – you don't want to be trying to buy new underwear on your first morning in Vientiane.
◇ Medicines. The above advice applies for anything you take regularly. A few painkillers are a good idea, as flying is very dehydrating and headaches are common. Air sickness is not unusual: if you know you suffer, dose yourself with your favourite medication. If you don't know, but fear you might, put some in your hand baggage – they take a while to work, but it's better to take them late rather than never.
◇ A pen, for filling in immigration forms.

Some people fly with far more; a Game Boy and/or Walkman, an inflatable neck pillow, and snacks or more substantial food in case of foodless delays, but also in case your appetite goes haywire on arrival (see p.182), causing you to venture out at 3am looking for munchies. Consider including swimwear, should you happen to be routed via one of the flashier airports – Singapore's Changi Airport for example, which has a swimming pool.

Checking in

At check-in you'll present your ticket and passport to the airline for checking and hand over your main baggage, which should weigh very little if you take our advice in Chapter Seven. When you check in your bag a baggage coupon will be clipped to your ticket or handed to you. Keep this safe. In the event that the worst happens, and you have lunch in London and dinner in Delhi but your baggage goes to Bangkok, you will need this counterfoil to complete the paperwork at your destination. You may also need the counterfoil if officials want to check that you are the owner of the baggage – this tends to happen in, among other places, Hanoi in Vietnam and Lhasa in Tibet.

Most airlines specify that for intercontinental flights you should check in a minimum of two hours before departure – there are exceptions to this (eg Air India and El Al both require longer), so you should ask your travel agent, or call the airline in advance. Whatever the minimum time given, it is advisable to check in as far ahead as possible.

Though it's a pain having to wait around for a couple of hours after you've checked in, you will be more likely to get your preferred seat, and that can make all the difference to your state of mind – and body – on arrival. If the plane isn't full, it is possible to change seats once you're on board, but it's much better to ask for what you want initially.

◊ If you have long legs, then go for the aisle seat, or make a special request for an exit-row seat where there are no seats immediately in front of you. Alternatively, the seats at the front of the cabin also have plenty of leg room, but you're likely to find yourself in amongst the babies as that's where the cot-seats are. Aisle seats have the advantage that you can get up and stretch your legs as often as you like without disturbing anyone, but you do get disturbed by everyone else in the row going in and out.

◊ A window seat, on the other hand, guarantees you extra in-flight entertainment. You get good views during takeoff and landing, and the views at 30,000 feet can be extraordinary, particularly at sunrise or sunset, or during flights over mountain ranges (like those that dominate western Iran), or azure-fringed archipelagos (such as the islands of Indonesia) during daylight hours.

◊ Even if you are a smoker, you might want to waive your right to a seat in the smokers' section simply because the air is stale and fuggy enough on the plane as it is, without being choked full of fumes. If you want the occasional cigarette it's nearly always possible to sit, or stand, in the smokers' section for ten minutes before returning to the cleaner part of the plane. Note that an increasing number of flights are totally non-smoking.

◊ If you haven't yet ordered your special food, such as a vegetarian or diabetic option (see p.86), this is your very last chance, though don't bank on a positive outcome.

Enjoy the flight

One way to ensure that the flight passes happily is to make full use of the in-flight bar service, offered free on most long-haul flights into Asia. Free drink can make the time go quickly, help you to sleep and calm your nerves if you're scared of flying. However, anyone who's ever got seriously drunk on a plane will know just how magnified the usual side effects become. Your head aches violently, your heart pounds incessantly, and your body temperature soars to an unnatural high – not much fun.

Whether or not you get drunk, dehydration is a major cause of discomfort on long flights, so you need to combat this by drinking lots of soft drinks and water.

It's a good idea to use the toilet on the plane before you get off at your destination. Tackling foreign public toilets with some or all of your baggage to worry about, and possibly having to pay for the facilities in local currency, is an avoidable extra hassle.

The transit experience

Should you be turfed off the plane for a couple of hours' refuelling en route, or have to wait for a connecting flight, the transit experience doesn't have to be an unpleasant one.

◇ Singapore's Changi Airport has a highly browsable English-language bookshop stocked full of books on Asia that you rarely see in the West. There's an Internet centre so you can email your friends to let them know you're nearly there, and the departures hall facilities include a swimming pool as well as showers.

◇ Jakarta's Soekarno-Hatta Airport is pleasingly laid out in pagoda-style buildings, connected by walkways that lead you through tropical gardens. There's a well-priced Asian food court and a *McDonald's* too.

◇ In the transit lounge at Osaka's Kansai International Airport you can rent therapeutic chaise longues that vibrate gently to massage away your in-flight stiffness; a bargain at $4 (£2.50) per hour, or $10 (£6) including use of the showers.

◇ Dubai is also a good one – a huge white dome dominated by dramatic fountains, with shops selling reasonably priced duty-free electrical goods.

◇ Bangkok Airport sells gorgeous orchids by the boxful – worth remembering for the homeward trip.

On the other hand, you might find yourself holed up for hours in the transit lounge from hell:

◇ Moscow offers hard seats, dim lighting, no refreshments in the middle of the night, the most miserable cleaners in the western hemisphere and, on occasion, resident refugees inhabiting cardboard boxes.
◇ Athens Airport has all the clutter, chaos, discomfort and dearth of information of a local bus station.

Landings can also be memorable:

◇ Flights into Kathmandu of necessity make their descent within spitting distance of soaring Himalayan peaks.
◇ After flying across Sichuan's western mountain ranges, the landing at Lhasa seems like a miracle of faith over logic as the ground appears to rise up to meet the plane instead of the plane making a normal descent.
◇ Flying in to the Philippines, you get a great view of the sparkling South China Sea and the seven thousand plus atolls that make up this island nation.
◇ No one who has ever arrived at Hong Kong's Kai Tak will ever forget the near-death approach through the towering sky-scrapers. However, with the new airport scheduled for 1998, you won't get the chance to experience this much longer.

Arriving at the airport

Whilst some Asian international airports – eg Tokyo – have the look and seamless efficiency to match anything in Europe, North America or Australasia, others, such as Tribhuwan in Kathmandu, are more basic. However, the days of grass landing strips and tin shacks operating as international airport terminals are largely extinct in Asia. Remember that airports the world over, even in your own country, can be soulless, confusing, intimidating places

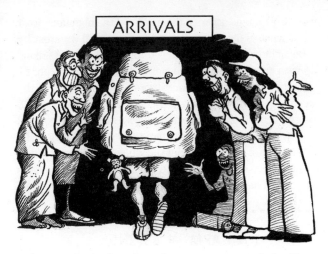

and certainly don't reflect the country as a whole. They are, literally, a rite of passage to be gone through by every traveller – ideally as painlessly as possible.

New arrivals are prime tout fodder and you'll be amazed just how many services you can be offered in the short walk between customs and the taxi rank – hotels, hash, sex, diamonds, tour guides, you name it. The slightest flicker of interest, or even friendly eye contact, is encouragement enough to continue the encounter and, if this is your first time in Asia, it will be written all over you, from your face to the way you walk. Not only do you feel vulnerable, but this is the time when you *are* most vulnerable. Much as you may hate to be unfriendly, in arrivals you should keep your eyes angled unflinchingly forwards, rucksack strapped firmly to your back, and your plan of action bleeping loudly inside your head. It's a mad zone out there and right now you can't afford to be soft-centred.

Hopefully you have already followed our advice and planned to arrive in daylight (see p.85), so that you have plenty of time to sort out your ride into the city and your accommodation before it gets dark. A lot of the lowlife of any city emerges after sunset; with your senses and fears heightened by the shadows it is perfectly possible, and even sensible, to assume that absolutely harmless and helpful people are out to rip you off. If the worst comes to the worst and you do arrive in the middle of the night and don't know what to do, just wait in the airport until daybreak.

Daylight or not, if you're on your own, think about linking up with other travellers who look as if they might be on the same budget as you and may therefore be heading to the same area of town – there's usually plenty of time to size people up in immigration and baggage collection queues. This will save money on taxi fares and will probably make you feel more confident about the whole arrivals procedure. Nonetheless, it makes sense to retain some of your healthy scepticism in encounters with fellow travellers, too.

● ●

NO HARM IN ASKING . . .

I was nervous about doing the big cross-Asia trip on my own, but as there was no one else to go with, off I went. Standing by the luggage carousel at Denpasar Airport in Bali (my first port of call), I got chatting to a couple of hip-looking American women, and asked if I could share a ride with them into town. It turned out we got on really well and we spent the next two weeks together, travelling as a threesome all round Bali. After that I was much more confident and happy to continue through Indonesia on my own.

Debbie King

● ●

Formalities

In general, the order of airport formalities is immigration, baggage collection, customs, and then into the arrivals hall. If you have followed the advice about paperwork given in Chapter Three, you shouldn't have too many problems, but the thing to bear in mind is that, whatever happens, keep your cool: the queues may be a mile long, the officials may be obstructive and rude, the bags may take ages to arrive, but keep calm, be polite and don't get angry – it rarely works in Asia in any case. And, remember – you're on holiday!

It goes without saying, but we'll say it anyway. You shouldn't be trying to bring anything inappropriate into the country. Most countries stipulate a duty-free allowance for alcohol or tobacco, some countries do not allow the import of certain food items (eg chewing gum into Singapore), and all prohibit the import of hard and soft drugs. In some Asian countries the penalty for smuggling drugs is death and, in the remainder, lengthy jail terms are the norm. It is up to you to find out what the regulations are in each country and obey them.

Solo travellers should be especially vigilant when collecting baggage. Many a lone traveller has left their hand baggage on a trolley while lunging for their pack on the carousel only to turn around and find their precious hand baggage has gone. Keep at least one hand on your hand baggage at all times – even if it means sacrificing your trolley.

••••••••••••••••••••••••••••••••••••••

ANARCHISTS FROM THE UK

The only time I've ever had trouble at immigration is when I went to Japan with my friend John. John is an archivist, which is what he told immigration officials when they asked. Unfortunately, they misheard, or at least misunderstood, and, thinking he'd said "anarchist", hauled us both off for a thorough baggage check behind closed doors. Moral of that story: either give a simple version of your job title or make one up.

Bob Williams

••••••••••••••••••••••••••••••••••••••

Changing money

Unless you have managed to buy some local currency before you left home (see Chapter Five), you'll need to change money before you leave the airport.

◇ Keep your eyes peeled for exchange facilities as soon as you get off the plane, as some airports keep them hidden away on the air side of Immigration; in other words, between the runway and passport control.

❖ Rates will probably be less favourable at the airport than at more competitive places in town, so you might only want to change enough for the first couple of days.

❖ Make sure you get plenty of small-denomination notes; you don't want to end up arguing with a taxi or bus driver who has no change.

❖ Make sure you get and hold onto your exchange receipt. Because of the proliferation of black-market money changers across Asia, you will probably be asked to show at least one official exchange receipt when you want to change back left-over money at the end of your stay.

❖ Stash your cash in an easily accessible place so that you do not have to unzip your clothes and bare all to half the population of Kathmandu while trying to retrieve a taxi fare from your money belt.

Finding a place to stay

If you haven't pre-booked a place from home (see p.170) it's not too late! Many international airports have a counter for booking local hotel rooms. They tend to deal in mid- to upper-range hotels and charge a booking fee. The booking clerk rings the hotel and makes the reservation, then issues you with a voucher, which will either be the receipt for payment made at the counter or specify the price you will pay at the hotel. He or she should also be able to advise you on the best way of getting to your hotel. The main drawback with this option is that only certain hotels feature on these official booking lists and they may not be described in your guidebook, so you won't have any idea of what the place is like until you get there.

If you are up to tackling the local telephone system and language, there is nothing to stop you ringing hotels yourself and finding a bed, although you should come armed with a list of options together with phone numbers – most public phones don't sport directories. Remember to establish the price and make sure you get them to hold the room for long enough for you to get there and claim it.

Probably the least desirable situation on your first night is to be tramping the streets with your pack on your back looking for a place to stay. If, for whatever reason, this happens, then you should head for an area where there is plenty of accommodation so you'll have a few alternatives and short distances to tramp between places. This means that you won't be unduly concerned if your first is full and your second closed down – particularly crucial if you arrive late in the day or if your visit coincides with peak tourist season or a local holiday. For full details on accommodation, see Chapter Eleven. If there are two or more of you travelling together it is easier if one stays in a café, bar or restaurant with the bags while the others do the trailing around to find a place.

Getting into town

The golden rule here is to put personal safety above everything, and that includes price. If you do not feel comfortable waiting an hour for a bus in a dark underground car park or sitting in an unlicensed cab on your own for forty minutes, then don't do it. You will have plenty of chances to save money later. On your first night do what feels safe.

Airports always seem to be a long way from where you want to go. The possibilities for getting into town obviously vary depending on where you are. In a few cases there is a rail link (eg from Don Muang in Bangkok and from Narita in Tokyo), but more likely you'll be looking at road transport. The variety can be overwhelming: you might find motorbike taxis and three-wheeled sidecar taxis, air-conditioned limos and special luxury six-seaters, vans and family cars, and even cycle-rickshaws, and it'll be up to you to decide! Guidebooks are probably the best way to weigh up, and budget for, your options. For example, it's useful to know that in Tokyo a ninety-minute taxi ride into town will cost no less than $320 (£200), whereas the ninety-minute train trip costs $13 (£8).

Your most likely options are as follows:

◊ **Official taxis**. In some cases you join the taxi queue and get the next metered cab from the rank. In others there are pre-paid taxi counters: you tell them where you're going, the price is fixed, you pay your money, get a coupon and they find an official cab to take you. This is generally the most expensive but most reliable method: the cabs and drivers are licensed and, in theory at least, know the area well.

◊ **Unofficial cabs**. Touts for these hang about at most major airports and try to entice customers away from the official cabs. They may well be cheaper – providing you can haggle effectively over the price – but you'll end up at the mercy of a car and driver with no official recognition and uncertain local knowledge. *Always* agree the price before you get in.

◊ **Courtesy buses**. Many of the upmarket hotels operate courtesy bus services for their customers. If you are booked into a more expensive hotel, check whether this service is available.

◊ **Airport buses**. Many airports operate bus services. Sometimes you prepay your ticket inside the arrivals hall and sometimes you pay on board. They are slower than taxis but their routes are often conveniently close to the main tourist and hotel areas and they usually have plenty of space for luggage. If available, these are probably the most hassle-free and cost-effective means of getting into the city.

◊ **Local buses**. These are the slowest but the cheapest of the lot. Make sure you know where to get off. You'll need to have small change to pay the fare and you should be prepared to be rather unpopular if you're hauling a mountain of luggage, even a small mountain, while commuters are trying to get to or from their workplaces. Some bus conductors might refuse entry if you've got piles of stuff; others may charge extra. Our advice is to leave your first brush with Asian buses until the next day – at least then you'll have a better chance of seeing the funny side (there's more on the delights of local buses in Chapter Ten).

Jet lag for beginners

If you're wide awake and feeling peckish at 3am, chances are you've got jet lag. Try as you might, your body just does not seem to understand that it's time for sleep right now. Though it's dark and most right-minded citizens of Manila are fast asleep, you're just not tired. In days of old when travellers went by land or sea nobody suffered from the effects of zooming across lots of time zones and arriving at a strange time of day or night with their body clock still operating on the time at home. It happens because we travel too far, too fast.

Some of the possible effects are disturbed sleep patterns, hunger pangs at weird times and severe fatigue and lethargy for several days. In general, the more time zones you go through, the worse the effects are likely to be. Received opinion says that for every hour of time change it takes a day to adjust (in other words, flying from London to Delhi should theoretically take you five and a half days to adjust). If you are exhausted before you leave home the effects are likely to be worse. The younger you are the more adaptable you're supposed to be and, if your home life is not rigidly timetabled, adapting may be easier.

Some people find that flights leaving home at night are better and that eastbound flights are worse than westbound (thought to be because your natural body clock adapts more easily to a longer rather than a shorter daily cycle). Also, being obliged to disembark during middle-of-the-night refuelling stops makes readjustment harder – try to find out if you'll be subject to this when booking your flight.

To combat jet lag you might want to try doing one, or all, of the following:

⬦ Adopt the timetable of your new country as soon as you land there. In other words, go to bed at 11pm Manila time, not 11pm Eastern Standard Time. If you're dozy at 3pm, have an espresso or go for a run round the block, but whatever you do don't lie down and have a nap. It will only take you longer to adjust.

⬦ Take a couple of strong sleeping pills an hour before local bedtime.

⬦ Try melatonin tablets (currently illegal in the UK because they haven't undergone official tests), an active herbal remedy treatment that dupes the body into believing it's night.

◇ Eat high-protein foods at breakfast and lunch (to keep energy levels high), and high-carbohydrate (low protein) foods such as pasta at dinner.

◇ Try the aromatherapy method. Geranium and lavender oils should help you sleep, whereas eucalyptus and rosemary keep you awake. For further advice, consult Jude Brown's *Aromatherapy for Travellers* (Thorsons).

◇ Switch on Star TV, the less-than-riveting Asian cable station.

◇ Soothe yourself with the thought that you'll be fully adapted in a couple of days, and meanwhile lie back and enjoy the coolness of the (very) early morning.

CHAPTER NINE

CULTURE SHOCK

Do not be surprised if you don't enjoy your first few days in Asia. You might feel self-conscious, paranoid or just plain exhausted. You might even find yourself wishing you'd never come, hating the heat, sickened by the smells and appalled by the poverty. This is quite normal and is called culture shock. Everyone experiences it in some form and anyway it's all part of the challenge of dropping yourself into an alien environment.

⋄ Be kind to yourself for a few days after arrival. You may well be jet-lagged (see p.182), extremely tired, and overwhelmed by the unbearably hot and humid climate. Check out the acclimatization guidelines in Chapter Twelve.

⋄ Venture out gradually. It takes time to find your bearings and get used to the ways of a new country. Start off by exploring the closer, more accessible places you want to see and save the more adventurous outings for later.

⋄ Buy a decent map of your new city; you'll feel far more confident if you know where you are.

⋄ However halting, try speaking a few words of the local language. It will make you feel much less alien and you might even make some friends. (See Chapter Six for some language-learning tips.)

✧ Do not feel obliged to have a completely "authentic" experience right from the start. If you feel like drinking milkshakes and eating nothing but cheese sandwiches for the first few days, then why not? There'll be plenty more opportunities to experiment with local cuisine, so ease yourself in slowly.

●●●

TRAVEL TALK

Once you have arrived in Asia, you'll find that the most useful, up-to-date information about where to go, what to see, where to stay, how to get there and what to avoid – in fact, stuff about pretty much every aspect of your trip – comes from other travellers. Sitting chatting in the guest house or over a beer you'll hear the latest from people who have already done it. They'll be more clued in than a guidebook, more impartial than the tourist office and they won't be getting commission for sending you to cousin X's restaurant, shop or hotel.

However, it pays to assess the person you are talking to fairly carefully. Sooner or later, you'll bump into the long-time-on-the-road-been-there-done-it-all-on-one-cent-a-day-macho-man (yes, most of them *are* men), who gets his jollies by insisting to newcomers that the only way to have a really authentic Asian experience is to stay in a particular rat-infested, fleapit tottering on stilts over a mosquito swamp where breakfast is a grain of rice and a lentil, if you are lucky, and the toilet is guarded by a pit of writhing black mambas who can kill with a droplet of venom from twenty paces.

This kind of traveller also loves to assure you that whichever place you thought of heading for is now spoilt, you should have been here five, ten, fifteen or twenty years ago to see the real Asia. In addition, you really need to speak the local dialect to get even a glimpse of the local culture, and any fool with half a brain could have bought whatever you've just purchased for a tenth of the price. He never takes precautions against malaria, drinks the water from the tap, doesn't believe in travel insurance and has never had an inoculation or day's illness in his life. He's also a dangerous liar who will spoil your holiday if you let him – avoid and/or ignore as necessary and watch out that you don't fall into the same sad trap of self-aggrandizement after a few months on the road.

●●●

And now for something completely different

Though your first brush with Bangkok, Beijing or Jakarta may well be disappointingly banal – a Western-style cityscape of neon Coca-Cola ads, skyscrapers and middle-class office workers – it won't be long before you realize that the *McDonald*-ization of Asia is only cosmetic.

Traditions run deep in Asia and, though urban fashions come and go, community life continues to revolve round religious practices and family units. From a Western point of view, traditional Asian values can seem stiflingly conservative, especially in relation to gender roles and social conformity. Many Asians find travellers' behaviour just as strange, not least because the whole idea of an unmarried youngster sloping off around the world seems bizarre if not downright irresponsible.

Women in the traditional Muslim and Hindu communities of India, Nepal, Pakistan and Indonesia are encouraged to be economically dependent on fathers and husbands, and to keep a low profile in public, often hiding behind veils or scarves. This can be a shock to Western travellers, who will miss having contact with local women – and of course it has an effect on how local men see Western women, too. Asian men often address all conversation to a Western woman's male companion (if she has one), while solo women may be jeered at or worse. Advice on coping with sexual harassment is given in Chapter Fourteen.

Asia is the most populous continent in the world and your first bus ride in China or India will etch that fact indelibly in your mind. Crowds and queues are the norm and there's no point protesting when five more people try to cram onto an already overloaded share-taxi. Time to dust off your sense of humour and start a section on "quaint local customs" in your journal.

The same goes for the bureaucratic tangles involved in simple transactions like cashing a travellers' cheque, and for the haphazard timetables of most Asian buses. Indonesians have a great phrase for Asian timekeeping that translates as "rubber time" – sometimes it stretches, sometimes it doesn't.

Being an alien

As an obvious outsider (or "alien", as foreigners are known in Japan), you will arouse a lot of interest, for your novelty value as well as your commercial potential.

In Asia it's just not rude to be nosy, so try not to get offended by the unflinching stares, or by women stroking your oddly coloured skin and feeling your strangely fine hair. And, if you're blond-haired or black-skinned, get ready for movie-star treatment!

Be prepared to answer endless questions about your marital status and also about your children (in most parts of Asia to be single is a calamitous state of affairs and to be childless a great misfortune). In fact, be prepared to answer questions about absolutely any private matter at all: how old you are, how much you earn and how much your air ticket cost are common conversational openers. People will read your letters over your shoulder, and eavesdrop quite blatantly too, even if they can't understand what's being said.

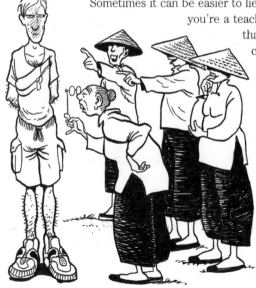

Sometimes it can be easier to lie about yourself – saying you're a teacher, for example, rather than a student, automatically engenders respect, as teachers enjoy a much higher status in Asia than in the West. Depending on who you're talking to, it may also be easier to pretend that you're a Christian (or whatever), as agnosticism is incomprehensible to many Asian communities and atheism almost offensive. Lies can sometimes get you into more trouble of course, as the box on p.190 illustrates only too well.

You may well be asked for your home address by complete strangers who like the kudos of collecting exotic Western pals, and you'll probably have your photo taken a few times too – now there's a cultural somersault to make you think. In short, you're as fascinating to them as they are to you – and that must have some positive influence on global relations.

• •

CURIOUSER AND CURIOUSER

We've all been stared at and had our hair stroked and muscles squeezed before, but I do remember a rather more significant experience on a long-distance bus journey in Vietnam. We had a toilet stop after about two hours, and this "toilet" just so happened to be a very large open field. Naturally I was rather surprised to find a man standing only 10cm away from me in such a spacious latrine. As I was going about my business he certainly wasn't minding his, and he saw nothing wrong in leaning over and staring directly at my penis during my efforts to relieve myself. "That's OK," I thought and looked straight ahead as if I hadn't noticed. It was only when he bent over and started touching it and wiggling it that I really had trouble ignoring him. This unbridled curiosity and complete absence of the concept of privacy is one of the hardest things to adjust to.

Chris Humphrey

• •

"Where are you going?"

It's amazing how quickly you tire of being in the public eye so much. One surprising irritation is being asked the same question – in English – again and again. In India the line is nearly always "What is your mother country?", while in most parts of Southeast Asia it becomes "Where are you going?". The questions aren't meant to annoy, but are intended as friendly greetings: "Where are you going?" is simply the literal translation of "Hi!" or "How're you doing?". Just as in the West no one expects a full run-down on your state of health, no one in Asia really wants to know where you're heading; they just want to make contact.

Instead of getting irked by the constant chorus and more incensed still when they ignore your answer, try responding as local people do. In Indonesia, for example, you should reply "jalan jalan", which means "walking walking"; in Thailand "bpai teeo" means "I'm out having fun", and in Malaysia the even more cryptic retort, "saya makan angin", translates as "I'm eating the wind".

● ●

TELLING TALES

Charles and I talked a lot about his travels in Indonesia. As in most parts of Asia, English-speaking Indonesians almost always ask the same four questions of every tourist: "(1) Where are you from? (2) How old? (3) You married? (4) How many babies?" Charles, already 62, never married, and childless, sometimes got tired of these questions. So, one day, when someone came up to him at a bus station in Sumatra and started firing away, Charles decided to make sure the guy would go away. He told him, "Yes, I *was* married, and sir, the reason I'm in Sumatra now is that I murdered my wife and I'm running away from the police!" The guy looked at him in awe and quickly left. Charles was satisfied, almost thrilled; he had found a way to avoid more personal questions.

An hour later the same guy came back with his whole family – about fifteen people in all – and he said to Charles, "Now you're going to tell me the story of how you murdered your wife, and I'll translate for my family!". Unfortunately, Charles' bus was delayed for ten hours, not the one hour he'd expected, and he was trapped there making up stories for most of the day.

Laura Littwin

● ●

On your best behaviour

However much you dislike the notion of being an ambassador for your country, that is how local people will see you. Similarly, your view of their country will almost certainly be coloured by how they treat you. So it pays for everyone to respect everyone else. No one expects you to traipse around Asia dressed in a local fashions, but it is polite – and in some places expedient – to adapt your Western behaviour to suit the local culture. Because social rules tend to be more rigid in Asia, it's relatively easy for tourists to do the wrong thing – nine times out of ten, you'll be forgiven for being ignorant of the niceties, but there are a few behaviour codes you should definitely follow.

◇ Asian men and women dress modestly and find exposed flesh an embarrassment anywhere but the beach (and even when swimming they plunge in fully clothed). For more detail, see the box on p.149. Shoes are never worn indoors (except in hotels and offices), so remember to take them off in religious buildings and when entering people's homes – this includes some small guest houses.

◇ Getting angry at anything is a very un-Asian thing to do. In fact, it's considered to be a loss of face and therefore an embarrassment both for the perpetrator and the recipient – a bit like being heard farting loudly in a posh restaurant.

◇ Canoodling in public is frowned upon in most parts of Asia (even Japan). It's quite common for friends of the same sex to wander about with their arms round each other, but passionate embraces with the opposite sex are considered rather gross, regardless of marital status.

◇ Throughout Asia, the head is considered the most sacred part of a person's body, and the feet the most profane. Try not to touch anyone on the head (even kids) or to point at anyone, or anything, with your feet.

◇ Avoid making eye contact with members of the opposite sex – in some Asian cultures it's seen as an unabashed come-on.

◇ Be sensitive when discussing religion and politics with local people. In most parts of Asia, a person's faith is inviolable and should not be questioned. Censorship is rife in some Asian countries and penalties can be severe for a resident who goes public with unfashionable views. This is very much the case in Indonesia at the moment, and in Burma, China and Tibet. Even in happy-go-lucky, Thailand anyone who makes disrespectful remarks about the king is liable to be put in jail. In India, on the other hand, opinionated political debate is standard fare on train journeys and in newspaper columns.

◇ For tips on avoiding embarrassing situations in Asian bathrooms, see Chapter Eleven.

● ●

BITTER MOON

Full moon over Hoi An, an ancient port town in Central Vietnam. I gazed off into the heavens from my café table; Hoi An had me feeling mystical. I smiled dreamily at nothing. Enter Don, all energy and intellect, clever not merely for his mastery of the English language, but for his sharp wit and precocious insights. He plopped into the empty chair across from me and I waited for the standard shoeshine pitch. Instead this beautiful 12-year-old boy asked me if I was in love. I pulled the picture of a new boyfriend (my "fiancé" for the trip) from my notebook. I kept the picture handy to ward off prospective suitors.

After twenty minutes of fluent chatter about Vietnam, America and tourism, it was clear that little Don had a crush. In the following days we shared discussions, lunches and laughs; he enjoyed practising his English and I enjoyed his energetic company. He took me to drink my first sugar cane and insistently paid for both drinks. It never occurred to me to ask Don where he got the money.

Later in my stay, I was out with a friend when we noticed Don. "Here comes my conscience," I laughed. My friend grimaced. "Don't look now, your conscience just disappeared with that German man." It was in that moment of rage and close-to-the-bone pain that I realized Don was a prostitute. He resurfaced a little while later with a fistful of money and disappeared into the night.

Andrea Szyper

● ●

Eating and food

Strange foods and bizarre eating habits are a major feature of the Asian experience, and can often be one of the highlights. After all, Asia is home to two of the world's greatest cuisines – Indian and Chinese – and you can be sure that tandoori chicken and Peking duck taste nothing like they do in the curry houses and takeaways of the West. Then there's the prospect of sampling real Thai food, regarded by nearly all travellers as one of Thailand's greatest assets. You will also probably encounter your fair share of unappetizing dishes and gut-wrenching cooking methods, but so long as you heed the advice on healthy eating and drinking given in Chapter Twelve you shouldn't go far wrong.

◇ Lots of Asian food is eaten with the hand (rather than a knife and fork). Sticky rice in Thailand is rolled up into tiny balls and then dunked in spicy sauces, and most meat and veg dishes in India, Nepal and Pakistan are scooped up with pieces of flat bread. Local people always use their right hand for eating because the left hand – which is used for washing after going to the toilet – is considered unclean (see Chapter Eleven). There's often a wash basin in the restaurant for diners to use before and after eating, or at least a pail of water and a scoop.

◇ Japanese and Chinese food is eaten with chopsticks, as are noodles in all parts of Asia. But don't panic! Though it's a good laugh to watch a hapless tourist wrestling with the equivalent of two pencils and a slippery piece of spaghetti, most restaurant owners take pity on foreigners and offer spoons and forks as well.

◇ Asian dishes can be unbearably spicy – just one mouthful of a Lao chicken salad or a green Thai curry could be enough to send you hopping round the room in a blaze of oral agony. Water won't cool your palate down, but yoghurt is a great palliative, and so is beer, as both contain chemicals that dissolve the chilli oils. It is possible to retrain your taste buds to actually enjoy chilli-rich food, but if you can't face that, be sure to learn the local phrase for "not spicy, please".

◇ Despite the strong religious culture, vegetarians get a mixed reception across Asia. With nearly all its restaurants categorized as either "Veg" or "Non-Veg", India is by far the most veggie-friendly nation. Chinese chefs, on the other hand, regard meat-free meals as unbalanced and lacklustre. The best approach is to learn the phrase for "without meat or fish" and to be prepared either to compromise when it comes to stocks and soups (which are nearly always made from fish or meat) or to eat mainly fresh market produce.

Some harsh realities

Poverty is a lot more visible in most parts of Asia than it is in the West, and in some places a lot more prevalent too. Asia is home to some of the poorest people in the world, destitute people who live in slums or on street corners, who sometimes disable their own children so that they can be sure of earning something from street-begging. It is also home to some of the wealthiest people in the world, and the rich–poor divide is distressingly pronounced in many Asian cities – beggars always congregate outside the most upmarket hotels, for example, and in Hong Kong it's hard not to be shocked by the sight of glossy banking headquarters built right next door to squalid tenement slums.

For Hindus, Buddhists and Muslims of all wage brackets, the giving of alms to the sick, the disabled and the very poor (as well as to monks and holy men) is almost an obligation, a way of adding credit to your karma. These donations serve as an informal welfare system, as in most parts of Asia there's no national health service or financial support for the unemployed.

Western tourists tend to be less used to dealing with beggars, and you would not be the first one to mask your discomfort with averted eyes and a purposeful stride. Giving is a personal decision, of course; you might prefer to donate to a charity instead or, better still, get actively involved with a local charity for a few days – see Chapter Two for some suggestions. Supporting local small businesses is also a positive way of preventing the encroachment of poverty; see the section on p.196 on responsible tourism for more about this. And it's always worth going out of your way to pay for small services – like giving kids in India a few rupees to stand in your bus queue for an hour, or agreeing to have your shoes shined by an elderly Malaysian man even though they don't really need a clean.

● ●

THE BOMBAY SHUTTLE

The airport shuttle bus between Bombay International and Bombay Domestic drives through mile after mile of shantytown slums, a whole suburb constructed out of cardboard boxes, rice sacks and corrugated iron. As the bus slows down at traffic lights, the noses and outstretched arms of the people who live in these slums press against the bus window, chorusing "one rupee mister, one rupee". Travellers lock the windows shut and turn the other way. It's a distressing experience – and one that you'll have again and again in Asia.

Lucy Ridout

● ●

Being a wealthy tourist

All over Asia, people will express amazement at the price of your air ticket – it will seem an absolute fortune to them. Regardless of how impecunious you are, or feel, to an Indian factory worker on less than a dollar a day or a Thai waiter on the daily equivalent of $3, you are quite literally a millionaire. And your camera, watch and sunglasses will do little to change his or her opinion. Small wonder that Asians can't understand why travellers dress in torn and dirty clothing – surely if they can afford an air ticket they can stretch to a new outfit?

It's always worth trying to put money matters in context when people ask the price of your ticket, and to emphasize how hard you had to save to buy it. For example, your ticket probably cost you the equivalent of three months' rent, or about three weeks' wages. On the other hand, there's no question that you are comparatively rich – and that was probably one of the reasons why you chose to go to Asia (just as Arabs and Japanese choose to do their shopping in Europe).

Be aware that as a person with cash you can easily pump up local inflation just by paying over the odds for a taxi ride or even a mango. Traders then overcharge the next customer and so prices rise and rise. The worst-case scenario is when goods and services then become so expensive that local people can no longer afford them and so traders start catering solely for foreigners. Ask local people about prices before buying, and do some bargaining – this is an age-old Asian practice and there's advice on how to do it in Chapter Five.

●●●●●●●●●●●●●●●●●●●●●●●●●●●●●●●●●●●●●●●

JUST SAY NO

One of the main tourist attractions in southern India is a six-hour boat trip along the narrow waterways of Kerala. Local kids are so used to the tourists that they now race, in relays, along the river banks yelling "one pen, one pen" at the boats. What began as a game on the boat that I took soon turned into a depressing case of bear-baiting as the tourists started to chuck pens into the water just so the little boys would dive in to grab them. The kids were just normal village boys, not destitute slum-dwellers, but they knew they could get some trinkets if they "performed" for the tourists – and that's how a demeaning relationship between locals and tourists begins. Though it's natural and generous to want to give little presents, the last thing you want to do is *create* a culture of beggars.

Lucy Ridout

●●●●●●●●●●●●●●●●●●●●●●●●●●●●●●●●●●●●●●●

Responsible tourism

Culture shock works both ways and, with Asia playing host to tens of millions of tourists every year, it's impossible to overestimate the impact that the tourist industry is having on indigenous cultures. One of the most alarming things is the way in which big businesses and multi-national companies have taken over local enterprises and begun mopping up all the profits. It's not uncommon for villagers to be forced off their land because a major investor wants to build a hotel or a golf course there. Hotel complexes make a massive demand on local infra-structures and regularly wipe out village water supplies. In some cases, as in Burma, it is government officials who are forcing villagers to cooperate with their tourist pro-jects. Many politically aware tourists are choosing to boy-cott Burma for this reason.

As a budget traveller, you're unlikely to be patronizing the *Hiltons* and *Sheratons* of Asia – but you may be stop-ping off at *McDonald's* and *KFC*. Try to support local restaurants, shops and hotels instead. That way, profits stay within the community, local residents still have power in their own neighbourhoods and the place keeps its original character – which is, after all, what you've come all this way to experience.

Try to eat local food too, so that you're not promoting a two-tier culture: one for the tourists, another for the locals. It's in your interest, anyway, as local produce is always much cheaper than imported brands. If you're very saintly you will also avoid buying bottled water – which creates tonnes of unrecyclable waste every year – and filter your own from tap water instead (see Chapter Twelve).

It's also important to support local initiatives when it comes to visiting ethnic villages, so that the people you go to see – such as the hill tribes of Thailand and Vietnam, the Dayaks of Borneo and Sarawak, or the Torajans of Sulawesi – profit from your curiosity. All too many tour companies advertise trips to see "the primitive people" without giving travellers any chance to communicate with them. The ethnic communities then become little more than human zoos and exotic photo opportunities (many Thai hill-tribe villages are a classic example of this).

If possible, try to organize a tour with someone from within the community, or at least make a big effort to meet the people you've travelled so far to see. Tourism has a huge effect on these remote communities, thrusting them suddenly into a cash economy they have existed without for centuries.

It's not all bad, however. Some minority groups – like the Sakkudai of the Mentawai Islands off the coast of Sumatra – see tourist interest as a way of keeping traditions alive, of encouraging young people to learn the old ways. In Bali, too, young and old can now make a good living out of traditional performing arts. The difficult thing is for them to keep control of their own cultural heritage in an increasingly voracious tourist industry.

As a responsible tourist, you should also try to minimize your impact on the environment. In practice, this can mean anything from being careful about rubbish disposal – in particular, don't dump non-biodegradable stuff like plastic bottles and dead batteries in rural areas – to sticking to marked trails when you're hiking. The Himalayas have suffered a lot from inconsiderate trekkers, and the same is true of coral reefs throughout Southeast Asia, where snorkellers and divers have broken bits off, and souvenir-buyers have encouraged local fishermen to do the same on a larger scale. For more information on organizations tackling global tourism issues, see *Basics* p.305.

CHAPTER TEN

GETTING AROUND

T ravelling in Asia can be both wonderful and frustrating, often at the same time. Just as the entire continent is teeming with people, so it is teeming with the means of getting them around. It's not so much a matter of discovering whether the journey you want to do is possible or not, but a question of deciding if it's better by plane, train, high-speed ferry, slow boat, share-taxi, tourist bus or local bus. Within some cities you'll even have the option of rickshaws and bullock carts. However, this exciting variety should be set against discomfort, lateness, some of the most terrifying driving on the planet, and unreliability, which are all enduring characteristics of Asian transport.

Look on the travel itself as part of your adventure and you'll stand a better chance of keeping it in perspective. One way to do this is to allow plenty of time to get around. Hold-ups and delays are almost inevitable at some point, and you'll be far less stressed if you've allowed for them in your schedule.

Whilst the huge plains of India and China are ideal for rail systems and the mountains of Nepal and northern India dictate road and air travel, the island states of the Philippines and the huge Indonesian archipelago, the mountainous jungle rivers of Borneo, and the mighty Asian waterways of the Mekong and Yangzi are served by ferries and boats in all shapes and sizes.

Even within individual countries the variations can be huge and you shouldn't make too many assumptions – there may not always be a direct service between two points; instead your journey could involve two painfully slow local buses, a ferry and a rickshaw journey. On the other hand, trips that you assume will be mundane can turn out to be extremely memorable. The Shimla Toy Train, for example, winds its way through the Himalayan foothills in northern India from Kalka up to the hill station of Shimla while you sit aboard in armchairs, reading the morning newspapers and sipping tea served by uniformed waiters. The golden rule is that distance does not equal time.

Despite initial impressions in some cities, car owner-ship is not widespread. Instead, bicycles are common, but most Asians rely on public transport. Although systems may appear hideously complex and grotesquely over-crowded, they are cheap and often far more comprehen-sive than services at home.

Planes

Most countries have an internal air network of some sort. This is the fastest, but also the most expensive, way of get-ting around, with the added disadvantage that you are fly-ing over the country rather than exploring it. Still, when the bone-rattling 1800-kilometre Trans-Sulawesi Highway from Manado in the northeast to Ujung Pandang in the south, somewhere from sixty to a hundred hours by bus (if you're lucky), is too much to contemplate, a few short hours in the skies looks decidedly appealing, and excellent value at

$105 (£65). It's worth bearing in mind that air fares are generally a lot lower than at home, so don't rule out buying plane tickets once you've arrived, especially if time is tight.

It's also worth remembering that in some countries a short plane ride can flip you into the wilderness which might otherwise take days or weeks to reach on foot. For example, the forty-minute flight between Kathmandu and Lukla in the Everest region can save you an extra five to seven days' walking, and access to many of the highland valleys of Irian Jaya is virtually impossible without flying.

Several airlines offer internal air passes at good rates to tourists who have travelled into the country with them, such as Air Malaysia and Garuda in Indonesia (see p.81). If you do buy an air pass, don't waste it on cheap journeys. For example, the Garuda deal is that each flight on the air pass costs $110, which represents a good saving if you're flying between Jakarta and Jayapura, in the far east of the country, but many of the shorter tourist hops, such as Bali to Lombok, only cost around $30 if bought locally. Similarly, at certain times, national airlines may offer a free internal flight or two to tourists travelling internationally with them. It's worth checking what deals are available at the time of booking your international tickets.

When using Asian airlines the following tips should make your trip easier:

⬦ Some of the airlines flying internal routes are small setups with minimal backup both on and off the ground. Don't expect quite the organization or efficiency of the airlines at home.
⬦ Make bookings in person and get confirmation in writing, especially if your ticket will be issued later. Take a note of the name of the person you dealt with, in case of problems later.
⬦ Don't let the booking office keep your passport overnight – a photocopy can be useful here.
⬦ Having booked a seat you often need to reconfirm with the airline before travel. Check the rules when you book.
⬦ If the airline seems to have lost your booking despite all the evidence you can produce, get them to look under your first or even your middle name, as misfiling is common.

- Some airlines find it virtually impossible to issue confirmed tickets for flights from a city other than the one you are in. If you get a ticket under these circumstances, be sure to reconfirm with the airline when you get to the place you'll be flying from.
- Flights are often overbooked, cancelled or delayed at short notice due to monsoons, typhoons, heavy snowfall and lack of aircraft. The more flexibility you can build into your timetable, the better.
- Check in as early as possible; if flights are overbooked, boarding passes are often given out on a first-come, first-served basis.
- Follow the advice on hand baggage on p.171 – just because a flight is internal doesn't mean you can't get delayed and/or your baggage lost.
- Certain items are banned on Asian planes – the stinking fruit called durian is the main one to remember. Penknives and Swiss Army knives are often confiscated from hand baggage and returned at your destination.

Long-distance buses

There are plenty of long-distance buses on offer throughout Asia, and in many cases your ticket includes a ferry crossing or two between neighbouring islands. Note that many cities have separate bus stations for local and long-distance destinations, and the larger the city the more likely it is to have several long-distance terminals, often on opposite sides of town far from the city centre – Bangkok, Ho Chi Minh City,

Jakarta and Beijing are among the most confusing. A good guidebook will provide you with enough information to orientate yourself and get into town, or vice versa.

Many drivers personalize their vehicles with pictures of their favourite gods and goddesses, flashing fairy lights and an incense stick or two on the dashboard. For some drivers the bus is their home and they eat and sleep on board when it's not in use. The quality of the buses, however, is very variable – the best ones have air-conditioning, comfortable reclining seats and bathrooms on board; the worst feature cracked or missing window glass, ripped seats and minimal suspension. Try to look at the bus before you book a seat, whatever the ticket-seller may tell you about his pristine, speedmobile that will whisk you to your destination faster, and more safely, than any other operator. The back seats are the bumpiest, the front seats give a grandstand view of the driver's technique and an earful of his choice of music and/or video.

It can sometimes appear totally impossible to get a ticket or seat on a bus – there are just too many people and they are all far more adept than you. Try booking through an agency for a small fee (often your accommodation will do this for you). As departure time gets close you could consider paying a small boy to climb through a bus window and occupy a seat for you until you can get to it.

Whilst tickets are extremely economical when compared to travel at home, for example $15–40 (£10–25), depending on the degree of comfort you want, for the 2200-kilometre, three-day, three-night trip from Medan on Sumatra to Jakarta on Java, don't underestimate the stamina needed to cope with several days and nights jammed on board. Asian buses are built for generally smaller Asian physiques. Consider booking two seats if you are quite large in any dimension and can afford it, although you'll have to be pretty assertive to keep both seats to yourself as the bus gets steadily more packed along the way. In countries with extensive train systems, India and China are prime examples, it's usually faster and far more comfortable to do long-haul trips on the train.

● ●

ROOM ON TOP

It is important to have the right attitude when travelling Burmese-style ie hanging from the side of a vehicle, teetering from the top like a flagpole in the wind or cramped in a fetal position with your knees in your face – if you are lucky enough to be inside. These situations need meditation; releasing the mind from the perils of travel is an absolute necessity for psychological survival.

We'd stepped on a few hands on the climb to the last free spaces – on the roof, but the other passengers didn't seem to mind. It took a few minutes to get the overstuffed truck moving at a reasonable clip down a one-lane road with barely a shoulder on either side and a sheer drop into the marshlands. I hoped the luggage I was holding on to was firmly attached to the roof. Several times as we moved over to the side of the road we tipped until I could see my reflection in the water all too clearly. I figured if the truck rolled over I'd be fine in the water – until the truck and other passengers landed on top of me. Swaying like a willow tree in the wind, the vehicle recovered again and again from potentially disastrous situations and continued on its way in its charmed state of existence.

Shannon Brady

● ●

Tourist buses

In some countries where the tourist infrastructure is developing, private companies have started operating special tourist bus services. The vehicles themselves aren't particularly different from regular buses – many aren't even air-conditioned – but they offer a direct, hassle-free, although more expensive, service between main tourist centres. Local people aren't allowed on board and there's always plenty of space for luggage. To get from Kuta to Ubud on Bali by public transport, for example, you have to change at least three times in a part of the island where routes are especially confusing, but a tourist bus will get you there in one go for around three times the ordinary fare. In Nepal, tourist buses ply between the main tourist destinations and are generally safer than local services and have bigger seats. It pays to do your research, though – on the more straightforward routes you'll be paying a lot for very little.

Is it safe?

There is no escaping the fact that much road travel in Asia is extremely hair-raising. Buses often travel far too fast for the conditions, overtaking on blind corners is a regular occurrence and drivers frequently take some form of stimulant to stay awake as a lot of long-distance services travel at night. Not surprisingly, accidents do happen. Remember that even once you've bought a ticket it's still your choice whether or not to climb on board any particular bus.

A pleasant journey

These suggestions may improve your journey:

◇ Baggage is often put on top of the bus where there may well be other passengers riding alongside it. As a security measure, you might consider chaining your pack to the roof rack so you won't be anxiously craning your neck out of the window at every stop to see if your stuff's still there.

◇ Make sure you have plenty of water, food and toilet paper. Stops are often at weird times when you may not want to eat and at places with limited facilities.

◇ Consider packing earplugs, as Asian buses usually travel with music tapes or videos turned up full volume for the entire journey.

◇ A neck-pillow is an excellent idea on long bus journeys – much better than jolting up and down on the shoulder of the person next to you.

◇ A blanket, sarong or jacket is useful for warmth, especially on overnight trips.

◇ However uncomfortable, you should keep your money belt on and well hidden: you are vulnerable when sleeping and theft isn't unknown.

Trains

Trains offer a memorable and often safer means of travel across large tracts of Asia. Although often distressingly crowded and rather dirty, especially in the cheaper classes, train travel thrusts you into the company of local people and you'll get brilliant views too: the sun setting over rice paddies in central Thailand and southern India; soaring cliffs and white-sand beaches along the coast between

Da Nang and Hué in Vietnam; and dizzying drops between the peaks en route from Peshawar to the summit of the Khyber Pass.

When booking a train ticket make sure you know whether the service is a stopping one or an express. Stopping services can literally stop at every sign of human habitation along the way with hawkers plying tea, snacks, books and toys continually hopping on and off even during the night. Whilst these slow trains are a lively experience with plenty to keep you entertained they can take twice as long as the express without a corresponding halving of the fare.

Tickets

Ticket options vary from system to system – Indian Railways has seven different classes – but you'll usually have a choice between hard and soft seats or berths and between carriages with and without fan and air-conditioning. Generally, the longer the trip the more advisable it is to go for a bit of comfort.

Fares are good value, with the very cheapest seats often the same price as the equivalent trip on a bus. For the nineteen-hour journey between Beijing and Shanghai expect to pay from $35 (£20) to $105 (£65) depending on class, while in Vietnam the two-day haul from Hanoi to Ho Chi Minh City costs between $40 (£25) and $95 (£60).

Actually getting hold of a ticket can be a major hurdle; for long-distance, sleeper and better-class travel, these invariably need to be booked several days in advance, and although foreigners' ticket offices can cut down hassle in larger cities in China, Thailand and India, and women-only queues in India can help, you'll may spend hours fighting in a mass of people only to find the train you want is already fully booked. Many travel agents and hotel staff can buy tickets for you for a small fee and this is money well spent. Short-hop and third-class tickets can often be bought on the train. You won't find many ticket barriers on Asian rail networks (Japan is an exception), but your ticket will be checked on board, often several times.

HARD SEAT HELL

We boarded the train to Chengdu and our expectations for the coming journey were high. We were well stocked with fruit, chocolate and enough biscuits to see us through the coming twenty hours. We were also naively optimistic about the chances of upgrading our seats.

Tickets for hard seats were the only ones available. No amount of charm, joviality or bare-faced begging could persuade our stony-faced ticket vendor to part with the more comfortable hard sleeper or even the ludicrously overpriced soft sleeper options usually reserved for party cadres. "No," he informed us, "no have."

Later we discovered that a hefty hard-currency "present" would have secured a comfortable passage. Instead I waited in vain for a non-existent legitimate bed to become available at the "next station . . . next station . . . next station". Sweat mingled freely with grime and smoke as the day turned into night and day again. My companions slept and my frustration and anger rose, aided by the neighbouring cherubic Chinese child clearing his sinuses, gulping and with an almighty hoik landing a dribble right on top of my big toe. His father looked on proudly.

Daniel Gooding

Sleepers

Remember that if you book a sleeper service you'll be saving on accommodation costs, so it can be worth splashing out to get a good night's sleep.

Sleeping areas usually consist of two or three tiers of bunks that may run the length of the railway carriage or be broken up into compartments by curtains or hard walls. Top bunks are marginally cheaper in some countries, China for example, and are the safest for your luggage, but cigarette smoke tends to gather up there and you may be next to a blaring radio, a light that stays on permanently, or right under a fan, which can be chilly. On the bottom bunks you'll often get people sitting along the edge and talking, smoking, eating and playing cards while you try to sleep. Thai trains are a pleasant anomaly: staff fold sleepers down out of the seats at night and make them up with fresh linen for you. Sleeping compartments can get surprisingly chilly at night, so remember to keep your warmer clothing handy. In India, though, you can rent extra bedding very cheaply on board.

Safety

The security issues on trains are pretty similar to those on long-distance buses, except that you'll have all your stuff with you and your fellow passengers have more chance to move around. The following may help:

◇ Lock your bags and padlock them to something immovable, like the berth or seat.

◇ Keep small bags away from windows so they can't get rifled at stations.

◇ Solo women travellers in India may feel more comfortable in the women-only compartments, especially on long trips.

Train passes

Train passes are available for travel in India, Thailand, Malaysia and Japan. You should check details before you leave home as the Japan Rail Pass, for example, is only available outside the country. You'll need to consider the individual passes carefully to work out whether they are good value or not. The Indrail Pass is available for periods of one to ninety days in first or second class. You'd need to travel a huge amount to make it financially worthwhile, but its chief advantage is that it saves you queueing for tickets, you get priority for tourist quotas on busy trains and you can make and cancel reservations free of charge. Similarly, the Thai and Malaysian passes are not worth the money for travellers intending to linger at places en route for a couple of days or more, because they are valid for a fixed period only. On the other hand, the seven-day version of the Japan Rail Pass pays for itself in just one return trip from Tokyo to Osaka.

Top train rides

◇ The Death Railway from Kanchanaburi to Nam Tok in Thailand (so called because thousands of the World War II prisoners of war who built it died during its construction) is a stunning feat of engineering. The track was blasted through mountains and rock faces and traverses numerous amazing bridges, passing along and over the River Kwai and stopping at flower-decked villages.

◇ The most scenic way of getting to Ooty, the former colonial outpost in India's Blue Mountains, is to take the Toy Train, a coal-fired, narrow-gauge, three-carriage antique that travels at around 11km per hour. The views of the hills are gorgeous, as you pass through forested slopes and tea plantations.

◇ If money's no object, you might consider treating yourself to a ride on the Eastern and Oriental Express. This deluxe train is modelled on the original Orient Express, with wood panelling, cordon-bleu meals and first-class service throughout the 41 hours it takes to travel from Singapore via Kuala Lumpur to Bangkok at a cost of around $1600 (£1000) per berth.

Boats

One of the highlights of travel in Asia is the opportunity to make some spectacular boat journeys. The island nations of Indonesia, with over thirteen thousand islands, and the Philippines with seven thousand, offer countless long- and short-distance trips, but in most Asian countries you'll have the chance to cruise on rivers and across lakes and lagoons as well as between islands. Boat travel is a convenient and economical alternative to flying, with the bonus of great views and the chance to see marine and river wildlife at close hand.

In some areas of Kalimantan, Sarawak and Laos, for example, river transport is the only way to get around, whereas in many cities, such as Bangkok, river ferries and taxis are considerably faster than road transport, as well as being a cooler and more pleasant way to travel.

Bearing in mind that long-distance trips can last several days, it pays to make some advance preparations:

◇ If you're travelling deck class, take a waterproof sheet to lie on as the floor gets very damp.

◇ Keep precious things, especially your camera and film, in waterproof bags. Particularly in smaller boats, ocean waves or wash from other river craft can sometimes drench you.

◇ Take your own food and water, even if they are available on board, as quality is often variable. Boats break down or get delayed or diverted due to bad weather conditions, and your journey may take longer than anticipated.

◇ It gets cold at sea – keep warm clothing near the top of your pack.

◇ Equally, the sun can be scorching, so keep sun protection, hats and lotion to hand.

◇ Put some sea-sickness tablets in your pack even if you don't normally suffer. The combination of big swells and deafening engines belching noxious fumes can affect even the most hardened stomach.

Best boat trips

◇ The Star Ferry across Hong Kong Harbour gives you the city's best views of the skyscraper skyline.

◇ Arriving at Puerto Galera on Occidental Mindano in the Philippines. The ferry operates from Batangas City and, although most of the two-hour journey is unspectacular, the approach to Puerto Galera is incredible – a tiny entrance through tropical palms opens out into a huge and picturesque bay.

◇ Backwater trips in Kerala, South India. The two-hour public ferry service between Allappuzha and Kottayam takes you along lily-choked canals and across lagoons, slicing through farmland and coconut plantations, past temples, mosques and waterfront houses. It's much more interesting than the eight-hour tourist ride from Allappuzha to Kollam.

◇ Across the Brahmaputra (Tsangpo) River to Samye Monastery in Tibet. Set amidst stunningly cold, high-altitude scenery, a noisy, smoky flat-bottomed boat weaves between sandbanks for well over an hour. Unforgettable.

◇ The Bangkok *khlongs*. Inky-black and stinky, a ride on these canals gives an unsurpassed insight into Bangkok's watery suburbs, including teak houses with longboats as the family car, half-submerged temple grounds, kids playing in the water, men bathing and women doing the washing-up as you swish past.

◇ The towering limestone outcrops in Ha Long Bay, Vietnam: sixteen thousand islands in 1500 square kilometres of water.

• •

MONSOON MIRACLE

Thai ferries are always full and always run on time, or close to it. Broken gadgets are usually repaired with random pieces of wire, shoelaces or just held together manually. This is the miracle of Thai transportation. You're always going somehow – storms, rain and floods be damned.

I hopped on the boat headed for Ko Tao. As we waited for passengers to board, I established myself on a wooden bench and watched a Thai official remove all the life jackets on board. I breathed deeply. My blind faith in Thai efficiency kicked in – we'd get there somehow, some time.

It began to rain and off we went. We dipped and trundled into the open sea, away from land, warm hotel beds and everything safe. After half an hour we encountered not waves anymore, but swells the size of two-storey buildings which rocked and crashed our little ferry from side to side, playing with us as a cat might bat a mouse around the room. We were reassured by the crew when the engines cut for a spell, that it was only engine trouble, nothing more. I sat on my bench and attempted to read as water crashed through the doorways on to backpacks and eventually on to me.

The swells grew higher, meaner and quicker. Book forgotten, I looked at my white knuckles, straining to keep my body on board and in an upright position. Around me, the other passengers held on as I did to whatever they could to prevent themselves from being catapulted out of the boat. I thought of my mother. She'd be devastated to learn of my demise. No glory, no excitement. Another drowning in a raging sea. My story would end up in the obscure international section of newspapers.

Our prospects looked grim. So I began to pray and remembered, as words failed to flow, that I knew no prayers whatsoever. I wished I had been raised in some religious setting. Nonetheless, I continued: "Holy Mother of God," I chanted, "please save us." And after one hour she did. I watched the swells change from assaulting us head on, to broadside, to coming in from the stern as we slowly turned to Ko Pha-Ngan, an island between Ko Samui and Ko Tao. I was alive and thankful to walk on land.

Nicole Meyer

• •

City transport

It's in the cities that you'll see the full and glorious range of Asian transport, and here that you can witness the incredible juxtaposition of traditional and ultramodern. As well as buses, taxis and subway systems, be prepared for minibuses, motorcycle taxis, rickshaws, three-wheelers and even horse carts. You'll be flung into close, sometimes very close, proximity with your fellow passengers, who'll possibly be travelling together with their vegetables, goats and chickens for market, babies for the clinic and kids for school. A sense of humour is a prerequisite for travel this way.

Finding out how to get around a city is a great way to increase your confidence in a place and helps you begin to feel less alien. You may adore Calcutta but be daunted by Delhi purely because you've worked out a couple of the central Calcutta bus routes, whereas the Delhi system remains a mystery, resulting in constant aggravation with taxi and rickshaw drivers.

Local buses

Most Asian cities operate with a mixture of large and small buses supplemented by a whole host of smaller minibuses, vans or motorized three-wheelers. The general rule seems to be that the smaller the vehicle, the less rigid the route and the greater the linguistic and geographical skills needed to find out where they are going. All these vehicles are cheap, but are very slow, packed solid with passengers, and the smaller ones stop wherever passengers want to get on and off. And, if the driver fancies a lunchtime break at the market en route, you will have to wait the twenty minutes or so it takes him to buy and eat his noodle soup. You'll see all of Asian life on the buses, and depending on your mood they are either great or intensely frustrating.

In some places, such as Bangkok, it is possible, and well nigh essential, to get a map of local bus services. Otherwise, get directions at the tourist information office, from your guidebook or at your hotel. Ask again when you're on board. The following tips will help you negotiate the confusion more easily:

◇ Find out the fare schedule (prices are generally incredibly cheap) and how you'll have to pay before you set off.

◇ Take a pocketful of small-denomination coins or notes as getting change is a nightmare.

◇ You'll find that drivers, conductors and other passengers are generally helpful and concerned to get you where you want to go, although rush-hour commuters the world over aren't the most patient of folks and Asia is no exception.

◇ Give yourself as much time as you can, keep calm and you'll soon be hopping around town like a local. Remember, it doesn't really matter if you get lost. You're on holiday!

◇ Be very wary of pickpockets and slashers with razor-sharp knives who cut through material, canvas and the straps of shoulder bags.

◇ Women travelling on crowded city buses are, unfortunately, prime targets for sexual harassment ("Eve teasing" as it is called in India), and you may well experience groping hands, men squeezing past and "accidental" touches and brushes against you.

●●●●●●●●●●●●●●●●●●●●●●●●●●●●●●●●●●●●●●●

BEWARE WOMEN!

Monks in Thailand, Laos, Cambodia and Vietnam are allowed no physical contact at all with women. If they accidentally touch or are touched by a woman they must engage in a lengthy series of purification rituals. On public transport monks often congregate in particular places such as on the back seat of buses. No matter how crowded the vehicle, women travellers should not sit next to a monk and should be very careful if passing close to one. Local people will give up their seat for a monk and you'll be appreciated if you offer to do the same.

●●●●●●●●●●●●●●●●●●●●●●●●●●●●●●●●●●●●●●●

Taxis

Most cities and built-up areas have official taxis and they are a convenient and usually very reasonably priced way to get from door to door. Find out what they look like and whether they should have meters or not, and you're ready to go.

There are, though, a few complications associated with using cabs. Most Asian taxis are supposed to have meters; however, these may or may not be a true indication of the full cost. Sometimes when prices go up the meters don't get adjusted until much later. In these cases, drivers carry official charts to convert from the meter price to the new fare. In other places there may be legitimate additional charges, such as entry to the central area of Singapore, tunnel toll charges in Hong Kong and surcharges after midnight, that many foreigners are unaware of. At many Asian airports the meter is officially suspended and taxis operate on a fixed price tariff to nearby destinations.

On occasions when the taxi meter is not working, drivers will negotiate a fare with the passenger. You may well experience taxi drivers claiming that the meter is not working or simply refusing to use it because they believe, usually correctly, that they can get a higher fare out of ignorant tourists than they can by using the meter. The situation varies from place to place: in some it is worth holding out and flagging down cab after cab until you get one to use the meter; in others you might as well start your negotiation with the first one that comes along.

Always negotiate the price before you get in. The price is per cab not per person and this is a good place to hone your bargaining skills (see p.117); the tactics are the same whether you're getting a ride or buying a mango. This is one area where a bit of research among other travellers is very useful indeed; but generally speaking, cabs in Indonesia, Thailand and India are so cheap, well under $5 (£3) to get across town, that if there are three or four of you with luggage, it's hardly worth bothering with a crowded bus. On the other hand, prices in Japan are sky high, around $130 (£80) for a sixty-minute ride from Central Osaka to Osaka International Airport, and in Singapore and Hong Kong you'll need to have plenty of spare cash to jump into them regularly.

Motorbike taxis

In many areas, motorbikes operate as taxis. They can be extremely convenient, but a high-risk, big-thrill way to get around. A few minutes screeching through the rush-hour Bangkok traffic on the back of one and you'll understand the real meaning of fear. Bikes are especially useful in busy cities as they can nip in and out of traffic jams and even zoom up one-way streets the wrong way. Drivers may or may not be able to manage a backpack. You might have to wear it, which is very uncomfortable after a while, or get it balanced between the handlebars. Negotiate the fare before you get on and, no matter how derisory the helmet offered or the means of keeping it on your head, you should still wear it.

Cycle-rickshaws

Rickshaws exist in a variety of different incarnations across Asia. The most ancient form, with a single man running on foot between two poles, pulling a seat perched above two wheels, has thankfully all but died out. Calcutta is the last outpost of such vehicles in Asia, and by the time you get there they may well have been replaced by cycle-rickshaws. It can feel morally uncomfortable sitting on the shaded, padded seat in a rickshaw while the wallah exhausts himself ferrying you around in the midday sun. Are you shortening

the poor chap's life, ensuring he suffers a chronically painful old age with wrecked joints or are you making sure his children at least get a meal to eat that evening?

Cycle-rickshaws have different designs and names depending on the country: *cyclo* in Vietnam and Cambodia, *samlor* in Thailand and *becak* in Indonesia. With all rickshaws, negotiate the price before you get in and make sure it's clear whether it is for the vehicle or per person. The price will depend not only on distance but also on the number of hills, amount of luggage and the effort the man thinks he'll have to put in. You can also negotiate an hourly rate if you plan to visit several places. Rickshaws are particularly useful for backroads where there is no other form of public transport and for finding obscure addresses – many of the drivers know every inch of their territory. They are also a lovely sedate way to travel, although you should be prepared to hop out at the foot of the most daunting hills.

BETTER YOU TAKE BUS

I had always refused the Calcutta rickshaws despite their bell-ringing blandishments every time I set foot outside my hotel. However, one day after wandering all over the backstreets of the city I was foot-sore, worn out by the heat and flies, and found myself well off the beaten track. I approached the nearest rickshaw driver and named my hotel. He looked me up and down, took in my height and likely weight at a glance, and looked at the sun blazing down. Then he raised an arm towards the nearest main road: "Better you take bus," he decided.

Lesley Reader

Motorized rickshaws

A more sophisticated version are motor-rickshaws, also known as auto-rickshaws (*auto* in India, *bajaj* in Indonesia, *cyclo mai* in Vietnam and *tuk tuk* in Thailand). They are noisy (*tuk tuks* are so named because of the sound they make), smelly, unstable three-wheelers with the driver in front and enough space for a couple of passengers behind (but that doesn't stop four or five crowding aboard on occasion). They are driven by a grossly underpowered two-stroke engine, and are extremely useful if you want wheels from A to B but balk at taxi fares. However, as with all rickshaws, if you're stuck in any traffic you'll be breathing in the exhaust fumes of every larger vehicle on the road.

Like taxis they are usually supposed to have meters and like taxis it's often difficult to get the drivers to use them. Rides can be hair-raising, as these little vehicles are very nippy. Received wisdom is to find an elderly *tuk tuk* driver in Bangkok, the theory being that in this notoriously manic profession he has survived to drive again. There's only one problem – it seems virtually impossible to find a single driver of these machines who looks more than sixteen.

Vehicle rental

Throughout Asia the law is variable on foreigners driving rental cars. In China, for example, foreigners may only drive in certain areas: Beijing, Shanghai, Hong Kong and Sanya on Hainan Island. However, in most countries an International Driver's Licence (get this before you leave home) will give you full access to the roads. Expect to pay the equivalent of $20 per day in India, $40 in China, $22 in Bali and $45 in the remainder of Indonesia (insurance and petrol not included). Most capital cities have international rental companies such as Hertz, Budget, Avis and Europcar, which means you can book your vehicle in advance, but these places are almost always more expensive than local firms.

Rules of the road

If you decide to drive yourself, the following tips may help:

◇ Make sure you know the legal speed limits and other requirements. In Indonesia you must carry the vehicle's registration

◇ Make sure you know the legal speed limits and other requirements. In Indonesia you must carry the vehicle's registration papers as well as your own. Balinese police love to stop tourists and issue on-the-spot fines if you are found without them.

◇ Inspect the vehicle carefully before you accept it and make a note, signed by the owner also, of any scratches or dents, or you may get blamed for these.

◇ Check things you would take for granted in a rental vehicle at home: the lights, horn, windscreen wipers/washers, door locks, petrol cap.

◇ Make sure you know how to get the bonnet up, check the spare wheel (is there one?), tool kit and jack.

◇ In some parts of Asia, insurance is not available for rental vehicles. If it is available, it's pricey. You should definitely buy insurance if you can, but make sure you know what is covered. In particular, check how much the excess is – the amount you will have to pay if there's a crash.

◇ Find out the local rules of the road. The official version should be in a comprehensive guidebook, but also spend some time observing what is going on around you. There's often a big gap between the legal and the habitual. In Beijing, nobody seems to obey red lights, while in Sumatra they are ignored if you are turning left.

◇ Be alert and considerate. Hardly a week goes by on the island of Phuket in Thailand without one foreign driver racing him or herself into a crumpled smash on the roadside. Island roads are not racetracks.

Cars

If you want to travel by car, you should consider the often minimal additional cost of hiring a local driver as well (although you'll have to pay his food and, if you're touring overnight, his lodging costs as well). The advantage of a local driver is that you can spend all your time enjoying the scenery, he'll probably know the way (or at least be better at asking if he gets lost), will often have good suggestions about side-trips and will hopefully offer a useful insight into the local area and people. And, if anything goes wrong, he carries the can: killing a cow in Nepal carries roughly the same penalty as killing a person – up to twenty years in prison. An alternative is to rent a local taxi for a day, a week or whatever – a popular and economical idea in India. It's a good way to see a lot quite quickly, visit outlying districts and do it all in a bit of comfort.

Motorbikes

Motorbikes are available for rent in many places and are a great way to travel independently for reasonable cost to out of the way places. All the comments above apply to motorbikes, with the additional proviso that, whatever the local laws dictate, drivers and passengers should both wear helmets and you should always cover up. However tempting it is to feel the wind on bare limbs, it's madness not to have some sort of protection in case you come off, and you also need to be especially careful of exhaust pipes – many a pillion passenger ends up with a nasty burn on their calf, which is no fun in the tropical heat. Be aware that unpaved roads can be unpredictable, varying from sand to mud depending on the weather conditions – motorbike riding in Asia is not for novices.

• •

RESPECT

To stay safe you must be respected. When I walked through the bazaar of one town in Pakistan, even fully robed, I was stared at, catcalled by giggly young men and felt a little vulnerable – a shameless foreign woman unaccompanied in male territory. The next day I rode into the same market on my motorbike. No giggles. No lechery. Previously disapproving old men decided I was worthy of a nod. Young men approached to make intelligent conversation and ask about the bike. Suddenly I became a person; I had respect again. The bike takes the focus off you and your marital status, opens doors and is a great conversation starter.

Nicki McCormick

• •

Bicycles

A bicycle is the only vehicle that millions of Asians will ever own, and they are available for rent pretty much everywhere. Levels of sophistication vary from mountain bikes to bone-shakers that barely hold together. If you want to rent a bike, ask at your guest house or at local shops – you'll get better rates for longer rents. Security can be a problem – the exception is Chinese cities where there are official bike parks – and you should always use a chain or lock.

A few words of warning:

◇ Try out the bike before parting with your money. Wonky front wheels, seats with springs sticking through and clunking chains get a bit wearing after an hour or so. Be especially careful to check the brakes. A working bell is essential for riding all over Asia.
◇ Be aware that most bikes come without a helmet and without efficient lights, so you must be home by dark.
◇ Most other road users will behave as though you don't exist.
◇ Carry plenty of water – cycling is thirsty work.
◇ Protect yourself from the sun.
◇ Don't be overambitious in tropical conditions and overdo it. In Beijing, where distances are enormous, some taxis will carry you and your bike back to your accommodation if you get too exhausted.

Hitch-hiking

The cost of travel in Asia is so low that hitching isn't really necessary for tourists, although in out of the way places, with the last bus gone, not a taxi in sight and still 40km to go to your hotel, it sometimes becomes the only option. Most drivers will expect payment from their passengers. Hitch-hiking carries the same risks wherever you are, and just because you're on holiday don't suspend the instincts that keep you safe at home. If you do decide to hitch a ride, bear in mind that in some areas drivers of trucks and other private vehicles are not legally permitted to carry foreigners (Tibet is one example), and risk heavy penalties if they are caught.

Walking

With the dizzying range of forms of transport, don't forget the pleasures of simply walking around – just get out of the guest house and wander where the fancy takes you. Asian life is lived on the streets – yes, there are beggars, hawkers and hustlers galore, but there are also millions of people going about their everyday lives, commuting to work, shopping at street markets, praying at tiny shrines, having a snack at food stalls, gambling or simply watching the world go by. Bear in mind that:

◇ Asian roads can be terrifying to cross. Put a local person between you and oncoming traffic. When they move, you move; when they stop, you stop.

◇ Jay-walking is illegal in many places – Singapore is one; Indonesia, another. You must obey pedestrian signs and use footbridges and underpasses if they exist.

◇ Pedestrian survival can depend on knowing the rules of the road: remember which way oncoming traffic is approaching from and be aware that drivers may interpret stop signs differently from you.

Tours

Just as tourist bus services can take the strain out of complicated connections, so there are plenty of travel agents and tour companies in Asia offering organized trips, which can make things a lot smoother. You may leave home vowing to see it all and do it all independently, but it's worth bearing a few things in mind:

◇ A day or half-day city tour can be an excellent way to orient yourself. You'll see far more than you could on public transport and it'll help you decide what you do and don't want to spend more time exploring on your own.

◇ In some places, such as Tibet, a tour is very often the only way to get to certain parts of the country.

◇ Not all tours are super-luxury – there are plenty of less expensive trips aimed specifically at backpackers.

◇ Going on a tour with a group can be an economical way to see harder-to-reach regions, eg the Mentawai Islands off the west coast of Sumatra. You can take an all-inclusive, five-day tour for around $150 (£95) from the mainland. Arrange individual porters, guides and some charter boats, and you'll be looking at around double this figure.

◇ With longer trips, make sure you find out the full details of the itinerary and what is included as well as departure and arrival times. One common complaint is that a "three-day trip" turns out to leave after lunch on Day One and arrives home in the early morning on Day Three.

CHAPTER ELEVEN

ACCOMMODATION

Accommodation in most parts of Asia is astonishingly inexpensive. It's quite feasible to set aside $5 (£3) a day or less for your accommodation budget in India, Nepal and many of the countries in Southeast Asia – though you'll get little more than a single bed and four walls for that money. You can scrape by on less if you share a double room, and less still if you sleep in dormitories with several others.

Although making the most of your money is important, you'll probably find that you're willing to pay a little more than rock-bottom rates in return for extra comforts like an attached bathroom, a quieter location, air-conditioning or more attractive surroundings. After a day-long bus ride in the sweltering heat or a marathon tour of every last Kathmandu temple, a comfortable room can restore your mental health faster than a bottle of Kingfisher beer. Good value for money is a factor right up the scale in Asia – for $40 (£25) in Vietnam you'll get a double room with TV and mini-bar as well as shower and air-conditioning, while for $75 (£45) you can stay in an Indian maharajah's palace.

Some hotels in China and Vietnam are not allowed to take foreign guests, simply because they haven't submitted the requisite paperwork, so don't take offence if you're rejected on sight. Hoteliers in other countries, however, can be prejudiced. Some mid-range and upmarket hotels in India won't take backpackers, regardless of how much cash you have; the suitcase-style travel sack is a useful disguise in such instances (see Chapter Seven). Putting on your smartest gear helps too.

Accommodation in Asia is not confined to hotels. You may well find yourself sleeping in a raft-house on the infamous River Kwai, dossing down in pilgrims' *gurudwaras* at the Golden Temple in Amritsar, or even sharing a tent with other trekkers at the foot of Mount Everest. More prosaically, major Indian train stations all offer "retiring rooms" for early-morning travellers and there's always sleeper-car accommodation on the trains themselves.

In some countries, it's also possible to organize a homestay with a local family. You can do this officially, through tourist offices in India, Korea and Malaysia, for example, through specialist travel agents, or for women, via the Women Welcome Women network (see *Basics* p.301 and 302 for details on these last two). Or you can do it on the spur of the moment, simply because you have no alternative, as in remote reaches of Tibet, or in Sarawak, where tribespeople welcome overnight visitors at their longhouses.

● ●

LOWERING THE TONE

The staff at the five-star Bombay hotel took one look at my scruffy T-shirt and well-travelled rucksack and said, "Sorry sir, the hotel is fully booked." I'd just finished a five-year contract in Bhutan – a country not noted for its designer clothes shops, or even its laundrettes – and was desperate for a few days of luxury. Though I waved wads of cash at the receptionist and flashed my credit card, he was just not willing to lower the tone of the establishment by admitting a backpacker: "Sorry sir, the hotel is fully booked." So I strolled down the street, found a public phone and called him up from round the corner. He didn't recognize my voice and answered, "Yes, sir, we have a room; how many nights?" Ten minutes later, I was back at the five-star, picking up the keys to my deluxe accommodation.

Gerry Jameson

● ●

Finding somewhere to stay

Any decent guidebook will list a range of accommodation, and these recommendations are useful starting points – bearing in mind that prices go up, hotels change managers and guidebook writers have preferences that you may not share. For your first few nights in Asia we strongly recommend reserving a hotel room before you leave home (advice on how to do this is given in Chapter Eight). After that, you'll probably do what every other traveller does and trawl the streets yourself, especially if you're looking for budget places.

Because accommodation is so inexpensive, youth hostel culture barely exists in most parts of Asia, and most backpackers head instead for traveller-oriented budget hotels known as guest houses. There is usually quite an obvious distinction between places that call themselves guest houses and those in the same price bracket that call themselves hotels. Inexpensive hotels are generally set up for local travellers (usually businessmen and sales reps), rather than foreign ones, which can mean that rooms are too soulless for any more than a one-night stop.

If you're in a city, start your search in an area that has several hotels or guest houses close together. That way you won't feel obliged to stay in the first fleapit you come across just because you've taken two buses to get there, and nor will you be unduly upset if your first choice is fully booked or has closed down. Get there by mid-morning, if you can, as most guest houses have a noon checkout time and, during peak season, will have an impromptu waiting list established by about 10am. If there are two of you, get one person to sit down and guard the packs while the other checks out two or three places to find the best deal.

Don't ignore a hotel just because it doesn't feature in your guidebook: it's not uncommon for some books' rec-

ommendations to be overflowing while the equally pleasant outfit next door is half-empty. If you don't have a
guidebook, or want to get right off the beaten track, then
the most obvious places to look for inexpensive hotels are
around bus and train stations. In some cities these may
well double as brothels, though business is generally discreet and you may not even realize that most of your fellow guests are booking in and out within the hour.

Finding a room in high season or at festival time can be a
real problem in some places, and prices always rocket
when demand outstrips supply. At Lovina in Bali, for example, accommodation is so scarce during July and August
that travellers often spend their first night there on the
beach. During the Sound and Light Festival at the River
Kwai in Thailand, rooms are so oversubscribed that travellers doss down on guest-house floors, in corridors and
even restaurant areas, while in Pushkar, northwest India,
the local authorities erect a special tent city to house the
thousands of visitors who come for the annual camel fair.

Lots of guest houses employ touts to bring in new customers and, though you might find their persistence
incredibly irritating, they sometimes come up with useful
leads, especially during peak season. Touts generally hang
around bus and train stations (though they have been
known to ride the most popular routes into town to get
the choicest pickings) and will flash various cards, photos
and brochures at you until you agree to go and see a place
with them. In some cases the tout's commission is invisi-
bly added onto your room rate. Before going off with a
tout, always get an assurance of price, facilities and, cru-
cially, its exact location on the map.

● ●

ALL THAT GLITTERS . . .

Looking for somewhere to stay in a small town somewhere
between Bombay and Goa, I was directed into a gloomy bar full of
tatty pin-up calendars and racks of bottles. "Aah," said the manager nervously, "this is, errmm, men's club."

With my short hair, androgynous clothes and large motorbike parked outside, no one dared to question my gender, so I took the room and hoped I wouldn't be asked to prove my manliness. In the brothel's communal bathroom next day, I kept my head low, grunting a deep "Mornin" to the night's revellers. However, I was soon spotted as female by a sharp-eyed client and the chatter of excited, astonished Hindi rattled through the corridors as I slipped away quickly, honour intact.

Nicki McCormick

The guest-house circuit

Most major tourist towns in India, Nepal, Thailand, Malaysia, Vietnam, the Philippines, Java and Bali have a backpackers' enclave where you might find anything from ten to a hundred guest houses packed cheek by jowl into a few hundred square metres. Such concentration ensures prices are kept low and gives you a range of options to check out without having to lug your rucksack too far. It's also a good place to meet new travel companions, especially if you're by yourself or in Asia for the first time. Travellers often say that the real highlight of their trip was the range of characters they met on the road and in the guest houses: an interesting crowd can transform a dull guest house into a memorable experience.

On the downside, backpackers' centres do tend to take on a peculiar ghetto character of their own, a strange medley of watered-down Asian practices and cheapskate Western ones, which not only insulates travellers from the real Bangkok/ Delhi/Kathmandu, but makes Bangkok, Delhi and Kathmandu seem

ACCOMMODATION

indistinguishable. The same is true of popular backpackers' beach resorts, where travellers may hang out for weeks, if not months, without even venturing to the nearest town.

A typical no-frills guest house (like the ones in Bangkok's Khao San Road) has about thirty rooms packed into three or four storeys, most of them little more than white-walled cells with one or two beds and a ceiling fan – some don't even have a window; bathrooms are shared with other rooms on the floor. Though basic, rooms are generally clean and functional and, best of all, cheap – from $3 (£2) a single (less if you share with several other people, dorm-style), so you can hardly complain about the decor. Some guest houses also have more expensive rooms with en-suite bathrooms and air-conditioning.

In smaller towns, guest houses can be far more appealing, with tropical gardens, cool central courtyards and much more spacious rooms. They're often more welcoming than hotels too, being family-run businesses offering just a handful of rooms. Beach accommodation is generally just as basic and cheap as city guest houses, but looks a lot more idyllic. A standard beach bungalow (the usual term for guest houses by the sea) on Malaysia's Pulau Tioman island, for example, is a rickety wooden A-frame hut built on stilts right on the beach, with a palm-frond roof and a verandah that looks out to sea.

Most people only use their rooms for sleeping and storing their packs, and spend their hanging-out time in the guest-house café. These cafés serve Western food like cheese sandwiches and milkshakes, but are used mainly as a common room, a place to write journals and postcards and to swap anecdotes and recommendations with other backpackers. A genial café or roof terrace with good views can do a lot to compensate for a depressing room.

Some guest houses also keep a noticeboard for travellers' messages and may offer a poste restante service too. The most efficient ones operate like small hotels and will sell bus and train tickets, do your laundry and store left luggage as well (though beware of leaving credit cards and other valuables in these; see Chapter Fourteen for details).

A few great guest houses

Below is a very selective taster of some of our favourite places to stay, where you'll pay under $13 (£8) a night for two people:

◇ The tree-houses at *Our Jungle House* in **Thailand's** Khao Sok National Park make perfect romantic hideaways. They're all set in secluded spots beside the river, overshadowed by limestone cliffs, and have nothing but hooting gibbons for company.

◇ *Mount Davis Youth Hostel* boasts eye-popping views over **Hong Kong** harbour – a treat by day or night. It's set right on the top of a hill, so getting there's a trek, but you couldn't find a calmer or more panoramic spot on Hong Kong Island.

◇ A stiff two-hour climb from Altit village, *Eagle's Nest* is a no-frills dorm with stupendous views along **Pakistan's** Hunza Valley. Most people wake before sunrise to catch the first rays of dawn lighting up the surrounding peaks.

◇ Though the bungalows at *Puri Widiana* in Ubud, **Bali**, are simply furnished, each has its own verandah where you get served banana pancakes and coffee in the morning and can sit quietly and watch the birds flitting round the tropical flower garden.

◇ The twenty bamboo huts at *Abdul's*, on the island of Perhentian Besar off **Malaysia's** east coast, are built right on the beach, and each has an uninterrupted sea view from its rattan verandah. The beach is peaceful, and there's great snorkelling close to shore.

◇ In Dharamsala, northern **India**, the best rooms at the hillside *Kalsang Guest House* look down over the village, and from the roof terrace upstairs you get perfect views of the snowcapped Dhauladhar mountains.

◇ Set plumb in the middle of a spectacular valley of sculpted rice terraces, *Hillside Inn* is one of just a few perfectly located guest houses in the traditional **Philippines** village of Batad.

◇ At Tutuala on the extreme northeastern tip of **Indonesia's** East Timor, you can stay in an old colonial-style Portuguese villa that's perched on a clifftop some 300m above the ocean. Accommodation is basic (and you need to bring your own food), but the views are stupendous, and you can watch whales and dolphins feeding below.

Room rates

Standards of budget accommodation vary quite a lot across Asia, so it might take you a while to work out whether or not you're getting good value for money. Most travellers rave about the guest houses in Bali, for example, where it's quite normal to be housed in a pretty setting and to have a good breakfast included in the price; for around $7 (£4) a double, that's a great bargain. At the other end of the scale, Chinese hotels in all price brackets are generally a disappointment, being mainly faceless blocks lacking atmosphere or appeal; they're not that cheap either.

Expensive countries such as Singapore, Hong Kong, Japan and Brunei charge relatively large sums for even the most basic double room ($35/£20), so most budget travellers opt for dorm beds – although even these will set you back around $10 (£6) a bed. Youth hostels can be a useful alternative in these countries and camping is cheaper still, though official city campsites tend to be inconveniently located in the suburbs. Elsewhere in Asia, camping is only appropriate in national parks and on treks. See Chapter Seven for advice on whether or not to take camping equipment. The following tips will help you make the most of your accommodation budget:

⬦ A good way to save money if you're on your own is to use dorms, where a bed will be at least thirty percent cheaper than a single room. If no dorms are available you might want to split a double room with another traveller, again cheaper than a single room. Obviously you should only do this if you feel comfortable with the other person.

⬦ Beds in many Asian hotels (as opposed to guest houses) are very large, so it's quite acceptable for two people to book into a single room; a double room will have two double beds in it.

⬦ In some places you can bargain over the price of a room (especially in low season); others might offer discounts for stays of a week or more.

- ◇ If travelling long distance, you can save a night's hotel costs by taking the overnight train or bus and making sure you get a reclining seat. Second-class berths on trains usually cost about the same as a single room in a guest house.
- ◇ Watch out for "luxury" service charges and taxes in mid- and upmarket places (up to 21 percent extra in Indonesia, for example), and for ridiculous room-service charges as well as overpriced food in the hotel restaurant.
- ◇ Using the phone in your room is just asking to get ripped off, as most hotels add a huge surcharge to phone bills.
- ◇ Unless you pay by credit card in many upmarket hotels (in India, for example), you may have to put down a deposit against your possible phone bill and mini-bar tariff.
- ◇ An unorthodox way of finding cheap accommodation in Japan is to check in to a "love hotel" after all the lovers have departed for the night (usually around 10pm). These hotels are designed for secret and extramarital liaisons, but are definitely not brothels. They're completely legal and unsleazy, if a little kitsch – rooms tend to be plastered in mirrors, fake fur and romantic images – and are scrupulously clean. Because most clandestine liaisons take place during the day, overnighters get a huge discount.

Can I see the room please?

Always look at the room you're being offered before paying for it – this is normal practice throughout Asia and, though time-consuming, is definitely worth it. Once you've checked out a few places you'll be able to size up a room in five seconds, but for first-timers here follows a checklist of essential points to look out for.

If you like the hotel but aren't sure about the room, always ask to see another one: the view might be better, the neighbours quieter and, who knows, the fan might even be working in that one.

- ◇ Is the room clean? Check the sheets for blood spots (blood means fleas or bedbugs), the floor for cockroaches and the walls for squashed mosquitoes. Look under the bed for rat traps (squares of cardboard sprinkled with food and smeared with glue) and scour the window screens and mosquito nets

ACCOMMODATION

CHAPTER 11   231

for holes (which render them useless, unless you want to spend the whole night doing repair jobs with Band-Aids).

◇ Does everything work? Try out the lights, the fan/air-conditioning/heater, the flush toilet (if there is one) and the shower (ditto).

◇ Do the taps run fresh or salt water? If you asked for hot water, check that it works.

◇ Is the room secure? Can you put your own padlock on the door? (Not applicable in China, where hotel rooms are locked and unlocked for you by the floor attendant.) Are the windows safe? Are there any peepholes in the door or walls?

◇ Is it quiet? Rooms on the main road will be noisy, but so will any place near a morning market, a night market, a disco, a hotel kitchen or an electricity generator – which you may not discover until the next morning. The same goes for rowdy neighbours (snorers and squabblers), and 4am cockerels; even temples can be noisy if there's an all-night prayer session or festival.

◇ Is it comfortable? Check the bed for springs and the mattress for lumps. Are you certain it's worth saving a dollar a day by staying in a place with no window or somewhere with paper-thin walls and a creaking fan?

• •

PEEPING TOMS

Jill and Danny were lying naked in their room in Danang, Vietnam when they spotted a hole in the wall with a dirty great eye behind it, staring at them. Completely amazed, they told the person in so many words to mind their own business, and blocked up the hole with tissue and tape. Ten minutes later, they looked up to see a long pair of chopsticks penetrate the hole, free the space and the big eye return.

Chris Humphrey

• •

Checking in

In most parts of Asia, you'll be asked to register when checking in to any accommodation, however small. This usually entails writing your name, passport number and several other details in a ledger – a legal requirement in most countries which, in theory at least, enables the authorities to trace travellers in cases of emergency. For the most part, this should be quite straightforward, though registration forms in China are a notable exception, being painfully long-winded and sometimes written entirely in Chinese script.

Wherever you stay, you should avoid leaving your passport with hotel staff unless you absolutely have to do so. This is unavoidable in some parts of Vietnam, however, where hotel managers have to present their guests' passports at the police station. If you're asked to surrender your passport as security against your bill, offer to leave a monetary deposit instead. Your passport is your only official means of identity in a strange land and should be kept on your person at all times – besides which, you'll need it for changing money and other transactions.

Most people keep their passport, airline ticket and other valuables with them whenever they leave their hotel, not least because hotel security can be quite lax. However, you could also leave them in your room and use your own padlock on the door (if you can), or put them in a hotel safety box, again secured by your own padlock. Bear in mind, though, that sawing through a small padlock is not so difficult, and be aware that not all hotel staff are scrupulously honest.

Security should also be an issue when you're inside your hotel room with your valuables. Always lock the door from the inside, even when you're awake (people have a habit of drifting in for a chat at the most inopportune moments, as shown in the box on p.281). And check on window access too, in case a thief decides to climb in while you're asleep.

Bathrooms and how to use them

Though many guest houses and hotels have Western-style showers, the traditional scoop-and-slosh method of bathing is also common right across Asia. Known in travellers' speak as a *mandi* (Indonesian for "to wash"), this basically involves dipping a scoop, jug or small bowl into a large bucket or basin of water and then chucking it over yourself. Very refreshing in a chilly kind of way. The cardinal rule of the *mandi* is never to put your soap or shampoo into the basin of water and, though it often looks like a big stone bathtub, *never, ever* to get into it as this water might have to supply the next two weeks' worth of guests.

Washing in cold water is the norm throughout most of Asia, but in the high altitudes of Nepal, northern India, Tibet, Pakistan and north China, you'll definitely need a hot shower, so make sure it's operational before paying for your room. Some places only turn on the water heaters at certain times of day. You'll come across some intriguing bathing habits depending on where you are in Asia:

◇ In rural parts of Asia, the local river, lake or well doubles as the village bathroom and everyone congregates there at the end of the day for their evening wash. Men and women nearly always have separate bathing areas and, though they may be within sight of each other, there's absolutely no ogling or communication between the two groups. Both sexes wear sarongs in the water and no one strips off to wash. If you bathe in the local river, you should do as they do, or find a place much further upriver.

◇ Traditional Japanese hotels generally have old-fashioned bathtubs. These have no running hot water, but work instead by heating up the full tub with an element, like a kettle – enabling you to sit in the water and keep warm for hours on end. The same bath water is used by several hotel guests one after the other (not as unhygienic as it sounds if you think of it like a public jacuzzi), so it's essential to wash yourself clean, using the scoop-and-slosh method, before hopping into the tub.

◇ In Bali, the most stylish guest houses and hotels have beautifully designed "garden bathrooms" with roofs that are open to the sky, sculptured water flues and tropical plants growing round the *mandi* area.

◇ Most small towns in Korea have public bathhouses – a national institution that should definitely be experienced. In these you wash yourself on the side of the main pool and then climb in for a soak and a chat with your neighbours. Most have separate pools for men and women.

◇ Traditional Bhutanese baths are heated with huge stones, which are first cooked to a high temperature in the embers of a fire and then thrown into the tub.

Toilet habits

Flush toilets and toilet paper are relatively new concepts in most parts of Asia and, apart from in tourist hotels and the wealthiest homes, it's usually a question of hunkering down over a squat toilet like everyone else does. Asians wash their bottoms rather than wipe them, using the bucket of water provided and their left hand. This explains why eating, shaking hands and giving things is always done with the right hand – see Chapter Nine for details.

Traveller-oriented guest houses often provide sit-down toilets that are plumbed in but don't flush. In these

you're expected to do the flushing manually by pouring a bucket of water down the bowl. These plumbing systems are very sensitive and get blocked up easily as, unlike Western ones, they're not designed to take paper or tampons. Many guest houses have signs telling you to throw your waste in the bin instead and it's selfish not to obey the rules. Even if there's no sign and no bucket, you should chuck any paper waste into a plastic bag: a blocked drain in your en-suite bathroom will attract mosquitoes and all sorts of germs, and the stink will permeate your dreams.

The obvious way round all this is to adopt the Asian habit and wash instead of wipe. If that sounds too unpalatable, then travel with your own roll of toilet paper as most places won't provide it. The one situation where it's hard to either wipe or wash is when you're out trekking in the wilderness. If you don't want to use leaves, either burn your paper with a lighter or dig a little hole and bury it – there's nothing like a ribbon of pink toilet paper for ruining a spectacular view.

Be prepared to come across a good percentage of gut-wrenchingly vile public toilets, particularly in bus and train stations, and on trains in China and India. Try and get into the habit of using hotel and restaurant facilities when you can, and don't be surprised by the following:

◇ Indoor bathrooms are considered unhygienic by many rural Asian communities, for whom the idea of having a toilet just a metre or so from the kitchen is quite disgusting. Indian villagers, for example, will set off for the fields every morning to do their ablutions away from the home or, if they live near the sea, they will do them on the shoreline so that the sea washes everything away. With that in mind, it pays to be careful where you swim and sunbathe on Indian beaches.

◇ Public toilets in China are often very public indeed – with only a low partition between squatters, and sometimes no partition at all.

◇ All Chinese and Japanese hotels provide special plastic slippers for wearing in the bathroom.

◇ Some public toilets in Japan play piped music to mask the sound of pissing, which is considered embarrassing for Japanese women. If you're lucky, you might even come across a singing toilet-roll holder, which plays *Für Elise* every time you yank the paper.

◇ In Thailand, toilet attendants in upmarket restaurants massage your neck and shoulders while you stand at a urinal.

◇ In Singapore, there's a S$500 fine for failing to flush a public toilet and, should you be caught urinating in a public space, you get your picture splashed over the front page of the national newspaper.

CHAPTER TWELVE

STAYING HEALTHY

There's no advice that we can give and nothing that you can do that will absolutely guarantee you do not fall sick in Asia. You are subjecting your body to different food and water, extreme heat or cold, tropical sun and a whole host of new creepy-crawlies. Even the air you breathe will be carrying different cold and flu viruses from those at home. This chapter presents the straightforward facts that every visitor to Asia should know, gives advice on precautions and has suggestions to help you to cope should you get ill.

These points may help to put things in perspective and prepare you before you travel:

◇ Millions of travellers go to Asia every year and millions return home safely, the vast majority having suffered nothing worse than a few days of travellers' diarrhoea.
◇ Almost everyone gets sick at some time during a lengthy Asian trip and the last thing you'll feel like doing at that time is boarding a massively overcrowded bus for an overnight journey or subjecting yourself to any other forms of travel. Make sure you build enough leeway into your itinerary to allow you to rest up for a few days if you need to.
◇ Read up about diseases prevalent in Asia, as symptoms that probably just indicate flu at home may be something far more

serious in the tropics. There are several good books on the market aimed at travellers' health – some people take them along, and they can make interesting if gory reading while you are squatting over the toilet for the twentieth time that day. Check out Dr Richard Dawood's *Travellers' Health: How to Stay Healthy Abroad* (OUP/Random House), an extensive and detailed book intended for those living overseas, but full of invaluable information for travellers, and Dr Jane Wilson Howarth's *Bugs, Bites and Bowels* (Cadogan/Globe Pequot), a splendidly titled book, small enough to carry easily, outlining simply and clearly the illnesses you may get in the tropics, likely symptoms and what to do about them.

✧ Have a dental checkup before you leave home and have any recommended treatment. Dental pain is unpleasant at the best of times and finding dental treatment in Asia on a par with that at home is even more difficult than other medical care.

✧ Carry a first-aid kit (see p.242). It will probably be bulkier and more extensive than you have at home and hopefully will be used very little. But it will be worth its weight in gold if you do actually need it. Also, take with you any medication you use regularly.

✧ Make sure you have adequate medical insurance (see p.86).

✧ Some Asian illnesses don't show themselves straight away – if you get sick within a year of returning home from Asia, make sure you tell the doctor treating you where you have been.

Vaccinations

You should get advice about which vaccinations you require for your trip as soon as possible. Even if your itinerary is not finalized, compile a list of places you are planning to visit (as well as any others you may visit) and think about whether you are planning to stay in tourist resorts, in the countryside, to travel during the monsoon and whether you'll be camping. All of these will affect the advice you are given.

Whilst your family doctor will be the cheapest for injections (many of them are free), you may want to contact a private specialist travel clinic to make sure you get the most specific information available. Many travel clinics have telephone information lines, are quick and convenient and, although they are expensive, their information is up-to-date and extensive (see *Basics* p.302 for contact details).

You need to get started early, as many vaccinations are given as a course of two or even three jabs to be maximally effective. Some cannot be given within a certain time of others because they cancel each other out and, in any case, you won't really want to subject your arm to four needles in one sitting. Be prepared for some pain, discomfort and possible fever after certain types of typhoid jab – unpleasant but much better than getting the disease. Similarly, you need to find out early about the type of malaria prophylaxis that is recommended for the areas you are visiting; you'll need to start taking the tablets in advance of departure.

Different countries vary in what inoculations they insist upon for visitors, but the only time you are likely to be asked for documentation is if you have recently travelled to a country where yellow fever is endemic (South or Central America). In this case, you must have had a yellow fever jab (and have the certificate to prove it).

The diseases you should know about

Below is a rundown of diseases you might be exposed to and what vaccinations are available. Don't be unduly alarmed, however, as some of these are seasonal (usually more prevalent during monsoon time) or confined to limited regions only:

◇ **Cholera**. Vaccine against this extremely severe diarrhoeal illness transmitted via contaminated food and water used to be recommended for travellers, but is now thought to be too ineffectual and short-lived. The best advice is to follow the guidelines given in this chapter regarding water and food, and steer well clear of any areas where you hear of an epidemic.

◇ **Dengue fever**. A mosquito-borne virus causing fever and joint and muscle pain, spread by mosquitoes which, unusually, bite during the day. There is no vaccination – see precautions for avoiding mosquito bites, p.243.

◇ **Hepatitis**. There are several strains of this disease (Hepatitis A, B and E) in which viruses attack the liver, causing a yellow colouring of skin and eyes (jaundice), extreme exhaustion, fever and diarrhoea. It is one of the most common illnesses that afflict travellers and can last for many months. The most effective vaccine against Hepatitis A, which is transmitted via contaminated food, water or saliva is the Havrix vaccine, a course of two injections giving ten years' protection. The shorter-lived gamma globulin injection is cheaper, gives three months' protection and is useful if you haven't time to fit in the Havrix course. The more serious Hepatitis B is transmitted through contaminated blood, needles and syringes and by sexual contact, and the vaccine is given as a course of three injections over six months and needs boosting every five years. There is currently no vaccine against Hepatitis E.

◇ **Japanese encephalitis**. This is a viral illness resulting in inflammation of the brain and is endemic across Asia, although largely restricted to rural areas. It's transmitted via mosquitoes from infected animals and is very dangerous – the death rate is high. Inoculation provides some protection and involves two injections one week apart which need boosting every five years.

◇ **Malaria**. There are several strains of malaria, most causing recurring bouts of fever, headache and shivering. All are serious, debilitating and difficult to treat successfully. Malaria parasites are carried by night-biting mosquitoes and all travellers to Asia should consider taking a course of preventative tablets and do everything to stop themselves being bitten, as none of the drugs available is one hundred percent effective. See pp.243–245 for more details.

◇ **Meningitis**. Caused by airborne bacteria, this disease attacks the lining of the brain and can be fatal. The vaccine (different from the injection given to children in the West) is given by a single injection and does not protect against all types of meningitis.

◇ **Polio**, **diphtheria** and **TB**. Most people will have been inoculated against these in childhood and, whilst they are rare in the West, they are still common in Asia. You should make sure

CHAPTER 12   241

FIRST-AID KIT

Many of the items listed here are available in Asia, but it's better to have them to hand and replace them later. You'll save money and get a more individualized pack if you put your kit together yourself rather than opt for a commercially packaged one. If you're trekking you should consult a specialist guide/trekking book for additional items.

Anti-diarrhoea tablets.
Anti-fungal cream.
Antiseptic cream.
Aspirin/paracetamol.
Band-Aids, small and large (if you take the fabric ones they work well for blisters also).
Bite cream. (Tiger Balm, available throughout Asia is a good soothing alternative; it is also useful for aching muscles and headaches.)
Cold remedy.
Gauze pads.
Insect repellent.
Lip salve/sun block for lips.
Rehydration salts.
Scissors.
Sterile dressings.
Sterile needles and syringes.
Surgical tape.
Thermometer.
Throat lozenges.
Tweezers.

Prescription drugs

The following items will need to be discussed with your doctor as they are only available on prescription in the West. He or she may be willing to give you a course of tablets to take with you if you explain where you are going. Make sure you know how and when to use them:

Antibiotics, for throat and bronchial infections, and for intestinal bacteria.
Diamox (acetazolamide), for the treatment of mild altitude sickness. However, this is somewhat controversial and medical opinion varies.
Tinidazole, for giardia (see p.250).

you are still covered – you need a booster injection every ten years.

◇ **Rabies**. Spread via the saliva of infected cats, dogs and monkeys, rabies is prevalent throughout Asia. You'll probably want to take specialist advice on this one as, although there is a vaccination, you'll need a course of three injections spread over at least eight months before leaving home, and a booster is required every three years. Even then, you'll still need urgent medical help and more injections should you get bitten by an animal suspected of carrying the disease.

◇ **Tetanus** (also known as lockjaw). Contracted via open wounds (for example, stepping on a rusty nail), you should make sure your jabs are up-to-date before you leave home – you need a booster every ten years.

◇ **Typhoid**. Spread by contaminated food and water, typhoid is characterized by extremely high fever, abdominal pains, headaches, diarrhoea and red spots on the body; patients need urgent medical help. Protection (which lasts for three years) is either given by injection or a course of more expensive capsules.

Mosquitoes

Given the number of diseases carried by mosquitoes (malaria, Japanese encephalitis, dengue fever), not to mention the unpleasantness of mosquito bites, you should do whatever you can to avoid getting bitten. This means wearing long sleeves or sloshing mosquito repellent on exposed skin during the dusk and darkness hours when the malarial mosquito operates, sleeping in a screened room with any open windows covered by a fine wire mesh and/or sleeping under a mosquito net. It's a good idea to have a shower and get changed for the evening before it gets dark – mosquitoes adore sweaty skin.

You might decide to take your own mosquito net with you – they are light, compact and you can guarantee it's not full of mosquito-sized tears and cigarette burns. Some nets now come impregnated with Permethrin insecticide as an additional barrier against the bugs, and you can also buy Permethrin sprays to treat older nets.

Malaria tablets

You will need specific advice about the recommended malaria prophylaxis for the areas you plan to visit – in some places strains of malaria have become resistant to certain drugs. Commonly used are chloroquine (sold as Nivaquine and Avloclor in the UK, and Aralen and Resochin in the US), taken weekly together with daily proguanil (sold as Paludrine). In areas where resistance to these has developed, the antibiotic doxycycline is being used (especially on the borders of Thailand and Cambodia). Mefloquine (sold as Larium) has recently increased in popularity, but there have been worrying reports about side effects. You should always discuss your individual situation with an expert.

The drugs must be taken according to a particular timetable. You must start taking them a week before you arrive in a malarial area and, even more importantly, continue taking them for four weeks after you leave. It is quite possible to develop malaria back home if you ignore this regime.

Mosquito repellents

The most renowned mosquito repellent is called DEET (Diethyl Tolumide) and you can buy repellent containing up to 95 percent DEET. Wrist and ankle bands pre-soaked in the chemical are also available. However, it's strong stuff and can cause skin reactions after extended use. You also need to be careful of anything plastic (sunglasses, watch straps, shoes), as they tend to melt on contact with it. Locally bought repellents are often very good and much cheaper than ones bought at home. They may even be the same brand – Autan, for example, is widely available throughout Asia. One advantage of using a mosquito repellent is that it will ward off leeches, ticks and sandflies as well.

There's also a range of natural products that work fairly well

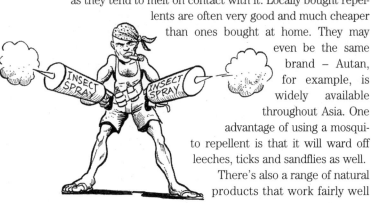

when applied to the skin. They are not quite as repugnant to mosquitoes, but avoid the disadvantages of DEET. Most commercially produced natural insect repellents are based around citronella, a substance found in certain plants, such as lemongrass. Eucalyptus oil is another natural repellent. Although there isn't much evidence for it, some travellers believe that vitamin B1 tablets or garlic capsules taken on a regular basis make the blood offensive to insects and so protect against bites.

At some point in your trip you'll encounter mosquito coils. These are bright green and chemically impregnated and are the main Asian way of deterring mosquitoes. You can buy them cheaply once you're there, in boxes of eight or ten coils. To be effective they need to be suspended above the floor (they come with a tin stand, the prong of which goes through the slit in the centre of the coil) and they need to be smoking, not burning. After you light them, let the flame burn for a second or two and then blow it out. Each coil will burn for about eight hours and they are useful for protecting your ankles if you are sitting out on a verandah at night, or you can put them beside the bed while you sleep. Thoughtful restaurants put lighted coils under tables. They are effective as long as you keep close to them, but you may find that after a few nights' sleeping near them you end up feeling suffocated by the pungent smell.

Several brands of plug-in electric machines are also available. They use vapour tablets that release a repellent into the air when they are heated up. The disadvantages are that they rely on having an electricity supply, need a fairly confined space and don't operate too well if there's a draught.

OTHER BLOOD SUCKERS

Any forays into the jungle, especially near the equator (or anywhere in the rainy season) mean potential encounters with leeches – tiny, thread-like blood-sucking creatures that attach themselves to your skin, zap you with an anaesthetic and anticoagulant, slurp away at the red stuff and, when they've had enough and expanded to many times their normal size, drop off and leave you dripping blood for a long time afterwards. The good news is they don't carry any nasty diseases; the bad news is that they can get through the tiniest holes, such as between the threads in most socks and they love the eyeholes of boots. One glimpse of your ankle with a dozen or so of them attached is a short cut to hysteria.

To stop them attacking, silk socks, insect repellent and tobacco leaves in your socks are all useful, plus regular checks of your feet when you are walking. If you do fall victim, dab at the creatures with salt, a lighted cigarette or chewing tobacco (widely available across Asia) to get them to let go. Don't just pull them off in a panic – easier said than done – as they're likely to leave their sucking parts embedded in your skin.

● ●

The heat

The opportunity to experience a tropical climate is one of the big attractions of a trip to Asia, yet exposure to extreme heat is one of the major causes of illness for many travellers. Once you arrive:

◊ Respect the heat. It isn't only mad dogs and Englishmen who go out in the midday sun, it's plenty of other travellers as well; but it's far better to stay in the shade during the extreme heat of the day, as most local people do.

◊ Dry yourself carefully after bathing – use medicated talcum powder (available throughout Asia) or anti-fungal powder if you fall victim to heat rashes, prickly heat or fungal infections that adore the damp, humid conditions of the tropics.

◊ Dress sensibly – see p.150 for ideas on clothing that will help you keep cool in hot climates.

◊ Protect yourself from the extreme sun and be especially careful at high altitude, where you may be cool but still exposed to huge amounts of sunshine. Use plenty of high-factor sunscreen, even if you are just walking around (don't forget the tops of your feet, tops of your ears and backs of your hands, especially if you are fair-skinned). A hat or umbrella can stop your brains frying.

♦ Drink plenty of water. The heat will make you sweat, so you need to increase fluid intake to compensate. If you stop peeing or your pee is becoming very dark, then you're not drinking enough.

♦ You also lose salt when you sweat, so increase your intake of this; many travellers add a pinch of salt to fruit juices and shakes (see rehydration advice on p.249). Muscle cramps are a sign that you are lacking salt in your diet.

♦ Be aware of the symptoms of heat exhaustion. It is common in hot, humid places and is characterized by exhaustion, cramps, a rapid pulse, red skin and vomiting. Anyone with these symptoms needs a cool place, plenty to drink and even wrapping in sheets or sarongs soaked in cold water. Hospital treatment is sometimes necessary.

♦ Get enough rest. It is very easy to get exhausted and run-down if you are racing round sightseeing in the heat all day and sampling the nightlife after dark. If you're tired you're more open to illness in general.

Water

With a couple of exceptions – Singapore and Japan – tap water in Asia is not safe for tourists to drink (and for this reason you should avoid ice in your drinks).

However, bottled water is widely available in all but the most out-of-the-way places. Check the seals of the bottles before you buy, as some unscrupulous dealers collect empty bottles and refill them straight from the tap. They have the seal missing or have obviously been tampered with. Bottled water can make a surprising hole in your budget and you'll need to allow for it in your pre-trip calculations. In the cheapest countries, a couple of litres of bottled water will only set you back a dollar or so a day, but this is $90 (£55) over a three-month trip, and you'll also have deposited a small mountain of unbiodegradable plastic bottles into the largely ineffectual Asian rubbish system.

One alternative is to boil drinking water to sterilize it – five minutes' boiling (more at high altitude) will kill off anything that is likely to harm you. Whilst this is fine if you are camping or have access to cooking equipment, it is not really convenient in most situations.

Another option is to sterilize the water using chlorine or iodine tablets (available from outdoor-equipment shops or travel clinics). Whilst these are cheap and easy, they are not effective against all the harmful organisms in the water (amoebic dysentery and giardia, to name a couple), and they leave the water with a definite chemical taste. Water filters also only do a partial job, and do not remove viruses (such as hepatitis). The most effective solution is to take a water purifier, which will both filter and sterilize the water. There are several on the market and you should compare their different sizes, weights, the speed at which they process water, and how often replacement cartridges are needed, before buying one.

Food

The sight, smell and taste of the massive variety of Asian food is one of the greatest pleasures of any visit to the continent. A few minutes among the fruit and vegetables of even the smallest town market and you'll be dying to try out the unfamiliar breadfruit, rambutans and mangosteens as well as the new variations on old favourites, such as red bananas. A walk through any Asian night market where cooks behind tiny stalls conjure up enticing, spicy meals of rice, noodles, seafood and soups, will set your taste buds tingling. Head down any Asian street and the chances are you'll stumble across carts selling tea, soup or ice cream, women peeling pineapples to order or tiny neighbourhood restaurants wafting succulent odours into the air. Whilst not everyone will want to tackle the crunchy cooked grasshoppers of Thailand, the liberal chilli-fest of Sumatran Padang cuisine or the dog-meat delicacies of southwestern China, we guarantee you will make some unforgettable culinary discoveries.

Whilst you should enjoy the new tastes and eating experiences to the full, it pays to exercise some control over what you eat and where you eat:

- Avoid food that has sat out in the midday heat assaulted by flies, and food that has had to be reheated. One of the reasons Indian food can have such a disastrous effect on foreign bowels is the cooking style: slow-cooked casseroles and stews are common, whereas in Thailand, for example, stir-fries are whipped up on the spot and have no chance to languish all day in the tropical heat.
- Western food is often the most hazardous. Ask yourself how long that cannelloni has sat around before its brief interlude in the microwave.
- Fruit that has been peeled for you or doesn't get peeled, such as pineapples, papaya or grapes, can be a hazard, but fruit you peel yourself should be fine.
- Similarly, raw vegetables, including salad, are suspect, either because of the water they have been washed in or the human excrement that is used for fertilizer in some parts of Asia.
- Surrounded by so many unfamiliar foods, it can be difficult to get a balanced diet, especially as in some places, such as Nepal and parts of China, fresh fruit and vegetables are scarce. You may want to consider taking vitamin tablets with you.

Diarrhoea and dehydration

There are numerous causes for the diarrhoea and vomiting that strike travellers in Asia, from a straightforward reaction to a change of water and diet to more unpleasant bacteria and viruses. Whatever the cause, the main problem you'll face is dehydration, which will make you feel exhausted, dizzy and will give you a splitting headache. It's important to focus on rehydrating the moment any stomach problems start; worry about a diagnosis later.

Just to cope with being in the tropics you should be drinking two or three litres of water a day, but if you get diarrhoea, you'll need a lot more. In addition, your body will be losing important minerals and you should always carry sachets of oral rehydration salts (ORS) with you. These just need dissolving in clean drinking water and are available under a variety of names (such as Dioralyte) in the West and throughout Asia. Even if you're vomiting, you should sip small amounts of the solution. If you can't get hold of commercial brands, dissolve one level teaspoon of salt and eight level teaspoons of sugar in a litre of water; the resulting mixture shouldn't be any saltier than the taste of tears.

Diarrhoea and vomiting caused by changes to diet and water should run their course in two to three days, and as long as you keep drinking you'll be OK until you can start eating again (start with bland food such as boiled rice). If the diarrhoea and vomiting are particularly severe, persist for more than three days without abating or are accompanied by blood or mucus in your faeces, or fever, then you should seek medical help. There are several illnesses you should be aware of, including bacilliary or amoebic dysentery, typhoid and a particularly common one called giardiasis (or giardia), which produces rotten-egg belches and farts – not guaranteed to help you make friends.

Anti-diarrhoea tablets should be used extremely sparingly. Diarrhoea serves a purpose in ejecting poisonous toxins from your body. These tablets, which effectively halt the action of your digestive system, stop the diarrhoea and block you up, don't attack the micro-organisms responsible for the problem and can actually make you feel worse. They are useful, however, if you absolutely have to travel and there is no alternative.

As bizarre as it may sound, after a few months on the road you'll be gleefully swapping stories with fellow travellers of "the yellow frothy diarrhoea I had in Nepal" – probably while tucking into a pizza in Thailand.

Altitude

The problem of altitude is a serious one for anyone planning to trek in the Himalayas or visit Tibet or other high-altitude regions such as Ladakh, some parts of Xinjiang, Sichuan and Yunnan in China, the Karakoram region in Pakistan or Mount Fuji in Japan.

The higher you go above sea level, the less oxygen there is in the air and the lower the air pressure that drives it from your lungs into your bloodstream. Your body needs time to adapt to this, and whilst this process is under way – probably for the first three days at altitude, especially if you have flown in – you can expect headaches, shortness of breath, tiredness, loss of appetite, aches and pains, sleeping problems and nausea (known as acute mountain sickness, or AMS). Relax totally and drink plenty of water and the symptoms should pass, although having acclimatized you must still ascend slowly – no more than 300m per day. If you go too fast the symptoms will return.

If your symptoms worsen, however, and especially if you start vomiting and experience loss of coordination, delirium, rapid heartbeat, breathlessness and blueness of tongue and lips, you must descend as rapidly as possible. Just a few hundred metres of vertical height can be life-saving and usually brings about immediate recovery. Serious cases are very rare, but anyone planning a trek over 3000m should inform themselves fully about the potential risks before setting off.

AIDS and contraception

Unprotected sex is as unwise in Asia as it is as home. Reliable figures are not easy to find, but HIV and AIDS are prevalent across the region. As an indication, there are an estimated 3.8 million HIV-positive Indians and 200,000 with AIDS. The level of AIDS education is very variable throughout Asia and all travellers should assume they will be the one taking responsibility for the supply and use of condoms in any sexual encounter.

Condoms, often locally manufactured, are widely available throughout Asia in pharmacies and supermarkets, although local brands have a fairly mixed reputation and you'd be well advised to check use-by dates and buy from air-conditioned suppliers as far as possible. Women travellers may feel very conspicuous asking for condoms, especially in traditional Muslim areas such as Indonesia, and may prefer to carry some from home, particularly bearing in mind the quality concerns. The disadvantage with this is that extreme heat can rot the rubber. Expatriate residents in Asia usually keep theirs in the fridge – not a service most budget hotels offer – but it is worth trying to keep them in the coolest part of your pack along with your films.

Not sure of the word in the local language? It may not be as tough as you think. While condoms are the fairly tongue-knotting *bao cao su* in Vietnamese, they are *kondom* in Indonesian and Malay, *kandom* in Hindi and Urdu, and are informally known as *meechai* in Thailand after the charismatic former Minister for Health, Mr Meechai.

Women travellers who are using the contraceptive pill should take a sufficient supply for the entire trip; your brand may not be available locally. However, the pills can be affected by the extreme heat and if you have diarrhoea or vomiting their effectiveness is reduced, so you'll need other protection.

Asian health care

Millions of people in Asia have only limited access to the good-quality, local, affordable health care that we take for granted. Of course, the situation varies from country to country, but don't be surprised if health facilities are few and far between, staff don't speak English, have only limited training and their equipment for diagnosis and treatment is woefully inadequate.

However, throughout much of Asia there are private hospitals that exist alongside the underfunded and overstretched public facilities, and these are most likely where you'll end up if you get sick. In some cities with a large expatriate population or plenty of tourists, such as Kathmandu, you'll find specialist travellers' clinics.

You should make it clear on arrival that you can pay (many hospitals accept credit cards) and set about con-

tacting your insurance company (see p.86 for more on medical insurance). In most cases, you'll end up paying the bill and reclaiming the costs later. In Singapore a visit to a general practitioner will cost you around $20 (£12), while in Vietnam, for example, a consultation in an international hospital will be about $40 (£25).

Throughout Asia there are plenty of pharmacies and even local corner shops selling drugs that in your home country would only be sold on prescription and/or by trained personnel. One advantage of this is that it is fairly easy to replace the drugs you've brought from home and used up, although you'll need to know how to take the drug, as the person who sells it may not. Be aware that in some places locally manufactured drugs may not be clearly marked with their strength. Always check the sell-by date on the drugs.

Traditional medicine

Many Asian countries have their own traditional health systems, and clinics are invariably willing to treat foreigners, although you may need to take an interpreter with you unless you're pretty fluent in the local language.

Ayurvedic medicine has flourished in India for five thousand years and is a holistic medical system that looks at the whole body and detects imbalances in the system. The body is believed to be controlled by three forces – *pitta*, the force of the sun, *kapha*, associated with the moon, and *vata*, linked to the wind – and an imbalance in these leads to disease. Treatment, often with herbal remedies, concentrates on restoring the balance.

Whilst the often apparently bizarre ingredients such as snake gall bladder and scorpion oil, not to mention the notorious rhinoceros horn, have served to give traditional Chinese medicine a somewhat besmirched reputation outside the country, this is another ancient holistic medical system with largely herbal remedies. Acupuncture, where needles are inserted at various vital points in the body, is available in clinics across China – make certain that sterile needles are used.

Tibetan medicine derives from ayurvedic medicine and health depends on the balance of the three humours – *beken* (phlegm), *tiba* (bile) and *lung* (wind). A diagnosis is made by examining tongue, pulse and urine and by diagnostic questioning; treatment may be by herbal remedies and/or changes of diet and activity.

Whilst opinions in the West vary about the efficacy of such treatments, there is a considerable body of anecdotal evidence that ayurvedic medicine can both provide useful relief of symptoms in travellers with hepatitis, whereas Western medicine can offer little.

CHAPTER THIRTEEN

KEEPING IN TOUCH

Not only is it fair and reasonable that your friends and family at home will want to keep in touch with you while you're away, but you may be surprised at the extent to which you are delighted by contact with them. Travelling abroad is huge fun and wildly exciting, but it can also be stressful, disorienting and at times depressing, and communication with familiar people is very comforting.

You'll find the quality of most mail and telephone services in Asia is very high. However, cost is variable – you'll notice a big difference in that six-minute phone call to your bosom chum at home from Singapore and from Thailand.

How will we know where you are?

Parents and friends are naturally concerned that there will be periods when, literally, they have no idea where you are. If you do some of the following before you go, it can help to reassure them that you have at least a tentative schedule and aren't as inaccessible as they fear:

◇ Provide them with a copy of your flight schedule (include carriers and flight numbers), and notify them of any changes as you go. If there should be an Asian plane crash while you are away, they will naturally assume you are on board unless they know otherwise.

◇ Give them a list of poste restante addresses and dates.

◇ Alternatively, give a few American Express office or hotel fax numbers and dates.

◇ Establish a phoning-in schedule; for example, every four weeks or so.

◇ Consider joining a voice-mail scheme. This gives you access to a private answerphone. You leave your message for callers, they call in and leave their own messages, which you can call in and listen to and change your own message at the same time. Most schemes rely on tone phones for access. When you enquire about schemes, make sure you check whether they are easily accessible from public phones in the countries you are visiting.

◇ Set up a free email account that you can access from Asia (such as Hot Mail; see p.266).

Post

To see Asian society in microcosm, get along to the post office. In Indonesia you'll see the hi-tech types heading upstairs to the public Internet access, whilst downstairs old men struggle to address letters to relatives a couple of islands away, parents queue to send cash to needy children studying away from home, and large businesses register piles of parcels to their overseas customers.

Essentially, Asian post offices perform pretty much the same functions as their Western counterparts and come in all sizes. In the larger ones, you'll find different services available from different counters, usually with a jostling crowd around them rather than a queue. It helps to know what the word for "stamp" looks like in the local language, as few counters are labelled in English and staff will generally speak little English. Even the tiniest villages have some system of postal collection and delivery, albeit sometimes bizarre.

Mail is quicker and more reliable from towns and cities, although variability in speed is a common complaint amongst travellers. Why should my postcard to the UK take three weeks when another traveller reliably reports that his took four days? Such things remain one of the mysteries of the East. Generally, mail does seem to reach its destination (although avoid posting anything other than letters from Nepal). However, it pays to be vigilant – stick your own stamps on and ask for them to be franked while you wait, as there is a danger they might be steamed off and reused.

• •

BHUTAN POSTAL RUNNERS

I lived for some time in a remote village in the Himalayan Kingdom of Bhutan. There was no road to the village and mail was delivered every two or three weeks by a "runner" whose job was literally to run between the nearest post office and all the outlying villages, delivering and collecting mail. He operated on a two-week circuit, travelling across mountain passes, over rivers, through sparsely populated forest, and sleeping wherever he was given hospitality at night. In the old days, runners carried spears to fend off bears (still a reasonable fear in the area), but these days they are more likely to carry transistor radios for company. These also have a bear-scaring purpose, as it is widely believed if a bear hears voices approaching it will run away. You only get attacked if you scare a bear that hasn't heard you coming.

Lesley Reader

• •

Poste restante

To receive mail you've got a few options. Most convenient is to use the poste restante service available at post offices throughout Asia – consult your guidebook for details in specific countries. Mail can be addressed to you at post offices in most Asian cities: you just turn up with your passport for ID, and collect it. In most countries the service is free, although, in China for example, there is sometimes a small charge.

The actual system varies enormously across the continent. In some places you get to look through the entire batch of mail that has arrived for any foreigner over the last two years; in others you ask for a particular letter of the alphabet to trawl through. Sometimes you give your name to the clerk who hunts through the mail for you, and some post offices even keep a record of all mail logged in a book or on a computer. Generally the post offices in the more popular tourist destinations are the most reliable and organized – Bangkok, Singapore, Kathmandu and Kuta (Bali) are some of the better places to receive mail.

You should be able to get the precise address of the post office you want to use from a good guidebook; otherwise your name followed by "Poste Restante, General Post Office" and the name of the city should get to the main post office. Anyone who writes to you should print your surname in capital letters and underline it. Most places file mail alphabetically by surname, but it pays to check through under your first name as well, or any other name, title or pet name that your nearest and dearest may have used.

Generally post offices only keep mail for a month or so before either returning it or junking it. This means you have to tread a fairly careful line between getting there too early or too late for your letters. The best plan is to get mail sent to a few key places on your itinerary which have reasonably fixed dates rather than try anything too complicated. Some post offices operate a forwarding system for mail that arrives after you've left. You must go in person and register, but it's generally not very reliable.

An alternative to GPO services is to use American Express offices. They accept and hold mail on behalf of their clients and also accept faxes. The branch offices in your home country will have a worldwide list of offices and representatives detailing the services they offer. You qualify if you have an Amex card or carry Amex travellers' cheques. You could consider taking an Amex travellers' cheque or two if you want to use the service but are carrying the bulk of your money in another brand of travellers' cheque.

Generally, getting mail addressed to you at hotels is the last resort. It'll be coming through the post office in any case, so it's just as easy and probably safer to collect it from there. You can't rely on hotels to have an efficient system and your letters could easily end up in someone's desk drawer, the waste-paper basket or winging their way back home to the sender.

Receiving parcels

It'll save some grief if you remember that parcels and packages are generally less reliably received by travellers than straightforward letters. So many go missing en route that it's better to tell people at home not to send them. If you really must get stuff sent out to you, it's better to use courier companies.

Courier companies specialize in getting stuff moved around the world reliably and quickly, but at a price. Because they operate door to door, they will not deliver to poste restante addresses – your best bet is to arrrange to collect it in their local office. They charge by both weight and size of the package, which should take between four and seven working days to arrive from the US or UK. Whilst it's handy to know it can be done, it probably isn't something you'd want to do very often.

Sending letters

Sending letters and postcards from Asia isn't difficult. Address them clearly, writing the destination country in the local language and script, if you can, to speed up processing. Label as airmail, get them weighed at the counter, stick on the stamps or franked label (some post offices use a franking machine) and drop them in the appropriate box. Usually an express service and registered service is available at extra cost. A few correspondence tips:

◇ Warn those at home that mail can take three weeks or so in each direction. Nepal is notoriously slow, and airmail to the West from Vietnam varies between four days and four weeks, whilst post from Singapore is among the fastest in Asia.

◇ If there has been a big disaster in your area, then, as well as a letter, a quick phone call home will set minds at rest.

◇ Don't make rash promises to write to people that you are then going to break. If you tell your parents you'll write daily/weekly or whatever, then you really should stick to it or they'll panic about your safety. If you're an irregular and unenthusiastic letter writer, then don't forget that just a signed postcard is enough to stop people worrying. Faxes can be useful; cheaper than phoning but more immediate than letters.

◇ If your personal stereo has a record button you can send tapes of you describing your experiences as well as or instead of letters.

◇ Don't write to close friends and family in the midst of a bout of dysentery or the day before a bungy-jump and then not contact them again for a few weeks.

◇ Ask whoever is your most regular correspondent to keep your let-ters – they make vivid reading when you get back. Some travellers don't write a diary but keep copies of the letters they write as a record of the trip (take carbon paper with you or buy it en route).

◇ If you send a huge number of postcards the cost can add up, so include it in your budget. The postage rate for cards is often equivalent to that for an aerogramme, which can carry much more news. For example, in China it costs the equivalent of around 20 cents for a postcard or aerogramme, but around 50 cents for a letter of 20g, whilst from Vietnam you'll pay 50 cents for a postcard and just under $1 for a letter to the West.

◇ Number the letters to people you are writing to regularly so they know if any have gone missing. Get them to do the same if they are writing to you.

◇ Take some stamps from your home country with you – you may well meet other travellers from home at the end of their trip who'll be happy to drop a few letters in the box for you when they land.

Shipping stuff home

Sending parcels home is rather more time-consuming than sending off letters. You should probably set aside at least half a day to get the formalities completed, but this is definitely preferable to carrying a Sri Lankan mask or Indian rug with you on the rest of your six-month trip. Basically, your choices are to send them airmail (the most expensive option), surface mail or via cargo agents.

Many post offices in tourist areas sell boxes and tape for packing your goods; others, such as Hong Kong, even have a packing service. In Vietnam it is obligatory that the parcel is wrapped for you. The Indian system involves a time-consuming process whereby the customs desk at the post office first needs to examine the goods you are sending. You are then required to have them stitched into white linen parcels (the stitchers operate outside all post offices) before they will be accepted for mailing. Charges for parcels sent through the postal system, whether airmail or surface, are calculated by weight.

Most cargo agents, on the other hand, ship by volume, with one cubic metre the minimum amount. This is the best option if you have something very heavy to send. Delivery times will be much faster if you're sending from port cities than from inland towns where the goods will have to be transported to the coast first.

Whichever method you opt for, it makes sense to send fewer larger amounts rather than many small ones. Always make sure that, *including* the packaging, you are just under the maximum of the weight/volume band rather than just over into the next band. Also bear in mind that whatever you send home is subject to examination by customs in your own country. They are not only looking for illegal substances, but are entitled to charge import duty/taxes on new goods that you are bringing into the country. For example, for parcels sent back to the UK, the value of goods is limited to £18 per parcel, although you can send as many parcels as you like.

Finally, classier souvenir stores the world over will always offer to arrange shipping for you. You'll be paying them extra for the service and there are always some rip-off merchants who take your money and send nothing, so try to go by personal recommendation if you can.

••

SUITS YOU, SIR

The tailors in Khao San Road, Bangkok, said they could make me a suit in two days for the equivalent of £30. Despite my ten-month backpacking itinerary still stretching ahead of me, I decided that a made-to-measure silk suit was something I must have. In fact, I ordered two.

The process itself was fascinating: after just two fitting sessions the assortment of pieces of fabric tacked inside out, draped around my body and marked up deftly with chalk lines were transformed into two superb suits – a pale cream one and a rich, deep brown one.

I packaged them up at the main post office, labelling them merely as clothes being returned home – two pairs of trousers and two jackets. In hindsight, parcels like this containing clothes from Bangkok are probably viewed fairly suspiciously, or else I was just unlucky. The box was opened when it arrived several months later at Liverpool docks, and duty of £60 was imposed on these imported items. Despite costing me twice as much as I had expected, my suits were still bargains.

Jonathan Tucker

••

Photographs

One thing worth thinking about is what to do with your photographs on a long trip. Quite apart from the hassle of keeping exposed film with you for months on the road (it deteriorates fast after exposure, and heat and humidity are particularly bad for it), prints weigh a lot and you don't really want to keep negatives and prints together just in case your stuff gets stolen. Sending your pictures home is a good way of keeping friends and family informed.

One option is to send the undeveloped film back to them for processing. A list of pictures with each film sounds extremely anal, but if you are trying to remember which Thai temple, Malaysian island or Tokyo skyscraper your shots are of after another six months' travelling, it'll prove invaluable and it gives your folks regular up-to-date information about what you're seeing and doing. There are intermittent scares about the theft of exposed film in the post – it is supposedly repackaged and sold as new film – but by sending them one at a time, packing them carefully and registering the package, you'll cut down the danger. Alternatively, send the prints and keep the negatives, or vice versa. Some clued-up email bureaus (see p.265) can even scan your holiday snaps adding suitable captions – "Look Mum, this is me in the jungle" – and send them along with an email. It's a pretty neat personalized postcard.

Phoning home

You'll be able to call home from pretty much any city or large town in Asia and the wide availability of direct dialling means you don't have to cope with an operator in a foreign language. Don't forget the time difference when you phone, though. You'll probably get a better reception from your loved ones if you don't wake them at 3am.

You'll find public telephones throughout the continent, both coin- and phonecard-operated, and some countries (Thailand and Singapore, for example) have phones, that accept credit cards. However, with public phones, don't count on having instructions in English. In most cases, if you're calling home, it's easier to phone from post offices or telephone offices rather than phones on the street, if only to avoid the noise.

When calling from a post office or telephone office you'll be directed to a booth, in some cases having paid a deposit, and you can then dial your call directly. The length of the call is logged and the price calculated automatically and you pay the balance or get change from your deposit when it's all over. It's worth checking whether there is a cheaper discounted time to call (typically at weekends and in the middle of the night), if calls are charged by the minute (in which case you'll be charged for the full minute even if you just use ten seconds of it), or by the second, and whether there is a minimum call time (typically 3min). Avoid making international calls from hotels as they not only charge higher rates for the call, but often slap a service charge on top too.

Reverse-charge calls and charge cards

Many telephone offices allow you to make reverse-charge calls or have a Home Country Direct facility, but you may pay a nominal charge for these. With a reverse-charge call the person you are calling is contacted and asked to accept the charges for that call before you are put through. Home Country Direct is a system that allows you to call the operator in your home country and then use a credit card to pay for the call or arrange a reverse-charge call through them.

In theory, you can use charge cards issued in your home country in Asia. These cards enable you to bill the cost of the call to your home number or put the cost onto a previously authorized credit card account. However, it can be difficult to get hold of the right local number to access the system when you're on the road. Get a list of these from your issuing company for every country you intend to visit.

Fax

Facilities for faxing are widely available across Asia, but will take a bit more hunting out than phones. Try post offices, telephone offices and the business centres of international-class hotels (the most expensive option). You'll be charged by the page or minute (find out which before you send the message) and you will also pay a charge if you receive faxes. Charges for faxes are in line with the telephone charges of the country, so, for example, in China expect to pay around $5 (£3) a minute to send a fax and about $2 per page to receive.

Email

Access to the Internet is pretty much global these days and public facilities are increasingly available. There are already cybercafés on Bali and in major tourist centres in Thailand, a brilliant Internet centre in the departure lounge at Changi Airport in Singapore, public email services in major post offices across Indonesia, and even in Kathmandu you'll find private companies offering email access. However, outside the major population and tourist centres don't expect too much.

Cybercafés charge by the minute and costs work out a lot cheaper than sending a fax or making a phone call. If you're going to be passing through cyber-friendly towns and tourist centres on a fairly regular basis, email can make a good alternative to post office poste restantes – even if you're not on the Internet at home. There are three different ways of doing this.

Using your existing account

Unfortunately, the most unreliable option is to use your existing, home-based email account. Though international Internet Service Providers (such as Globalnetwork and Uunet) and Online Service Providers (such as AOL and Compuserve) pride themselves on having local connection numbers all over the world, the reality is that in Asia these local numbers (when they do exist) are nearly always confined to the capital city – not at all useful if you're sitting in a cybercafé hundreds of kilometres from the capital. Bali, for example, is an expensive long-distance phone call away from Jakarta and, worse still, the long-distance lines are so oversubscribed that it is almost impossible to get a line to major Jakarta ISPs at any time of the day or night. Do not be duped by ISP staff in your home country who assure you that the local number is very local – it's unlikely they've tried it out for themselves.

Even if you have an existing account, you're much better off subscribing to a free email account (such as Hot Mail) for the duration of your trip and relying on that instead. It's relatively cheap and easy to set up a forwarding system from your home-based account to the new account.

Setting up a free email account

Even if you don't already have an email account, you can establish a free, private and personal account either before you leave home (using someone else's system or through a local cybercafé) or in a cybercafé somewhere in Asia. Several companies offer this service, but by far the most popular is Hot Mail. Hot Mail is completely free to join as it's financed by advertising. Any cybercafé will have Hot Mail bookmarked for easy access and will help you set up a new account. All you need to do is access *www.hotmail.com* and follow the instructions.

Give friends and family your new Hot Mail address and they can send you email any time – it will stack up in a nice pile in your in-box, ready for you to access whenever you can. You can of course use your Hot Mail account to send out email as well. Other free email accounts can be found at *www.yahoo.com* and *www.mailcity.com*. There's also one run by *TNT* magazine (*www.tnt.co.uk*), for which you need to pay a small registration fee.

Using cybercafés as poste restantes

The third option is to use local cybercafé addresses as email poste restantes. This involves getting a particular cybercafé's email address and giving it to your correspondents, so it's only really viable if you're staying in one place for a while. For a list of cybercafés in the countries you're planning to visit, check out *www.cybercaptive.com*. Public Internet centres, such as Indonesian post offices, don't offer this service. Many cybercafés have an efficient system whereby they print out the day's emails and keep them in a file for a few weeks, much as a post office would with letters; others just let you scroll through their in-box. The important thing to remember when using cybercafés' addresses is that your correspondent should write your name in the subject field box. These cafés let you use their accounts to send email as well, so it doesn't matter that you haven't got your own.

The media

You won't have to rely solely on contact with your friends and family for news from home. Western newspapers from Europe, Australia and North America are often available a few days late in capital cities and tourist centres. However, the supply is unreliable and the price high. Most Asian countries also publish good-quality English-language newspapers of their own for English-speaking local people, tourists and expatriates. Several of the magazines mentioned in Chapter Six, such as the *Far Eastern Economic Review* and *Asiaweek*, as well as the Asian editions of *Time* and *Newsweek*, are available locally – airports are usually a good source if you have any difficulty finding them.

Television

Satellite and cable television have reached some very remote corners of Asia, and you'll find league soccer from England and Italy is a great favourite throughout Indonesia and Malaysia. Most mid- to top-range hotels offer CNN and Asian satellite networks such as Star or MTV, while some restaurants use them to lure in customers. In India you'll also find BBC World, a TV version of the BBC World Service radio network.

Radio

Worldwide radio networks, including the BBC, Voice of America and the Australian Broadcasting Corporation, broadcast across the globe 24 hours a day, whilst many countries have an indigenous English-language radio station or schedule. A radio is a great way of getting up-to-the-minute news in the more remote areas and it's well worth considering travelling with one. A pair of earphones will mean you can listen when people around you, on buses, in dorms, etc, are sleeping.

Buy a radio with the greatest number of short-wave bands you can afford, as most stations change their frequency during the day and you'll want to be able to follow them through the changes. Get hold of a copy of the programming schedule for your country's international network before you leave home – it'll tell you which frequencies to pick them up on at which times across Asia. The BBC World Service publishes its monthly Asia schedule on the Internet at *www.bbc.co.uk/worldservice/*

Coming home

Everyone expects to suffer from culture shock when they go away to distant places, but it can be an even greater shock when you arrive back home. People's lives have moved on, the dog has had puppies and Uncle Toby really doesn't want to hear in graphic detail about Delhi Belly or cosmic enlightenment on Mount Fuji. You may feel that your experiences have totally changed your life and the direction you see yourself moving, while those closest to you hope you've "got it out of your system" and are now ready to settle down. The following tips may help you cope:

◇ Make sure you have kept in touch with people at home and tried to paint a realistic picture about your experiences and thoughts.

◇ Get in touch with other travellers you've met on the road who are probably going through similar experiences at the same time.

◇ Keep in touch with local people you have met – if you haven't yet sent them the photographs you promised, then do it as soon as you get home.

◇ Whilst you are still travelling, make some plans, however rudimentary, for the immediate future after you get home. The worst possible homecoming is to come back to nothing. Even if it's only a plan to get work and save up to travel some more, at least it's a plan of action.

◇ Think about writing up your experiences for magazines (see p.112).

◇ Don't forget your resolution to learn Hindi, Thai, Japanese, Mandarin or whatever language fascinated or beat you while you were away. Local evening classes are the most sociable way of doing this, or if you've a university near you with foreign students you may be able to arrange one-to-one tuition or exchange English lessons for the language you want to learn.

CHAPTER FOURTEEN

CRIME, SAFETY AND SLEAZE

Whilst it is news of tragic accidents, violent weather conditions, kidnappings and fatalities that reach the world's media, most people who run into trouble in Asia are the victims of far more ordinary petty theft, robbery and con tricks. However, getting your stuff stolen is no joke, getting taken for a ride leaves a nasty taste in the mouth, and losing your passport, travellers' cheques and credit cards can land you with major inconvenience and possibly ruin your trip. The information in this chapter should help to steer you away from the pitfalls that await the unwary in Asia, and help you to cope if disaster strikes.

The underlying rule is to travel with the instincts you use to keep you safe at home. If it's your first time in Asia it can be difficult to establish the norm; it's easy to over-react and get spooked without real reason. However, it is better that way than blithely marching into danger with eyes fixed wonderingly on the blue horizon, white-sand beach and glittering sunshine. Just because you're on holiday, the crooks aren't.

Nobody should set foot in Asia without adequate insurance. Health insurance is vital in case the worst happens and you are faced with serious illness or an accident. Some policies aimed at backpackers exclude baggage cover to keep costs down, but we would advise you to consider taking out a policy that also covers your belongings. You may only be taking your oldest, tattiest clothes with you, but the cost of replacing everything, including rucksack and perhaps sleeping bag and camera, can be very high. See p.86 for more information and p.303 for recommended insurance agents.

Read up, find out, calm down

Supplement your guidebook reading with up-to-the-minute information from newspapers and magazines. Travellers' newsgroups and bulletin boards on the Internet are an excellent resource (see *Basics* p.308 for a list of some of the best). Even the most dramatic civil war isn't going to find its way into a guidebook for several months at the least, but it'll be splashed across the world's media in a couple of hours.

Most Western governments are concerned about keeping their citizens safe abroad. They each have a department at home to advise on safety issues across Asia and you should contact them before you leave to find out the current local situation in the places you are heading for (see *Basics*, p.304). They will also have a list of embassies or consulates abroad, which you can contact in the event of an emergency. They can:

◇ Issue emergency passports.
◇ Contact friends and family and ask them to help with money or tickets.
◇ Help you get in touch with local doctors, lawyers and interpreters.
◇ Advise on local organizations which help trace missing persons.
◇ Contact and visit their citizens in local prison.
◇ Arrange for next of kin to be informed about serious illness or death.

They cannot:

◇ Give you money (they may be able to cash a cheque or give you a repayable loan against very strict criteria).
◇ Pay your bills or pay to get you home except in very exceptional circumstances.

◇ Intervene in legal proceedings or give legal advice.
◇ Get better treatement for you than other prisoners or hospital patients.
◇ Get you out of prison.
◇ Arrange employment, accommodation or work permits.

Get it in perspective

Aside from the hazards that travellers will find anywhere in the world, Asia has its own more specific ones. These include land mines in Cambodia, Vietnam and along the Cambodian–Thai border; the violence that usually precedes elections in India; active volcanoes right across the continent; riptides on many Indian Ocean beaches; and cerebral malaria on the Thai–Cambodian and Thai–Burmese borders. However, you should always put the information you receive into geographical perspective. If you read about rioting in Xinjiang province in China and you're heading for Shanghai, it's a good idea to stay alert, but at almost 4000km distance the chances are you'll be out of the line of fire. If, on the other hand, one of the larger Indonesian volcanoes erupts fairly exuberantly on a small island just 20km across a stretch of ocean from where you were planning a fortnight by the sea, it may be an idea to think again.

Karma armour

Most Asian religions have a rather more fatalistic approach to accident and misfortune than we do in the West. We are increasingly of the view that we can, and indeed have the right to, control anything nasty happening to us. Buddhists and Hindus believe in karma, whereby a previous existence influences the events in their current life. Thus a traffic accident is more likely to be seen as a preordained karmic retribution than as a direct result of irresponsible driving. Muslims presage most plans with the word *Inshallah* (by the will of Allah), showing they accept that they do not have ultimate control over the future. This can be infuriating or even downright terrifying if you're on a bus with a maniac driver who seems intent on killing you all.

Theft

Most crime involving tourists is oppor- tunistic theft of one sort or other. A few guidelines will help you cut down on the chances of it being you that gets robbed. It's worth mentioning that a small percentage of trav- ellers fund their own journeys by thieving from others, so don't automatically trust other West- erners, and be just as careful in dor- mitories as you are in other situations.

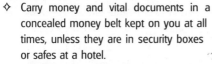

- ◇ Carry money and vital documents in a concealed money belt kept on you at all times, unless they are in security boxes or safes at a hotel.
- ◇ Never leave your valuables on the beach while you swim – most travel shops sell waterproof money belts or plastic canisters that you can wear round your neck.
- ◇ Never leave your passport, travellers' cheques and credit cards in a guest-house safe "for safekeeping" while you go off trekking. Many a visitor has returned a week or so later to find everything intact, only to realize, when their credit card bill comes in, that the card has been used right up to its credit limit while they've been slogging through the jungle.
- ◇ Keep photocopies of important documents (e.g. passport, trav- ellers' cheque numbers, airline tickets, insurance policy) in a separate place, plus a small stash of cash in case of robbery.
- ◇ Don't flaunt what you've got. Avoid wearing a lot of jewellery, use a cheap watch and carry your camera in your daypack.
- ◇ Use padlocks to lock your pack and attach it to immovable fit- tings on long-distance journeys. This also protects against unwanted items, such as drugs, being stored in your pack.
- ◇ Use your own padlock to supplement or replace the one on your guest-house door.
- ◇ Never carry important stuff in rucksack pockets on your back; they are especially vulnerable to theft. You can always carry a small pack on your front where you can keep an eye on it.

The natural world

Asia is full of volcanoes that erupt, winds that transform themselves into typhoons, snakes that bite, rivers that flood, land that slips, and earth that moves and cracks asunder at regular intervals. Or so it appears if you have a disaster mentality and don't manage to temper what you read with reality.

Volcanoes and earthquakes

Being at the confluence of several of the world's largest tectonic plates, which are constantly shifting, the level of volcanic and earthquake activity in Asia is much higher than many travellers are used to. Seismologists are notoriously unable to predict when and where the next big event will take place, but realistically the chances of being caught in a severe earthquake or a volcanic eruption are extremely slim.

If you are unfortunate enough to be involved in a strong quake, you should stay indoors if possible (corrugated-iron sheets flying off roofs are a common cause of fatalities) and shelter in a doorway if the building looks in danger of collapse (the lintel that supports the wall above the door is the strongest part of the structure).

Typhoons

If you know that a typhoon is expected in your town, the best advice is to get yourself established in a guest house or hotel that feels safely and solidly built – don't be stingy about paying up and moving to a better place for the night – and to stay indoors. Ideally you should sleep in a room that is not on the ground floor as it could get submerged. Keep all windows closed and move your bed away from them if possible – flying debris might smash the glass. Expect to be stranded in your room for up to 24 hours after the typhoon hits, while you wait for the flood waters to subside, so get yourself enough drinking water, some food and a good book before you tuck yourself away.

TYPHOON LINDA

I arrived in Chumphon, South Thailand, to find preparations in full swing. Typhoon Linda was on her way, due in around 1am, and was expected to cause more damage than her predecessor who'd hit the town two months earlier. What happened then, I asked. "The water came up to here," said the guy in the restaurant, indicating a tidemark on his wall that was 1.5m above the floor, "and we all had to stay indoors for 48 hours because you couldn't get down the street without swimming." At the house next door, a lady was dragging her best teak furniture up to the first floor – she didn't want a repeat performance of the last time, she explained, showing off her own tidemarks, also a 1.5m high. Her husband, meanwhile, was storing his motorbike in a neighbour's upstairs loft.

Every downstairs room in the town seemed to have a tidemark. And Linda was set to be even more vicious. A crowd stood outside the TV shop, where all the sets were tuned to the weather station, and a loudspeaker van was circulating through the town, issuing official sounding instructions.

Faced with the prospect of spending two soggy days confined to my hardboard cell of a guest house, I decided to relocate, choosing a hotel room on the third floor, where the outside walls didn't seem likely to crumble in a Force 10. I stocked up on 48 hours' worth of food and water, battened down the window shutters, got my torch out in case the power lines went down, and fell asleep wondering how things would look in the morning.

Not very different, as it turned out. A few puddles, but no obvious devastation. The guest-house manager looked happy: Linda had diverted at the last minute, and had struck Prachuap instead, 170km up the coast. And so it was that the newspaper pictures of razed houses and submerged town centres, and the scenes of distraught families that filled the TV screens that evening, were of a town that I'd left the day before, and not of Chumphon after all.

Lucy Ridout

Dangerous animals

The chances of coming face to face with poisonous snakes and savage animals are obviously higher in the jungles of

Kalimantan than back home, but remember that local people are as terrified of these things as you are likely to be. Listen to local advice and take sensible precautions:

◇ Don't antagonize any snake, anywhere. They usually avoid human contact, but will strike if threatened.
◇ Trek with local guides who know the terrain and the hazards.
◇ Keep fires or lanterns burning at night if you are camping in the jungle.
◇ Never walk without shoes.
◇ Shake out your shoes each morning.
◇ If you get bitten, immobilize the limb and avoid all movement. The aim is to reduce your heart rate and the speed with which any toxin spreads through your body. Send someone for medical help.

Transport

Anyone who has spent even a few minutes on a bus hurtling along the Trans-Sumatran or West Bengal highways or, in fact, almost any main road in Asia, will have a very clear idea of the dangers of road travel on the continent. Driving is fast, furious and often heedless, with overtaking on blind corners the norm and horns rather than brakes the response to any surprise event or potential hazard. Vehicles are poorly maintained, road conditions horrendous and driving schedules very pressurized, so that drivers are often exhausted.

The trouble is that the other options are often no better. Ferries in Asia are regularly overloaded and lack even the most basic safety equipment, and many of the small domestic aircraft companies have dubious safety standards. For this reason, many travellers feel much safer on trains and, in countries where there *is* a rail network, it is often the least hazardous way to travel. Make safety rather than economy your main consideration, and if it means surrendering your ticket rather than boarding a certain death trap or simply getting off a bus halfway to your destination, then do it.

Wars and unrest

Gruesome as it seems, there is a new type of tourism prevailing today, known as "terror tourism". Some people, reading of civil unrest, war, conflict or other examples of the worst that human beings can do to each other, book their plane ticket and head off to the danger zone to view the proceedings at close quarters. For the rest of us, this type of news is an indicator to reroute ourselves, and fast. However, you might like to look at *The World's Most Dangerous Places* by Pelton, Aral and Dulles (Fielding Worldwide) which, despite its decidedly gung ho title, is a detailed and fascinating account of the wars, political upheaval and crime across the globe, putting the dangers to travellers into perspective.

The sad fact is that more than eighty armed conflicts have taken place in the world during the last three years. The big ones, new ones and ones that are particularly relevant to our economy hit the media big time; the others smoulder away, largely ignored by the rest of the world. Some of the most significant for travellers to Asia are:

◇ **East Timor** and **Irian Jaya**, where independence movements are in opposition to the Indonesian government. In January 1996 seven Western researchers and students were kidnapped in Irian Jaya while, in East Timor, the presence of Indonesian government forces tackling the armed East Timorese fighters makes it a tense and unhappy place.

◇ **Cambodia**. Civil unrest is prevalent throughout the country, and Phnom Penh and Angkor Wat are currently the only safe spots for visitors. Elsewhere, mines and roadblocks cause serious dangers. Check the situation carefully before you travel.

◇ **Kashmir**. Various militant separatist groups are fighting it out with government forces. Of five Western hostages taken in July 1995, one was beheaded and four are still missing.

◇ **Sri Lanka**. The Tamil minority are fighting for autonomy, making the north and east of the country too dangerous for visitors. The rest of the island is also affected with Colombo, the capital, the focus of an irregular bombing campaign.

It is also worth bearing in mind that democracy in many parts of Asia is often a very different creature to the familiar form in the West, and in the run-up to elections there can be a very high level of tension and violence. Every election in India brings several deaths and hundreds of injuries through fighting between the supporters of different parties. In some cases, violence follows elections – particularly in the case of disputed results. Unless you are a political science student there for a purpose, it is best to give Asian elections a wide berth. If you do get caught up up in one, obey any curfews imposed by the authorities.

Common scams

Many of the common scams perpetrated on hapless tourists in Asia are legendary. They change, evolve and become more sophisticated, but never really go away. They range from the ridiculous to potentially more serious ones, but the best source for up-to-date information on these is other travellers – they've been there, seen it, and probably been caught by it as well. Talk to people on the road and learn from their mistakes. Watch out for:

◇ Various miscalculation tricks when you're changing money, especially prevalent when dealing with hundreds of thousands of Indonesian rupiahs. There are even rigged calculators in some places. Work out what you should have and count it carefully before you leave the counter.

◇ Sleights of hand over the denomination of note you have given in payment in a shop or post office. Tricksters hide the note and produce one of a much lower denomination, telling you that you haven't paid enough. Keep your wits about you and know what you are handing over.

◇ Hotel touts and taxi drivers are sometimes desperate to get you to hotels where they either have an interest or will get a chunk of commission (it'll go on your bill, never fear), so beware if they tell you the hotel you want is full. Go inside and check at reception yourself; they sometimes have stooges on the steps outside, looking official and repeating the misinformation.

◇ Taxi drivers will sometimes tell you major sights are closed and you are much better taking a tour with them as your driver for the day. Again, go and check for yourself.

◇ The longtime classic scam in Thailand has been persuading gullible, and greedy, tourists that they are being offered an incredibly good deal on cut diamonds or other gems. Travellers are attracted by the prospect of hundreds, if not thousands, of dollars' profit to be made in their own country by selling the diamonds at home. So, despite knowing nothing about precious stones, they spend $100 on a handful of sparklers and ten times out of ten arrive home to learn their hands are full of pretty, but totally worthless, cut glass.

◇ At Delhi railway station the latest scam is for policemen to insist that you have to register with them and, needless to say, pay to do so, to remain in Delhi. The best way to tackle this is to offer to go to the police station and fill in the forms there.

◇ Beware of accepting food or drink from fellow passengers on journeys. Some rogues ply the unwary with drugged food and drink and, while they are sleeping off the effects, steal everything they own.

INDIAN SHOESHINE

At 6am on my first day in India, I arrived by airport bus in the centre of New Delhi. Not wishing to appear more vulnerable than my bloodshot eyes and untanned skin made me look, I shouldered my pack and began to walk as confidently as I could.

After a few minutes my worst fears were realized when I felt a tap on my shoulder and turned round to face a very dark, scrawny man with a glint in his eye. He was frantically pointing at my feet. I looked down to discover a neat pile of dung – about the size of a molehill and as perfectly formed – resting on the top of my right shoe. My immediate reaction was amazement: how on earth had this pile of shit managed to tread on me?

As I stood awe-struck, my Indian friend knelt down, produced a rag from the cloth bag slung over his shoulder, and started to wipe my shoe clean. He performed this task with a full-bodied, jerking action, which caused the bag to slip from his shoulder. When I saw its contents, the penny dropped and the mystery was solved.

This man had crept up behind me, scooped a portion of dung from his bag and skilfully dolloped it on top of my shoe as I walked. Now, of course, he demanded his fee for cleaning my shoes, holding up his soiled rag as evidence of his hard work.

Ross Velton

● ●

Sexual harassment

Much of the Asian continent is awash with Western films, videos and magazines that portray the West as sexually rampant, with Western women taking an active part. When you graft onto that a population of Western female travellers who relate to men in ways unheard of in the Asian population, dress in ways local people may consider highly provocative and, perhaps the greatest difference of all, actually have the freedom to travel around the world unchaperoned, it isn't surprising that misunderstandings and misconceptions are rife. Generally, the local perception of Western female travellers is of sexual availability and promiscuity. This means that harassment, both verbal and physical, is unfortunately alive and flourishing across the continent. The following tips may help:

◇ Always carry enough cash on you in case you need to take a taxi to get back to your hotel.

◇ Make sure your hotel room is secure. Be especially careful to check door and window locks. You may want to use your own padlock and/or wooden door wedge.

◇ Observe how local women dress – you may feel more comfortable and you'll attract less unwelcome attention if you cover up similar bits of flesh.

◇ Be aware of the different interpretations placed on some behaviour in other cultures. For example, smiling and making eye contact with a man in countries such as India, Pakistan and Indonesia is interpreted as a distinct come-on, as is a casual touch.

✧ Talk about a man's sister, equate yourself with her and ask how he would want her treated in similar situations.

✧ Adopt a mythical husband: some women travellers wear a ring, carry his photograph and pictures of the mythical kids with which to bore potential pests.

✧ Try not to let any hassles get you down to the extent where you close yourself to all local contact and friendliness – it isn't personal.

✧ Join up with other solo women travellers for some of your trip if it suits you. There's no right and wrong way to travel; don't stay alone out of mistaken pride.

✧ Don't automatically trust other Westerners because of familiarity and distrust local people because of their strangeness.

Don't forget it can work both ways: some men feel extremely uncomfortable with the upfront approaches of many Asian prostitutes. Whilst many women cope with sexual harassment as a part of everyday life, for many men the experience comes as a rude, and often distressing, awakening.

● ●

ROOM SERVICE

In a hotel in Danang, Vietnam, a woman walked straight into my room while I was lying there naked under my mosquito net. She didn't mess around: "Would you like sex, mouth, love, touch or massage with no clothes?" When I said a polite "No, thank you", she looked at me rather despondently and added, "Do you have any washing, then?"

Chris Humphrey

The only guest at the only hotel in town, I spent the evening on the verandah listening to tales of the days of the Raj. Charming and well educated, the manager was the perfect host, until he casually slipped into the conversation, "Do you need your own room tonight or would you prefer to share mine?" I acted suitably horrified and

haughty, demanded my own room and barricaded the door, just in
case. But the manager had already forgotten the incident.

Nicki McCormick

●●●

Drugs

Asian governments appear somewhat schizophrenic
about drugs. They openly condemn them but know they
are sold to tourists in certain places and seem to turn a
blind eye. However, the penalties are serious: Malaysia
enforces the death penalty for drug smuggling, and in
Thailand long prison sentences are the punishment for
attempting to get drugs out of the country. Even buying
drugs for your own immediate use isn't worth the risks;
set-ups by dealers and the police are common and much
of what is on sale is poor quality.

The situation is made more complicated by the fact that
in some areas of India, for example, drugs, typically mari-
juana and opium, are sold openly in *bhang* shops, princi-
pally for religious purposes, to help meditation, and are
smoked in public without any retribution. Unless you are
absolutely sure of the local situation, the best advice is
still to steer clear.

If disaster strikes

◇ Contact your embassy or consulate if you need a new passport or are in a serious situation.
◇ Contact the police. In the case of an insurance claim you'll
need a police report to support it, and if you are the victim of
crime they'll need to take your statement.
◇ Contact your insurance company. Carry the policy number and
emergency number with you and leave copies at home. There
are claims procedures that you must take care to follow in the
event of theft or your claim will be invalid. You will need
receipts for recently bought goods and for expenses you have
incurred. Similarly, in the event of serious medical emerg-
encies, the correct procedures must be followed; if you need

hospitalization you will have to inform your insurers within certain time limits.

◊ In the event of theft of credit cards, get them cancelled, and contact the issuing company if travellers' cheques have been stolen, to order your replacements (see p.120 for more details).

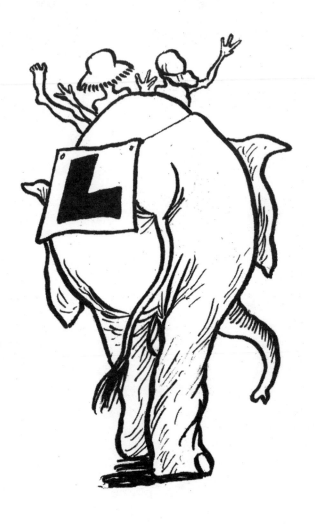

FIRST-TIME ASIA

THE BASICS

NATIONAL TOURIST OFFICES

Not all countries have a national tourist organization. Where no details are given, you should try contacting the embassy for information (see p.290 for embassy details). Also check out the online directory of tourist offices worldwide, at *www.towd.com/*

BANGLADESH
No national tourist office.

BURMA
No national tourist office.

CAMBODIA
No national tourist office.

CHINA including Hong Kong
UK and Ireland 4 Glentworth St, London NW1 (℃0171/935 9427).
US 333 West Broadway #201, Glendale, CA 91204 (℃818/545-7505); 350 Fifth Ave, Suite 6413, New York, NY 10118 (℃212/760-9700).
Canada 480 University Ave #806, Toronto, Ontario M5G 1V2 (℃416/599-6636).
Australia China: 19th Floor, 44 Market St, Sydney, NSW 2000 (℃02/9299 4057); Hong Kong: Level 4, Hong Kong House, 80 Druitt St, Sydney, NSW 2000 (℃1-800/251 071).
New Zealand Contact the Sydney office or the embassy in Wellington.

INDIA
UK and Ireland 7 Cork St, London W1X 1PB (℃0171/437 3677).
US 1270 Ave of the Americas #1808, New York, NY 10020 (℃212/586-4901, 586-4902 or 586-4903); 3550 Wilshire Blvd, Suite 204, Los Angeles, CA 90010 (℃213/380-8855).
Canada 60 Bloor St W #1003, Toronto, Ontario M4W 3B8 (℃416/962-3787).
Australia 46 Piccadilly Plaza, 210 Pitt St, Sydney, NSW 2000 (℃02/9264 4855).

New Zealand Contact the Sydney office or the embassy in Wellington.

INDONESIA

UK and Ireland 41 Whitehall, London SW1A 2BY (✆0171/493 0030).

US 3457 Wilshire Blvd, Suite 104, Los Angeles, CA 90010 (✆213/387-2078).

Canada Contact the embassy.

Australia DWI Tour Australia, Prince Centre, 8 Quay St, Haymarket, Sydney, NSW 2000 (✆02/9211 3383).

New Zealand Contact Garuda airline offices or the embassy in Wellington.

JAPAN

UK and Ireland Heathcote House, 20 Savile Row, London W1 (✆0171/734 9638).

US 360 Post St #601, San Francisco, CA 94108 (✆415/989-7140); 624 South Grand Ave, Los Angeles, CA 90017 (✆213/623-1952); Rockefeller Plaza #1250, New York, NY 10020 (✆212/757-5640); 401 North Michigan Ave, Chicago, IL 60611 (✆312/222-0874).

Canada 165 University Ave, Toronto, Ontario M5H 3B8 (✆416/366-7140).

Australia Chifley Tower, 115 Pitt St, Sydney, NSW 2000 (✆02/9232 4522).

New Zealand Contact the Sydney office or the embassy in Wellington.

LAOS

No national tourist office.

MALAYSIA

UK and Ireland 57 Trafalgar Square, London WC2N 5DU (✆0171/930 7932).

US 818 West 7th St #804, Los Angeles, CA 90017 (✆213/689-9702); 595 Madison Ave #1800, New York, NY 10022 (✆212/754-1113).

Canada 830 Burrard St, Vancouver, BC V6Z 2K4 (✆604/689-8899).

Australia 65 York St, Sydney, NSW 2000 (✆02/9299 4441).

New Zealand Contact the Sydney office or the embassy in Wellington.

NEPAL
Australia 10 Eagle St, Brisbane, QLD 4000 (℡07/3232 0336).
New Zealand Contact the Brisbane office.

PAKISTAN
UK and Ireland 52 High Holborn, London WC1 (℡0171/242 3131).

THE PHILIPPINES
UK and Ireland 17 Albermarle St, London W1 (℡0171/499 5443).
US 30 North Michigan Ave #913, Chicago, IL 60602 (℡312/782-2475); 556 Fifth Ave, New York, NY 10036 (℡212/575-7915).
Canada Contact the New York office.
Australia Wynayd House, 301 George St, Sydney, NSW 2000 (℡02/9299 6805).
New Zealand Contact the Sydney office or the consulate in Auckland.

SINGAPORE
UK and Ireland 1st Floor, Carrington House, 126 Regent St, London W1R 5FE (℡0171/437 0033).
US 8484 Wilshire Blvd #510, Beverly Hills, CA 90211 (℡213/852-1901); 590 Fifth Ave, 12th Floor, New York, NY 10036 (℡212/302-4861); 2 Prudential Plaza, 180 North Stetson Ave #1450, Chicago, IL 60601 (℡312/938-1888).
Canada Standard Life Center, 121 King St W #1000, Toronto, Ontario M5H 3T9 (℡416/363-8898).
Australia AWA Building, 47 York St, Sydney, NSW 2000 (℡02/9290 2888).
New Zealand Contact the Sydney office or the embassy in Wellington.

SOUTH KOREA
UK and Ireland 2nd Floor, Vogue House, 1 Hanover Square, London W1R 9RD (℡0171/409 2100).
US 2 Executive Drive #750, Fort Lee, NJ 07024 (℡201/585-0909); 3435 Wilshire Blvd #1110, Los Angeles, CA 90010 (℡213/382-3435).
Canada 480 University Ave, Toronto, Ontario M5G 1V2 (℡416/348-9056).

Australia 17th Floor, Tower Building, Australia Square, 264 George St, Sydney, NSW 2000 (℡02/9252 4148).

New Zealand Contact the Sydney office.

SRI LANKA

UK and Ireland 22 Regent St, London SW1 (℡0171/930 2627).

Australia Level 1, 91 York St, Sydney, NSW 2000 (℡02/9244 1813); 439 Albany Highway, Victoria Park, WA 6100 (℡09/362 4579).

New Zealand Contact the Sydney office.

THAILAND

UK and Ireland 49 Albemarle St, London W1 (℡0839/300800).

USA 303 East Wacker Drive, Suite 400, Chicago, IL 60601 (℡312/819-3990); 3440 Wilshire Blvd, Suite 1100, Los Angeles, CA 90010 (℡213/382-2353); 5 World Trade Center, Suite 3443, New York, NY 10048 (℡212/432-0433).

Canada 55 University Ave #1208, Toronto, Ontario M5J 2H7 (℡416/364-3363); 2840 West 6th Ave, Vancouver, BC V6K 1X1 (℡604/733-4540).

Australia 255 George St, Sydney, NSW 2000 (℡02/9247 7549); 2 Hardy Rd, South Perth, WA 6151 (℡08/9474 3646).

New Zealand 2nd Floor, 87 Queen St, Auckland (℡09/379 8398).

VIETNAM

UK and Ireland 12 Victoria Rd, London W8 5RD (℡0171/937 3174).

EMBASSIES AND CONSULATES

BANGLADESH

UK 28 Queen's Gate, London SW7 (℡0171/584 0081).

US 2201 Wisconsin Ave NW, Washington, DC 20007 (℡202/342-8373); consulates in New York (℡212/599-6767) and Los Angeles (℡310/441-9399).

Canada 275 Bank St, Suite 302, Ottawa, Ontario K2P 2L6 (℡613/236-0138).

Australia 35 Endeavour St, Red Hill, Canberra, ACT 2600 (℡02/6295 3328).

New Zealand Contact the embassy in Canberra.

BURMA
UK 19a Charles St, London W1 (✆0891/600306).
US 2300 South St NW, Washington, DC 20008 (✆202/332-9044,
332-9045 or 332-9046); consulate in New York (✆212/535-1311).
Canada 85 Range Rd, Suite 902, Ottawa, Ontario K1N 8J6
(✆613/232-6434).
Australia 22 Akuna St, Yarralumla, Canberra, ACT 2600 (✆02/6273
3811).
New Zealand Contact the embassy in Canberra.

CAMBODIA
UK None.
US 4500 16th St NW, Washington, DC 20011 (✆202/726-7742).
Canada Contact the embassy in Washington.
Australia 5 Canterbury Crescent, Deakin, Canberra, ACT 2600
(✆02/6273 1259).
New Zealand Contact the embassy in Canberra.

CHINA
UK 31 Portland Place, London W1 (✆0891/880808).
US 2300 Connecticut Ave NW, Washington, DC 20008 (✆202/328-
2517); consulates in Chicago, Houston, Los Angeles, New York
and San Francisco.
Canada 515 St Patrick's St, Ottawa, Ontario K1N 5H3 (✆613/789-
9608); consulates in Toronto and Vancouver.
Australia 15 Coronation Drive, Yarralumla, Canberra, ACT 2600
(✆02/6273 4780).
New Zealand 588 Great South Rd, Greenland, Auckland 1
(✆09/525 1589).

INDIA
UK India House, Aldwych, London WC2B 4NA (✆0891/444544);
consulates in Birmingham and Glasgow.
US 2536 Massachusetts Ave NW, Washington, DC 20008
(✆202/939-9849 or 939-9806); consulates in Chicago, New
York, San Francisco and Houston.
Canada 10 Springfield Rd, Ottawa, Ontario K1M 1C9 (✆ 613/744-
3751, 744-3752 or 744-3753).
Australia 3 Moonah Place, Yarralumla, Canberra, ACT 2600
(✆06/273 3999); 25 Bligh St, Sydney, NSW 2000 (✆02/9223

9500); 15 Munro St, Coburg, Vic 3058 (℡03/9386 7399); India Centre, 49 Bennett St, East Perth, WA (℡08/9221 1485).

New Zealand FAI House, 180 Molesworth St, Wellington PO Box 4005, (℡04/473 6390).

INDONESIA

UK and Ireland 38 Grosvenor Square, London W1X 9AD (℡0891/171210).

US 2020 Massachusetts Ave NW, Washington, DC 20036 (℡202/775-5200); consulates in Chicago, Houston, Honolulu, Los Angeles, New York and San Francisco.

Canada 55 Parkdale Ave, Ottawa, Ontario, K1Y 1E5 (℡613/724-1100); consulates in Toronto and Vancouver.

Australia 8 Darwin Ave, Yarralumla, Canberra, ACT 2600 (℡02/6250 8600); 236–238 Maroubra Rd, Maroubra, NSW 2035 (℡02/9344 9933); 72 Queens Rd, Melbourne, Vic 3004 (℡03/9525 2755); 20 Harry Chan Ave, Darwin, NT 5784 (℡08/8941 0048); 134 Adelaide Terrace, Perth, WA 6001 (℡08/9221 5858).

New Zealand 70 Glen Rd, Kelburn, Wellington, PO Box 3543 (℡04/475 8697).

JAPAN

UK 101 Piccadilly, London W1V 9FN (℡0171/465 6500); consulate in Edinburgh.

US 2520 Massachusetts Ave NW, Washington, DC 20008 (℡202/939-6700); consulates in Agana (Guam), Anchorage, Atlanta, Boston, Chicago, Detroit, Honolulu, Houston, Kansas City, Los Angeles, Miami, New Orleans, New York, Portland, Saipan, San Francisco and Seattle.

Canada 255 Sussex Drive, Ottawa, Ontario K1N 9E6 (℡613/241-8541); consulates in Edmonton, Montréal, Toronto and Vancouver.

Australia 112 Empire Circuit, Yarralumla, Canberra, ACT 2600 (℡02/6273 3244); consulates in Melbourne, Sydney, Brisbane and Cairns.

New Zealand 7th Floor, Norwich Building, 3 Hunter St, Wellington (℡04/473 1540).

LAOS

UK None.

US 2222 South St NW, Washington, DC 20008 (℡202/332-6416).

Canada Contact the embassy in Washington.

Australia 1 Dalman Crescent, O'Malley, Canberra, ACT 2606 (℡02/6286 6933).

New Zealand Contact the embassy in Canberra.

MALAYSIA

UK 45 Belgrave Square, London SW1X 8QT (℡0171/235 8033).

US 2401 Massachusetts Ave NW, Washington, DC 20008 (℡202/328-2700).

Canada 60 Boteler St, Ottawa, Ontario K1N 8Y7 (℡613/241-5182).

Australia 7 Perth Ave, Yarralumla, Canberra, ACT 2600 (℡06/273 1543).

New Zealand 10 Washington Ave, Brooklyn, Wellington (℡04/385 2439).

NEPAL

UK 12a Kensington Palace Gardens, London W8 4QU (℡0171/229 1594).

US 2131 Leroy Place NW, Washington, DC 20008 (℡202/667-4550); consulate in New York (℡ 212/370-4188).

Canada 200 Bay St, Royal Bank Plaza, South Tower, Toronto, Ontario M5J 2J8 (℡416/865-0210).

Australia Level 3, 441 Kent St, Sydney 2000 (℡02/264 5909).

New Zealand Contact the embassy in Sydney.

PAKISTAN

UK 35 Lowndes Square, London SW1 (℡0891/880880).

US 2315 Massachusetts Ave NW, Washington, DC 20008 (℡202/939-6200); consulates in New York (℡212/879-5800) and Los Angeles (℡310/441-5114).

Canada Burnside Building, 151 Slater St, Suite 608, Ottawa, Ontario K1P 5H3 (℡613/238-7881).

Australia 4 Timburra Crescent, O'Malley, Canberra, ACT 2606 (℡02/6290 1676).

New Zealand Contact the embassy in Canberra.

PHILIPPINES

UK 9a Palace Green, London W8 (℡0891/171244).

US 1600 Massachusetts Ave NW, Washington, DC 20036 (℡202/467-9300); consulates in Chicago, Honolulu, Los Angeles, New York and San Francisco.

Canada 130 Albert St, Suite 606–608, Ottawa, Ontario K1P 5G4 (✆613/233-1121).

Australia 1 Moonah Place, Yarralumla, Canberra, ACT 2600 (✆02/6273 2535); 301 George St, Sydney, NSW 2000 (✆02/9299 6633).

New Zealand 8th Floor, 121 Beach Rd, Auckland 1 (✆09/303 2423).

SINGAPORE

UK 9 Wilton Crescent, London SW1X 8SA (✆0171/201 1804).

US 3501 International Place NW, Washington, DC 20008 (✆202/537-3100); consulate in New York (✆212/826-0840, 826-0841, 826-0842, 826-0843 or 826-0844).

Canada 999 West Hastings St, Suite 1305, Vancouver, BC V6C 2W2 (✆604/669-5115).

Australia 17 Forster Crescent, Yarralumla, Canberra, ACT 2600 (✆06/273 3944).

New Zealand 17 Kabul St, Khandallah, Wellington, PO Box 13-140 (✆04/479 2076).

SOUTH KOREA

UK 4 Palace Gate, London W8 (✆0891/444560).

US 2320 Massachusetts Ave NW, Washington, DC 20008 (✆202/939-5660, 939-5661, 939-5662 or 939-5663); consulates in major US cities.

Canada 150 Boteler St, Ottawa, Ontario K1A 5A6 (✆613/244-5010).

Australia 32 Martin Place, Sydney, NSW 2000 (✆02/9221 3866).

New Zealand 43 Manners St, Wellington (✆04/472 3865).

SRI LANKA

UK 13 Hyde Park Gardens, London W2 2LU (✆0171/262 1841).

US 2148 Wyoming Ave NW, Washington, DC 20008 (✆202/483-4025, 483-4026, 483-4027 or 483-4028); consulates in New York (✆212/986-7040), Los Angeles, Honolulu, New Orleans and Newark.

Canada 333 Laurier Ave W, Suite 1204, Ottawa, Ontario K1P 1C1 (✆613/233-8449).

Australia 35 Empire Circuit, Forrest, Canberra, ACT 2603 (✆02/6239 7041); 5 Elizabeth St, Sydney NSW 2000 (✆02/9223 8729).

New Zealand Contact the embassy in Canberra.

THAILAND

UK 30 Queen's Gate, London SW7 (©0891/600150); consulates in Birmingham, Cardiff, Glasgow, Hull and Liverpool.

US 1024 Wisconsin Ave NW, Washington DC 20007 (©202/944-3600); consulates in Chicago, Los Angeles and New York City.

Canada 180 Island Park Drive, Ottawa, Ontario K1Y 0A2 (©613/722-4444).

Australia Optus Gate, 10 Moore St, Canberra ACT 2600 (©02/6230 4200); consulates in Adelaide, Brisbane, Melbourne, Perth and Sydney.

New Zealand 2 Cook St, PO Box 17-226, Karori, Wellington (©04/476 8618).

VIETNAM

UK 12 Victoria Rd, London W8 5RD (©0891/171228).

US 1233 20th St, Suite 501 NW, Washington DC 20036 (©202/861-0694).

Canada 226 MacLaren St, Ottawa, Ontario K2P 0L9 (©613/236-0772).

Australia 6 Timburra Crescent, O'Malley, Canberra, ACT 2606 (©02/6286 6059).

New Zealand Contact the embassy in Canberra.

DISCOUNT FLIGHT AGENTS AND CONSOLIDATORS

UK AND IRELAND

Bridge the World, 47 Chalk Farm Rd, London NW1 8AN (©0171/911 0900; *www.bridge-the-world.co.uk*).

Campus Travel, 52 Grosvenor Gardens, London SW1W 0AG (©0171/730 8111); 541 Bristol Rd, Selly Oak, Birmingham B29 6AU (©0121/414 1848); 61 Ditchling Rd, Brighton BN1 4SD (©01273/570226); 37 Queen's Rd, Clifton, Bristol BS8 1QE (©0117/929 2494); 5 Emmanuel St, Cambridge CB1 1NE (©01223/324283); 53 Forest Rd, Edinburgh EH1 2QP (©0131/668 3303); 122 George St, Glasgow G1 1RS (©0141/553 1818); 166 Deansgate, Manchester M3 3FE (©0161/273 1721); 105 St Aldates, Oxford OX1 1DD (©01865/242067); *www.campustravel.co.uk*

Cheap Flights *www.cheapflights.co.uk* Online service that lists the day's cheapest flight deals available from subscribing UK flight agents.

Flightbookers, 177 Tottenham Court Rd, London W1P 0LX (℡0171/757 2444); 34 Argyle Arcade, off Buchanan St, Glasgow G1 1RS (℡0141/204 1919).

North South Travel, Moulsham Mill Centre, Parkway, Chelmsford, Essex CM2 7PX (℡01245/492882).

STA Travel, 86 Old Brompton Rd, London SW7 3LH; 117 Euston Rd, London NW1 2SX; 38 Store St, London WC1E 7BZ (℡0171/361 6262); 25 Queen's Rd, Bristol BS8 1QE (℡0117/929 4399); 38 Sidney St, Cambridge CB2 3HX (℡01223/366966); 75 Deansgate, Manchester M3 2BW (℡0161/834 0668); 88 Vicar Lane, Leeds LS1 7JH (℡0113/244 9212); 36 George St, Oxford OX1 2OJ (℡01865/792800); and branches in Aberdeen, Birmingham, Canterbury, Cardiff, Coventry, Durham, Glasgow, Loughborough, Nottingham, Warwick and Sheffield; *www.statravel.co.uk*

Trailfinders, 42 Earl's Court Rd, London W8 6FT (℡0171/938 3366); 194 Kensington High St, London W8 7RG (℡0171/938 3939); 58 Deansgate, Manchester M3 2FF (℡0161/839 6969); 254 Sauchiehall St, Glasgow G2 3EH (℡0141/353 2224); 22 The Priory Queensway, Birmingham B4 6BS (℡0121/236 1234); 48 Corn St, Bristol BS1 1HQ (℡0117/929 9000); 4 Dawson St, Dublin 2 (℡01/677 7888).

Travel Bag, 52 Regent St, London W1R 6DX; 373 The Strand, opposite the *Savoy Hotel*, London WC2R 0JF; 12 High St, Alton, Hampshire GU34 1BN (℡0171/287 5558).

The Travel Bug, 125a Gloucester Rd, London SW7 4SF (℡0171/835 2000); 597 Cheetham Hill Rd, Manchester M8 5EJ (℡0161/721 4000).

USIT, Fountain Centre, College St, Belfast BT1 6ET (℡01232/324 073); 10 Market Parade, Patrick St, Cork (℡021/270 900); 33 Ferryquay St, Derry (℡01504/371 888); 19 Aston Quay, Dublin 2 (℡01/602 1700); Victoria Place, Eyre Square, Galway (℡091/565 177); Central Buildings, O'Connell St, Limerick (℡061/415 064); 36 Georges St, Waterford (℡051/872 601).

US AND CANADA

Air Brokers International, 150 Post St, Suite 620, San Francisco, CA 94108 (℡1-800/883-3273 or 415/397-1383; *www.airbrokers.com*).

Council Travel, 205 East 42nd St, New York, NY 10017 (℡1-800/226-8624; www.ciee.org), and branches in many other US cities.

Discount Airfares Worldwide On-Line www.etn.nl/discount.htm

Educational Travel Centre, 438 North Frances St, Madison, WI 53703 (℡1-800/747-5551 or 608/256-5551; www.edtrav.com).

High Adventure Travel, 353 Sacramento St, Suite 600, San Francisco, CA 94111 (℡1-800/350-0612 or 415/912-5600; www.highadv.com). The web site features an interactive database that lets you build your own RTW itinerary.

International Travel Network/Airlines of the Web
www.itn.net/airlines

Skylink, 265 Madison Ave, 5th Floor, New York, NY 10016 (℡1-800/AIR-ONLY or 212/573-8980), with branches in Chicago, Los Angeles, Montréal, Toronto and Washington DC.

STA Travel, 10 Downing St, New York, NY 10014 (℡1-800/781-4040 or 212/627-3111), and branches in the Los Angeles, San Francisco and Boston areas; www.sta-travel.com

Student Flights, 5010 East Shea Blvd, Suite 104A, Scottsdale, AZ 85254 (℡1-800/255-8000 or 602/951-1177; www.isecard.com).

TFI Tours International, 34 West 32nd St, New York, NY 10001 (℡1-800/745-8000 or 212/736-1140), and offices in Las Vegas and Miami.

Travel Cuts, 187 College St, Toronto, Ontario M5T 1P7 (℡416/979-2406), and branches all over Canada; www.travelcuts.com

Travelocity www.travelocity.com

AUSTRALIA AND NEW ZEALAND

Asia and World Travel, corner of George St and Adelaide St, Brisbane (℡07/3229 3511).

Asian Travel Centre, 126 Russell St, Melbourne (℡03/9654 8277).

Budget Travel, 16 Fort St, Auckland, plus branches around the city (℡09/366 0061 or 0800/808 040).

Destinations Unlimited, 3 Milford Rd, Auckland (℡09/373 4033).

Far East Travel Centre, 50 Margaret St, Sydney (℡02/9262 6414).

Flight Centres Australia: 82 Elizabeth St, Sydney, plus branches nationwide (℡13 1600). New Zealand: 205 Queen St, Auckland (℡09/309 6171), plus branches nationwide.

Northern Gateway, 22 Cavenagh St, Darwin (℡08/8941 1394).

STA Travel, Australia: 702 Harris St, Ultimo, Sydney; 256 Flinders St, Melbourne; other offices in state capitals and major universities (nearest branch ℗13 1776, fastfare telesales ℗1300/360 960). New Zealand: 10 High St, Auckland (℗09/366 6673), plus branches in Wellington, Christchurch, Dunedin, Palmerston North, Hamilton and at major universities; *www.statravel.com.au*

Tymtro Travel, Level 8, 130 Pitt St, Sydney (℗02/9223 2211 or 1-800/652 969).

COURIER FLIGHT COMPANIES

UK

Bridges Worldwide, Old Mill Road House, West Drayton, Middlesex TW3 3JU (℗01895/465065). Flights to Bangkok, Tokyo and Seoul.

Flight Masters, 83 Mortimer St, London W1 (℗0171/462 0022). Flights to Bangkok and Tokyo.

International Association of Air Travel Couriers (UK), c/o International Features, 1 Kings Rd, Dorchester, Dorset DT1 1NJ (fax 01305/264710; *www.courier.org*). Agent for lots of courier companies; small membership fee required.

US AND CANADA

Air Courier Association, 191 University Blvd, Suite 300, Denver, CO 80206 (℗1-800/282-1202 or 303/279-3600; *www.aircourier.org*). Clearing house for over forty courier companies, with flights to China, Hong Kong, Japan, the Philippines, Singapore, South Korea, Taiwan and Thailand. For a small subscription fee you receive a list of freight brokers and their timetables.

Air-Tech, 588 Broadway Suite 204, New York, NY 10012 (℗1-800/575-8324 or 212/219-7000; *www.eideti.com/aerotech/cflights2.html*). Flights to China, Hong Kong, Japan, the Philippines, Singapore, South Korea, Taiwan and Thailand.

International Association of Air Travel Couriers, 8 South J St, PO Box 1349, Lake Worth, FL 33460 (℗561/582-8320; *www.courier.org*). Flights to China, Hong Kong, Japan, the Philippines, Singapore, South Korea, Taiwan and Thailand.

Now Voyager, 74 Varick St, Suite 307, New York, NY 10013 (℗212/431-1616; *www.nowvoyagertravel.com*). Flights to China, Japan, the Philippines, Singapore and Thailand.

SPECIALIST TOUR OPERATORS

UK

Dragoman, 14 Camp Green, Debenham, Stowmarket IP14 6LA (℡01728/861133; *www.dragoman.co.uk*). Extended overland journeys in purpose-built expedition vehicles.

Encounter Overland, 267 Old Brompton Rd, London SW5 9JA (℡0171/370 6845). Long-established organizer of overland expeditions.

Exodus, 9 Weir Rd, London SW12 0LT (℡0181/675 5550, brochure requests ℡673 0859; *www.exodustravels.co.uk*). Adventure-tour operators and overland-expedition specialist.

Explore Worldwide, 1 Frederick St, Aldershot, Hampshire, GU11 1LQ (℡01252/319448, brochure requests ℡344161; *www.explore. co.uk*). Big range of small-group tours, treks, expeditions and safaris.

RADAR (Royal Association for Disability and Rehabilitation), 12 City Forum, 250 City Rd, London EC1V 8AF (℡0171/250 3222, minicom ℡250 4119). Produces a holiday guide to help disabled travellers plan long-haul trips.

World Expeditions, 4 Northfields Prospect, Putney Bridge Rd, London SW18 1PE (℡0181/870 2600; *www.worldexpeditions.com.au*). Adventure tours, including mountain and jungle trekking, and cycling.

US AND CANADA

Above the Clouds Trekking (℡1-800/233-4499). Trekking and rafting.

Backroads (℡1-800/462-2848; *www.backroadsinternational.com*). Specialist adventures in Nepal, Indonesia and Thailand.

Directions Unlimited, 720 North Bedford Rd, Bedford Hills, NY 10507 (℡914/241-1700). Travel agency specializing in custom tours for people with disabilities.

Global Exchange (℡415/255-7296; *www.globalexchange.org*). "Reality tours" to the Philippines and Vietnam.

Himalayan Travel (℡1-800/225-2380). Trekking and rafting expeditions.

Journeys (℡1-800/255-8735; *www.journeys-intl.com*). Adventure and culture tours.

Mountain Travel-Sobek (US ✆1-800/227-2384; Canada ✆1-800/282-8747). Trekking and wildlife tours.

Worldwide Adventures (✆1-800/387-1483). Trekking, rafting, wildlife and cycling adventures.

AUSTRALIA

Exodus Expeditions, 8th Floor, 350 Kent St, Sydney (✆02/9299 8844). Extended overland trips through Asia.

Intrepid, 246 Brunswick St, Melbourne (✆03/9416 2655). Small-group tours with the emphasis on cross-cultural contact and low-impact tourism.

Peregrine Adventures, 258 Lonsdale St, Melbourne (✆03/9663 8611), plus offices in Brisbane, Sydney, Adelaide and Perth. Adventure travel.

Sundowners, 600 Lonsdale St, Suite 15, Melbourne (✆03/9600 1934 or 1-800/337 089). Overland train travel, including Trans-Siberian Express and the Silk Route.

VOLUNTARY WORK AND CONSERVATION PROJECTS

UK ORGANIZATIONS

British Trust for Conservation Volunteers (BTCV), 36 St Mary's St, Wallingford, Oxfordshire OX10 0EU (✆01491/839766; fax 839646). One of the largest environmental charities in Britain, with a programme of international working holidays (as a paying volunteer), including dry-stone walling in Japan.

Coral Cay Conservation, 154 Clapham Park Rd, London SW4 7DE (✆0171/498 6248; *www.coralcay.org*). Coral surveying in the Philippines and Indonesia.

Earthwatch, 57 Woodstock Rd, Oxford OX2 6HJ (✆01865/311600; *www.earthwatch.org*). Largest and longest-established voluntary-holiday organization, with sixteen different projects in Asia.

Frontier, 77 Leonard St, London EC2A 4QS (✆0171/613 2422; *www.mailbox.co.uk/frontier*). Rainforest surveys in Vietnam.

Indian Volunteers for Community Service (IVCS), 12 Eastleigh Ave, South Harrow, Middlesex HA2 0UF (✆0181/864 4740, evenings only). Three-week visitors' programme at a rural development project in India.

i venture, i to i International Projects, 1 Cottage Rd, Headingly, Leeds LS6 4DD (℮0113/217 9800; *www.i-to-i.com/venture*). Short-term voluntary English teaching in India and Sri Lanka.

World Service Enquiry (℮0171/737 7811, fax 737 3237). Umbrella organization for jobs with charities working overseas.

US ORGANIZATIONS

Council on International Educational Exchange, 205 East 42nd St, New York, NY 10017 (℮888-Council; *www.ciee.org/*). Two- to four-week volunteer projects.

Earthwatch ℮617/926-8200; *www.earthwatch.org* Largest and longest-established voluntary-holiday organization, with sixteen different projects in Asia.

Global Volunteers ℮1-800/487-1074. Projects in Vietnam, Indonesia and China.

AUSTRALIAN ORGANIZATIONS

Earthwatch 126 Bank St, South Melbourne, Vic 3205 (℮03/9416 1499; *www.earthwatch.org*). Largest and longest-established voluntary-holiday organization, with sixteen different projects in Asia.

ACCOMMODATION BOOKING AGENTS

HOSTELLING INTERNATIONAL

UK 14 Southampton St, London WC2 7HY (℮0171/836 1036).

US 733 15th St NW, Suite 840, PO Box 37613, Washington, DC 20005 (℮202/783-6161; *www.hiayh.org*).

Canada Room 400, 205 Catherine St, Ottawa, Ontario K2P 1C3 (℮1-800/663-5777 or 613/237-7884).

Australia 422 Kent St, Sydney (℮02/9261 1111); 205 King St, Melbourne (℮03/9670 9611); 38 Stuart St, Adelaide (℮08/8231 5583); 154 Roma St, Brisbane (℮07/3236 1680); 236 William St, Perth (℮08/9227 5122); 69a Mitchell St, Darwin (℮08/8981 2560); 28 Criterion St, Hobart (℮03/6234 9617).

New Zealand PO Box 436, Christchurch (℮03/379 9970).

HOMESTAYS

American-International Homestays PO Box 1754, Nederland, CO 80466-1754 (℮1-800/876-2048; *www.spectravel.com/ homes*). Stay with a local family in China, India or Nepal.

Women Welcome Women UK ✆ & fax 01494/465441; US ✆ & fax 203/259-7832; Australia ✆ & fax 03/843 1102. WWW is an organization of women living in all parts of the world who are happy to meet, show round and usually accommodate women travellers. There are members in nearly all parts of Asia, with a particularly large number in Japan. To join, you pay a minimal membership fee.

ONLINE HOTEL FINDERS

Asia Hotels *www.asia-hotels.com/aboutlg.asp* Small selection of online hotels in Asia, with prices from $25 (£15).

City Net *www.city.net/* Links to individual Asian countries, many of which have online hotel reservation sites.

Online tourist information *www.efn.org/~rick/tour* Call up a links list for the country you're interested in, then choose the online hotel finder.

Travel Web *www.travelweb.com/* Hotel reservations in major Asian cities and resorts, but nothing much under $35 (£20).

TRAVEL CLINICS

UK AND IRELAND

British Airways Travel Clinic, 156 Regent St, London W1 7RA (✆0171/439 9584). Also at Flightbookers, 177 Tottenham Court Rd, London W1P 0LX (✆0171/757 2504); 101 Cheapside, London EC2 (✆0171/606 2977); the BA terminal in London's Victoria Station (✆0171/233 6661); Gatwick and Heathrow airports; and about forty regional clinics (call ✆0171/831 5333 for locations).

Hospital for Tropical Diseases, St Pancras Hospital, 4 St Pancras Way, London NW1 0PE (✆0171/388 9600). Travel clinic and recorded message service (✆0839/337733).

MASTA (Medical Advisory Service for Travellers Abroad), London School of Hygiene and Tropical Medicine. 24-hour Travellers' Health Line (✆0891/224100).

Nomad Pharmacy and Travellers' Store, 3 Wellington Terrace, Turnpike Lane, London N8 0PX (✆0181/889 7014). Travellers' medical supplies and first-aid equipment, plus general advice on healthy travelling.

Travel Medicine Services, PO Box 254, 16 College St, Belfast 1 (℡01232/315220). Advice only.

Tropical Medical Bureau, Grafton St Medical Centre, 34 Grafton St, Dublin 2 (℡01/671 9200); Dun Laoghaire Medical Centre, 5 Northumberland Ave, Dun Laoghaire, Co. Dublin (℡01/280 4996); *www.iol.ie/-tmb* Offers travel vaccinations, up-to-date information and specialist advice for travellers.

US AND CANADA

Canadian Society for International Health, 170 Laurier Ave W, Suite 902, Ottawa, Ontario K1P 5V5 (℡613/230-2654). Distributes a free list of travel health centres in Canada.

Centers for Disease Control, 1600 Clifton Rd NE, Atlanta, GA 30333 (℡404/639-3311; *www.cdc.gov/travel/travel.html*). Advises on outbreak warnings, inoculations and precautions.

International Association for Medical Assistance to Travellers (IAMAT), 417 Center St, Lewiston, NY 14092 (℡716/754-4883); 40 Regal Rd, Guelph, Ontario N1K 1B5 (℡519/836-0102); *www.sentex.net/~iamat* Non-profit organization that can provide a list of English-speaking doctors in-country, climate charts and leaflets on various diseases and inoculations.

Travelers Medical Center, 31 Washington Square, New York, NY 10011 (℡212/982-1600). Consultation service on immunizations.

AUSTRALIA AND NEW ZEALAND

Travellers' Medical and Vaccination Centre, 7/428 George St, Sydney (℡02/9221 7133); 3/393 Little Bourke St, Melbourne (℡03/9602 5788); 6/29 Gilbert Place, Adelaide (℡08/8212 7522); 6/247 Adelaide St, Brisbane (℡07/3221 9066); 1 Mill St, Perth (℡08/9321 1977); Level 1, Canterbury Arcade, 170 Queen St, Auckland 1 (℡09/373 3531); *www.tmvc.com.au* In addition to administering inoculations, the centres sell first-aid equipment and water purifiers.

INSURANCE AGENTS

UK AND IRELAND

Columbus Travel Insurance, 17 Devonshire Square, London EC2M 4SQ (℡0171/375 0011).

Endsleigh Insurance, Cranfield House, 97 Southampton Row, London WC1B 4AG (☎0171/436 4451).

Marcus Hearne & Co Ltd, 65 Shoreditch High St, London E1 6JL (☎0171/739 3444).

Worldwide, The Business Centre, 1 Commercial Rd, Tonbridge, Kent TN12 6YT (☎01732/773366).

USIT, see p.296 for addresses.

US AND CANADA

Access America ☎1-800/284-8300.

Carefree Travel Insurance ☎1-800/323-3149.

Desjardins Travel Insurance Canada only ☎1-800/463-7830.

STA Travel Insurance ☎1-800/781-4040; *www.sta-travel.com*

Travel Assistance International ☎1-800/821-2828.

Travel Guard ☎1-800/826-1300; *www.noelgroup.com*

Travel Insurance Services ☎1-800/937-1387.

AUSTRALIA AND NEW ZEALAND

Cover More, 9/32 Walker St, North Sydney (☎02/9202 8000 or 1-800/251 881).

Ready Plan, 141 Walker St, Dandenong, Melbourne (☎03/9791 5077 or 1-800/337 462); 10/63 Albert St, Auckland (☎09/379 3208).

OFFICIAL ADVICE ON INTERNATIONAL TROUBLE SPOTS

The organizations listed below are official government bodies providing basic security information for citizens travelling overseas. You'll find details on war zones, internal conflicts, and particular crime or safety concerns. The UK web site includes a country-by-country list of current no-go areas in Asia and the rest of the world. If you use the MASTA Travellers' Health Line (see p.302) your printout will include a summary of FCO advice for the countries you have indicated you'll be visiting. The official Web site of the US State Department is extremely thorough and useful even to non-US citizens. As well as warnings on recent political dramas and disasters, it has sections on the health hazards, road safety and crime in every country, plus details on visa regulations (for US citizens only).

FCO Travel Advice Unit, Consular Division, 1 Palace St, London SW1E 5HE (©0171/238 4503; *www.fco.gov.uk/reference/travel_advice/*).

US State Department Travel Advisory Service, 2201 C St NW, Room 4811, Washington, DC 20520 (©202/647-5225; *travel.state.gov/travel_warnings.html*).

Canadian Department of Foreign Affairs and International Trade, 125 Sussex Drive, Ottawa, Ontario K1A 0G2 (©1-800/387-3124, 1-800/ 267-6788 or 613/944-6788; *www.dfait-maeci.gc.ca/graphics/cosmos \CNTRY_E.htm*).

Australian Department of Foreign Affairs and Trade, The RG Casey Building, John McEwan Crescent, Barton, Canberra ACT 2600 (©02/6261 9111; *www.dfat.gov.au/dfat/consular/advice/advices_mnu.html*).

New Zealand Department of Foreign Affairs, Stafford House, 40 The Terrace, Wellington, Private Bag 18 901 (©04/494 8500, fax 494 8512; *www.nz-high-com.org.sg/go-osea1.html*).

RESPONSIBLE TOURISM: FURTHER INFORMATION

BRITAIN AND IRELAND
Tourism Concern, Stapleton House, 277 Holloway Rd, London N7 8HN (©0171/753 3330; *www.gn.apc.org/tourismconcern*).

US AND CANADA
Rethinking Tourism Project, PO Box 581938, Minneapolis, MN 55458-1938 (©612/5210098; email *RTProject@aol.com*).

AUSTRALIA AND NEW ZEALAND
Responsible Tourism Network, PO Box 34, Rundle Mall, Adelaide 5000 (©08/8232 2727, fax 8232 2808; *www.caa.org.au/travel/*).

TRAVEL BOOK AND MAP STORES

UK AND IRELAND
Blackwell's Map and Travel Shop, 53 Broad St, Oxford OX1 3BQ (©01865/792792).

Daunt Books, 83 Marylebone High St, London W1M 3DE (✆0171/224 2295); 193 Haverstock Hill, London NW3 4QL (✆0171/794 4006).

Easons Bookshop, 40 O'Connell St, Dublin 1 (✆01/873 3811).

National Map Centre, 22–24 Caxton St, London SW1H 0QU (✆0171/222 2466).

Stanfords, 12–14 Long Acre, London WC2E 9LP (✆0171/836 1321); also at Campus Travel, 52 Grosvenor Gardens, London SW1W 0AG (✆0171/730 1314), within the British Airways offices at 156 Regent St, London W1R 5TA (✆0171/434 4744), and at 29 Corn St, Bristol BS1 1HT (✆0117/929 9966).

The Travel Bookshop, 13–15 Blenheim Crescent, London W11 2EE (✆0171/229 5260).

US AND CANADA

Adventurous Traveler Bookstore, PO Box 1468, Williston, VT 05495 (✆1-800/282-3963; *www.AdventurousTraveler.com*).

Book Passage, 51 Tamal Vista Blvd, Corte Madera, CA 94925 (✆415/927-0960).

The Complete Traveler Bookstore, 199 Madison Ave, New York, NY 10016 (✆212/685-9007).

Map Link, 30 South La Petera Lane, Unit #5, Santa Barbara, CA 93117 (✆805/692-6777).

The Map Store Inc, 1636 1st St, Washington, DC 20006 (✆202/628-2608).

Open Air Books and Maps, 25 Toronto St, Toronto, Ontario M5R 2C1 (✆416/363-0719).

Phileas Fogg's Books & Maps, #87 Stanford Shopping Center, Palo Alto, CA 94304 (✆1-800/533-FOGG).

Rand McNally, 444 North Michigan Ave, Chicago, IL 60611 (✆312/321-1751); 150 East 52nd St, New York, NY 10022 (✆212/758-7488); 595 Market St, San Francisco, CA 94105 (✆415/777-3131); call ✆1-800/333-0136 ext 2111 for other locations.

Sierra Club Bookstore, 6014 College Ave, Oakland, CA 94618 (✆510/658-7470).

Travel Books & Language Center, 4931 Cordell Ave, Bethesda, MD 20814 (✆1-800/220-2665).

Traveler's Bookstore, 22 West 52nd St, New York, NY 10019 (✆212/664-0995).

Ulysses Travel Bookshop, 4176 St-Denis, Montréal (©514/843-9447).

World Wide Books and Maps, 736 Granville St, Vancouver, BC V6Z 1E4 (©604/687-3320).

AUSTRALIA AND NEW ZEALAND

Bowyangs, 372 Little Bourke St, Melbourne (©03/9670 4383).

The Map Shop, 16a Peel St, Adelaide (©08/8231 2033)

Perth Map Centre, 891 Hay St, Perth (©08/9322 5733).

Specialty Maps, 58 Albert St, Auckland (©09/307 2217).

Travel Bookshop, Shop 3, 175 Liverpool St, Sydney (©02/9261 8200).

Worldwide Maps and Guides, 187 George St, Brisbane (©07/3221 4330).

ONLINE TRAVEL BOOKSTORES

Adventurous Traveler *www.AdventurousTraveler.com/*

Amazon *www.amazon.com*

Bookpages *www.bookpages.com*

Literate Traveler *www.literatetraveler.com/*

ONLINE TRAVEL RESOURCES

TRAVEL RESOURCES AND LINKS

City Net *www.city.net/* Not a bad place to start, with detailed links for individual Asian countries from Bangladesh to Vietnam, ranging from country information provided via the CIA factbook, to hotel bookings and sightseeing.

Internet Travel Information Service *www.itisnet.com* Specifically aimed at budget travellers, this fairly new site has the makings of a really useful resource. Its researchers send weekly reports from the road (Asia is well covered), so there's heaps of up-to-the-minute info on things like current air fares, border crossings, visa requirements, as well as hotel openings and closures. A travellers' bulletin board is planned too.

Online tourist information *www.efn.org/~rick/tour* Exhaustive online travel resource, with web links for more than 150 countries. Links go to both official web sites and travellers' homepages, so you can get your facts and your firsthand advice.

Rec. travel library *www.travel-library.com/* Highly recommended site which has lively pieces on dozens of travel topics, from a budget travellers' guide to sleeping in airports, to how to travel light and where to find a list of cybercafés across the world. Good links too.

Rough Guides *www.roughguides.com/* Updated daily, this travel site features news pages where you can catch up on what's happening in the world this week, original travel tips, musings and opinions from Rough Guide authors, ticket-booking facilities and competitions. Just key in a destination and get the lowdown on where to eat, where to sleep and the top ten things to do. In addition, Rough Guides publish their travel guides online, for free.

TRAVELLERS' NEWSGROUPS AND BULLETIN BOARDS

Fielding's Adventure Forum *www.fieldingtravel.com/blackflag* Travellers' question-and-answer forum on adventurous and "dangerous" places to travel, created by the people who produce *Fielding's Guide to the World's Most Dangerous Places* and other guidebooks. Especially worth checking out for the less-travelled places such as Cambodia, Pakistan and North Korea.

Lonely Planet Thorn Tree *www.lonelyplanet.com/thorntree/ thorn.htm* Highly recommended travellers' bulletin boards, divid-ed into regions (eg the Indian subcontinent, Southeast Asia). Ideal for exchanging information with other travellers and for starting a debate. Also a good place to look for travel companions and up-to-the minute first-hand advice.

Rec. Travel Asia *news:rec.travel.asia* A Usenet forum that deals specifically with Asian travel, this is a bit unwieldly compared to the Lonely Planet site, but gets a lot of traffic.

Rough Journal *www.roughguides.com/* New forum for travellers to share their news and views, exchange current tips, give advice and get free email.

ONLINE MAGAZINES

Asiaweek *www.asiaweek.com/* Good range of weekly articles, accessible without subscription, plus headline snippets from the archives.

Far Eastern Economic Review *www.feer.com/* The week's articles. Registration is necessary, but free.

New Internationalist *www.oneworld.org/ni/* Offers a selection of the month's articles without subscription.

TRAVEL EQUIPMENT SUPPLIERS

UK

Cotswold Outdoor Ltd, 42–46 Uxbridge Rd, London W12 8ND (℡0181/743 2976, fax 740 1490), and branches in Betws-y-Coed, Harrogate, Manchester, Reading, St Albans, South Cerney and Southampton; *www.cotswold-outdoor.co.uk* Sells a huge range of outdoor and adventure gear for pretty much any activity and climate. Mail order is available; to order a catalogue, call ℡01285/643434.

Field and Trek Branches in Brentwood, Canterbury, Chelmsford, Croydon, Gloucester, London, Slough; *www.field-trek.co.uk* Stocks a massive choice of gear by a variety of manufacturers including their own-brand items. Mail order is available, call ℡01277/233122 for a catalogue.

YHA Adventure Shops. Branches in Ambleside, Birmingham, Brighton, Bristol, Cambridge, Cardiff, Leeds, Liverpool, London, Manchester, Nottingham, Oxford, Plymouth, Reading, St Albans, Salisbury, Southampton. A good range of gear at competitive prices aimed at general outdoor activities. Adequate for most purposes, but lacks the variety and some of the specialist stock of other shops. Call head office (this is not a shop) for your nearest branch: ℡01784/458625.

US AND CANADA

Travel Medicine, 351 Pleasant St, Suite 312, Northampton, MA 01060 (℡1-800/872-8633). Sells first-aid kits, mosquito netting, water filters and other health-related travel products.

Campmoor, PO Box 700, Saddle River, NJ 07458-0700 (℡1-800/226-7667 or 201/825-8300, fax 1-800/230-2153 or 201/825-0274). Clothing plus outdoor and camping gear.

The North Face. Twelve stores in the US and one in Canada selling camping equiment and clothing. For your nearest store, call ℡1-800/362-4963, fax 1-510/618-3532.

Recreational Equipment Inc, Sumner, WA 98352-0001 (℡1-800/426-4840, fax 1-206/891-2523). Sixty stores selling outdoor gear and clothing. Extensive mail-order catalogue.

Sierra Trading Post, 5025 Campstool Rd, Cheyenne, WY 82007-1802 (℡1-800/713-4534, fax 378-8946). Clothes, shoes and small equipment.

Travel Smith, 60 Leveroni Court #1, Novato, CA 94949 (℡1-800/950-1600, fax 950-1656).

AUSTRALIA AND NEW ZEALAND

A-Roving, 112 Toorak Rd, Toorak, Vic 3142 (℡03/9824 1714). Suppliers of travel luggage and accessories, maps and travel guides.

Bivouac 5 Fort St, Auckland 1 (℡09/366 1966). Several stores in New Zealand stocking a full range of backpacking and camping gear.

Katmandu, PO Box 1191, Collingwood, VIC 3066 (℡03/9417 2480 or 1-800/33484). A mail-order company, with outlets in all major Australian and New Zealand cities, offering an extensive range of quality outdoor and climbing gear.

Mountain Designs, 105 Albert St, Brisbane, QLD 4000 (℡07/3221 6756); branches also in Sydney, Melbourne, Perth, Adelaide, Canberra, Hobart and Auckland. Australian-designed, lightweight mountaineering and adventure equipment, specializing in sleeping bags, Gortex and fleeces.

Mtn Equipment Pty, Ltd, 491 Kent St, Sydney, NSW 2000 (℡02/9264 5888), and branches in Chatswood and Hornsby. This shop has a comprehensive range of lightweight, functional gear for outdoor and sporting activities. For mail order, call ℡02/9264 2645.

Paddy Pallin, 507 Kent St, Sydney, NSW 2000 (℡02/9264 2685), and thirteen branches throughout Australia. One of the original designers and suppliers of hiking and camping gear specially designed for Australian conditions, but some may be of interest to people heading overseas. For mail order, call ℡02/9525 6829 or 1-800/805398.

FINAL CHECKLIST

DOCUMENTS

Full details on all the following items are given in Chapter Seven.

AIRLINE TICKETS

CREDIT CARD

GUIDEBOOKS

INSURANCE POLICY

INTERNATIONAL DRIVERS' LICENCE

INTERNATIONAL STUDENT CARD (ISIC CARD)

INTERNATIONAL YOUTH HOSTEL CARD

MAPS

PASSPORT

PASSPORT PHOTOS

PHRASEBOOK

PHONE CARD/ PHONE HOME CARD

PHOTOCOPIES OF ALL YOUR VITAL DOCUMENTS

TRAVELLERS' CHEQUES

THE BARE ESSENTIALS

BACKPACK/TRAVEL SACK

CLOTHES

DAYPACK

FLEECE JACKET OR SWEATSHIRT

MONEY BELT AND/OR NECK POUCH

PADLOCKS OR BACKPACK LOCKS

SARONG

SHOES

SUN HAT

WATERPROOF MONEY-HOLDER ("SURFSAFE")

BASIC ODDS AND ENDS

CAMERA EQUIPMENT AND FILM

CONTACT LENS STUFF/GLASSES

CONTRACEPTIVES AND/OR CONDOMS

FIRST-AID KIT

FLASHLIGHT (TORCH)

MINI-PADLOCKS AND A CHAIN

MOSQUITO REPELLENT

SUNGLASSES

SUNSCREEN

TAMPONS

TOILET PAPER

TOILETRIES

TOWEL

OPTIONALS

ALARM CLOCK/WATCH

BATTERIES

BOOKS

CIGARETTE LIGHTER

COMPASS

EARPLUGS

GAMES

GLUESTICK

HANDKERCHIEF

MOSQUITO NET

NOTEBOOK OR JOURNAL, AND PENS

PENKNIFE

PERSONAL STEREO

PHOTOS OF HOME

RAIN GEAR/UMBRELLA

SEWING KIT

SINK PLUG

SHEET SLEEPING BAG

SHORT-WAVE RADIO

SLEEPING BAG AND TENT

STAMPS FROM YOUR HOME COUNTRY

STRING

WALLET

WATER BOTTLE, WATER PURIFIER OR PURIFICATION TABLETS

INDEX

Stay in touch with us!

**ROUGH*NEWS* is Rough Guides' free newsletter.
In three issues a year we give you news, travel
issues, music reviews, readers' letters and the
latest dispatches from authors on the road.**

I would like to receive ROUGH*NEWS*: please put me on your free mailing list.

NAME . . . .

ADDRESS . . . .

Please clip or photocopy and send to: Rough Guides, 1 Mercer Street, London WC2H 9QJ, England
or Rough Guides, 375 Hudson Street, New York, NY 10014, USA.

direct orders from

		UK£8.99	US$14.95	CAN$19.99
Amsterdam	1-85828-218-7			
Andalucia	1-85828-219-5	9.99	16.95	22.99
Antigua Mini Guide	1-85828-346-9	5.99	9.95	12.99
Australia	1-85828-220-9	13.99	21.95	29.99
Austria	1-85828-325-6	10.99	17.95	23.99
Bali & Lombok	1-85828-134-2	8.99	14.95	19.99
Bangkok Mini Guide	1-85828-345-0	5.99	9.95	12.99
Barcelona	1-85828-221-7	8.99	14.95	19.99
Belgium & Luxembourg	1-85828-222-5	10.99	17.95	23.99
Belize	1-85828-351-5	9.99	16.95	22.99
Berlin	1-85828-327-2	9.99	16.95	22.99
Boston Mini Guide	1-85828-321-3	5.99	9.95	12.99
Brazil	1-85828-223-3	13.99	21.95	29.99
Britain	1-85828-312-4	14.99	23.95	31.99
Brittany & Normandy	1-85828-224-1	9.99	16.95	22.99
Bulgaria	1-85828-183-0	9.99	16.95	22.99
California	1-85828-330-2	11.99	18.95	24.99
Canada	1-85828-311-6	12.99	19.95	25.99
Central America	1-85828-335-3	14.99	23.95	31.99
China	1-85828-225-X	15.99	24.95	32.99
Corfu & the Ionian Islands	1-85828-226-8	8.99	14.95	19.99
Corsica	1-85828-227-6	9.99	16.95	22.99
Costa Rica	1-85828-136-9	9.99	15.95	21.99
Crete	1-85828-316-7	9.99	16.95	22.99
Cyprus	1-85828-182-2	9.99	16.95	22.99
Czech & Slovak Republics	1-85828-317-5	11.99	18.95	24.99
Dublin Mini Guide	1-85828-294-2	5.99	9.95	12.99
Edinburgh Mini Guide	1-85828-295-0	5.99	9.95	12.99
Egypt	1-85828-188-1	10.99	17.95	23.99
Europe 1998	1-85828-289-6	14.99	19.95	25.99
England	1-85828-301-9	12.99	19.95	25.99
First Time Asia	1-85828-332-9	7.99	9.95	12.99
First Time Europe	1-85828-270-5	7.99	9.95	12.99
Florida	1-85828-184-4	10.99	16.95	22.99
France	1-85828-228-4	12.99	19.95	25.99
Germany	1-85828-309-4	14.99	23.95	31.99
Goa	1-85828-275-6	8.99	14.95	19.99
Greece	1-85828-300-0	12.99	19.95	25.99
Greek Islands	1-85828-310-8	10.99	17.95	23.99
Guatemala	1-85828-323-X	9.99	16.95	22.99
Hawaii: Big Island	1-85828-158-X	8.99	12.95	16.99
Hawaii	1-85828-206-3	10.99	16.95	22.99
Holland	1-85828-229-2	10.99	17.95	23.99
Hong Kong & Macau	1-85828-187-3	8.99	14.95	19.99
Hotels & Restos de France 1998	1-85828-306-X	12.99	19.95	25.99
Hungary	1-85828-123-7	8.99	14.95	19.99
India	1-85828-200-4	14.99	23.95	31.99
Ireland	1-85828-179-2	10.99	17.95	23.99
Israel & the Palestinian Territories	1-85828-248-9	12.99	19.95	25.99
Italy	1-85828-167-9	12.99	19.95	25.99
Jamaica	1-85828-230-6	9.99	16.95	22.99
Japan	1-85828-340-X	14.99	23.95	31.99
Jordan	1-85828-350-7	10.99	17.95	23.99
Kenya	1-85828-192-X	11.99	18.95	24.99
Lisbon Mini Guide	1-85828-297-7	5.99	9.95	12.99
London	1-85828-231-4	9.99	15.95	21.99
Madrid Mini Guide	1-85828-353-1	5.99	9.95	12.99
Mallorca & Menorca	1-85828-165-2	8.99	14.95	19.99
Malaysia, Singapore & Brunei	1-85828-232-2	11.99	18.95	24.99
Mexico	1-85828-044-3	10.99	16.95	22.99
Morocco	1-85828-169-5	11.99	18.95	24.99
Moscow	1-85828-322-1	9.99	16.95	22.99
Nepal	1-85828-190-3	10.99	17.95	23.99
New York	1-85828-296-9	9.99	15.95	21.99
New Zealand	1-85828-233-0	12.99	19.95	25.99
Norway	1-85828-234-9	10.99	17.95	23.99

UK orders: 0181 899 4036

around the world

Pacific Northwest	1-85828-326-4	UK£12.99	US$19.95	CAN$25.99
Paris	1-85828-235-7	8.99	14.95	19.99
Peru	1-85828-142-3	10.99	17.95	23.99
Poland	1-85828-168-7	10.99	17.95	23.99
Portugal	1-85828-313-2	10.99	17.95	23.99
Prague	1-85828-318-3	8.99	14.95	19.99
Provence & the Cote d'Azur	1-85828-127-X	9.99	16.95	22.99
The Pyrenees	1-85828-308-6	10.99	17.95	23.99
Rhodes & the Dodecanese	1-85828-120-2	8.99	14.95	19.99
Romania	1-85828-305-1	10.99	17.95	23.99
San Francisco	1-85828-299-3	8.99	14.95	19.99
Scandinavia	1-85828-236-5	12.99	20.95	27.99
Scotland	1-85828-302-7	9.99	16.95	22.99
Seattle Mini Guide	1-85828-324-8	5.99	9.95	12.99
Sicily	1-85828-178-4	9.99	16.95	22.99
Singapore	1-85828-237-3	8.99	14.95	19.99
South Africa	1-85828-238-1	12.99	19.95	25.99
Southwest USA	1-85828-239-X	10.99	16.95	22.99
Spain	1-85828-240-3	11.99	18.95	24.99
St Petersburg	1-85828-298-5	9.99	16.95	22.99
Sweden	1-85828-241-1	10.99	17.95	23.99
Syria	1-85828-331-0	11.99	18.95	24.99
Thailand	1-85828-140-7	10.99	17.95	24.99
Tunisia	1-85828-139-3	10.99	17.95	24.99
Turkey	1-85828-242-X	12.99	19.95	25.99
Tuscany & Umbria	1-85828-243-8	10.99	17.95	23.99
USA	1-85828-307-8	14.99	19.95	25.99
Venice	1-85828-170-9	8.99	14.95	19.99
Vienna	1-85828-244-6	8.99	14.95	19.99
Vietnam	1-85828-191-1	9.99	15.95	21.99
Wales	1-85828-245-4	10.99	17.95	23.99
Washington DC	1-85828-246-2	8.99	14.95	19.99
West Africa	1-85828-101-6	15.99	24.95	34.99
Zimbabwe & Botswana	1-85828-186-5	11.99	18.95	24.99

Phrasebooks

Czech	1-85828-148-2	3.50	5.00	7.00
Egyptian Arabic	1-85828-319-1	4.00	6.00	8.00
French	1-85828-144-X	3.50	5.00	7.00
German	1-85828-146-6	3.50	5.00	7.00
Greek	1-85828-145-8	3.50	5.00	7.00
Hindi & Urdu	1-85828-252-7	4.00	6.00	8.00
Hungarian	1-85828-304-3	4.00	6.00	8.00
Indonesian	1-85828-250-0	4.00	6.00	8.00
Italian	1-85828-143-1	3.50	5.00	7.00
Japanese	1-85828-303-5	4.00	6.00	8.00
Mandarin Chinese	1-85828-249-7	4.00	6.00	8.00
Mexican Spanish	1-85828-176-8	3.50	5.00	7.00
Portuguese	1-85828-175-X	3.50	5.00	7.00
Polish	1-85828-174-1	3.50	5.00	7.00
Russian	1-85828-251-9	4.00	6.00	8.00
Spanish	1-85828-147-4	3.50	5.00	7.00
Swahili	1-85828-320-5	4.00	6.00	8.00
Thai	1-85828-177-6	3.50	5.00	7.00
Turkish	1-85828-173-3	3.50	5.00	7.00
Vietnamese	1-85828-172-5	3.50	5.00	7.00

Reference

Classical Music	1-85828-113-X	12.99	19.95	25.99
European Football	1-85828-256-X	14.99	23.95	31.99
Internet	1-85828-288-8	5.00	8.00	10.00
Jazz	1-85828-137-7	16.99	24.95	34.99
Millennium	1-85828-314-0	5.00	8.95	11.99
More Women Travel	1-85828-098-2	10.99	16.95	22.99
Opera	1-85828-138-5	16.99	24.95	34.99
Reggae	1-85828-247-0	12.99	19.95	25.99
Rock	1-85828-201-2	17.99	26.95	35.00
World Music	1-85828-017-6	16.99	22.95	29.99

  US/International orders: 1-800-253-6476

Listen!

Your Rough Guides to World Music, Reggae, Classic Jazz, Salsa, and to the music of Kenya and Tanzania, West Africa, Scotland, Ireland, India and Pakistan, Zimbabwe, South Africa, Brazil, North Africa, Cuba, the Andes and many more!

  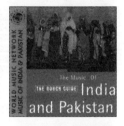

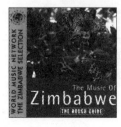  

'If you want to explore the music of another country you need a guide.
Like the useful Rough Guide travel books and television shows,
these discs delve right into the heart and soul of the region they explore'
Rhythm Music (USA)

'Intelligent, authoritative compilations' Folk Roots (UK)

Rough Guide CDs (and cassettes) are available worldwide through selected record and book shops.
Alternatively order direct at £9.99 per CD and £6.99 per cassette (+ £1.95 p&p per order).

WORLD MUSIC NETWORK, 6 Abbeville Mews, 88 Clapham Park Road, London SW4 7BX
Credit Card Hotline: 0171 498 5252 Fax: +0044 [0]171 498 5353 [UK]
Email wldmusic@dircon.co.uk Website: www.users.dircon.co/-wldmusic/

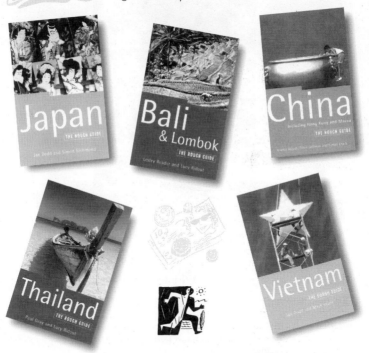

"I'm flat out."

Call them and really bring things home.

Calling from abroad needn't be hard work. With a BT Chargecard, just dial the access code for the country you're in and follow the voice prompts. To make it even simpler, find out the code before you go - **Free**fone 0800 **345 625**. Or, if you haven't got a BT Chargecard, dial **155** to find out how to call home. It's so easy, you could almost do it in your sleep.

For further information and dialling codes when you're abroad, call the local operator.

BT *It's good to talk*